Ross Coulthart is a Walkley award winning journalist, who presently works as an investigative reporter for Channel 7's *Sunday Night*. For 14 years he reported for the *Sunday* program on Channel 9, and for four years on *Four Corners* at the ABC. Most recently, he uncovered one of the biggest medical scandals in Australia, the story of the so-called 'Butcher of Bega'.

Duncan McNab is the author of *The Usual Suspects: The life of Abe Saffron* and *The Dodger: Inside the World of Roger Rogerson*. He is also a former policeman and private investigator.

DEAD MAN RUNNING

ROSS COULTHART AND DUNCAN McNAB

WITHDRAWN

ALLEN&UNWIN

First published by Allen & Unwin in 2008
This edition published in 2009

Allen & Unwin
83 Alexander Street
Crows Nest NSW 2065
Australia
Phone: (61 2) 8425 0100
Fax: (61 2) 9906 2218
Email: info@allenandunwin.com
Web: www.allenandunwin.com

Cataloguing-in-Publication details are available :
from the National Library of Australia
www.librariesaustralia.nla.gov.au

978 1 74237 027 9 (pbk.)

Typeset in 11.5/16pt Bembo by Midland Typesetters, Australia
Printed in Australia by McPherson's Printing Group

10 9 8 7 6 5

CONTENTS

PROLOGUE

I'm not becoming like them; I am them.
Stevan Utah

It's a still, sticky day in the lonely pine forests just below the Glasshouse Mountains on Queensland's Sunshine Coast. We are just five minutes up the road from one of the country's best known landmarks—the Steve Irwin-created Australia Zoo. A few minutes earlier, as we turned off the main highway up Roy's Road, two tour buses passed us, packed with tourists craning to get their first glimpse of man-eating crocodiles, the world's deadliest snakes and cuddly koalas. There's also a golf club nearby, popular with the many retired Queensland and New South Wales policemen who live in the area. This part of Australia is for some reason so popular with ex-New South Wales coppers the New South Wales Retired Police Association has a local branch for its members.

Ironic then, in view of why we take the empty tree-lined road to Beerwah cemetery. Established AD 1936, it is a bleak and forlorn place and today the air is thick with flies. Perfect weather to rot a corpse. Which is what we are here to find. It may seem more than a little absurd, searching for a body in a cemetery, but somewhere in the thick undergrowth, under the dense carpet of pine needles, no doubt tucked away off one of the myriad access tracks, we are told there is a body . . . waiting to be found.

We don't even know his name. We only know that one night, in a bloody act of homicidal rage fuelled by the suspicion that the victim was a police informant—a 'dog'—a Bandido bikie boss, Joseph 'Hombre' Jonker is alleged to have shot him twice outside the Caloundra clubhouse. Ironically, Hombre's trusted associate, who saw the murder happen, went on for a brief time to become one of Australia's most valuable witnesses to the organised crime networks inside outlaw motorcycle gangs. That witness's name is Stevan Utah. And the reason we are probing the undergrowth around this graveyard for a long-dead corpse is because Utah says Hombre Jonker told him he dumped the body somewhere in or around the graveyard in which we are now standing.

Utah is a self-confessed criminal, and he has seen and participated in some horrible things. He is an accomplice after-the-fact to a brutal murder, and a witness to numerous bloody bikie beatings—and he is a victim of a nasty attempted hit himself.

Inside the bikie gangs he witnessed extensive and highly profitable drug manufacture and dealing and he has himself been an underworld cook of the illegal methamphetamine drug 'ice', or 'crystal meth' as it's also known. From the inside, Utah has seen the bikies trading cash, chemicals and guns with notorious mafia drug families and other outlaw motorcycle gangs. He has also been a notable international wildlife smuggler and—courtesy of Her Majesty's Australian Army explosives technicians' course—not only does he know how to blow things up, he has also witnessed dealings in weapons stolen from supposedly secure army repositories.

Utah took on the personality, swagger and diction of the bikie world, becoming so much a fixture in the clubhouse he was offered 'full-patch' status (bikie parlance for full membership—denoted by the gang's distinctive 'patch' worn on their vest) if he got himself the essential Harley-Davidson. For the police, who had long been frustrated with their inability to penetrate the bikie gangs, especially the ultra security-cautious Bandidos, Utah was able to show the reality behind the public protestations of many bikie leaders that they are all law-abiding rebels unfairly persecuted by police. Not all bikies are criminals, but Utah's eyewitness accounts show that outlaw motorcycle gangs are a national menace, and they have become a haven for some nasty thugs.

His story is a wake-up call. It shows the big lie behind the charity bike runs and hospital fundraisers the outlaw motorcycle gangs organise to sanitise their public image. Utah's recordings and detailed reports to police showed them just how involved many senior bikies are in extensive organised crime both in Australia and overseas. And in an act that he believes was partly his undoing, he also fingered corrupt police who enjoyed the illicit and often salacious entertainment in gang clubhouses—the strippers and the prostitutes—and who, all too often, tipped off bikie leaders to forthcoming raids.

When we first listened to Utah's colourful account down a crackling phone line from the other side of the world, his story seemed preposterous. It all sounded too lurid, too cartoon-like to be true. The extraordinary failures and questionable decisions by state and federal police agencies seemed too ridiculous to be believable. But with even initial cursory enquiries, his tale began checking out. Court files showed Utah really had been charged with murder and that those charges had inexplicably been dropped. It was clear he must indeed have known something very valuable for police to make such calls.

Then there was a road trip to meet a well-respected Queensland lawyer who an intermediary had said would brief us on Utah's bona fides, a man who had witnessed Utah's negotiations with police from three different agencies. He refused to talk about his client on the phone and we met in the crowded bar–restaurant of a local country pub, where his office staff were farewelling a colleague. Pushing a package of computer disks and documents across the table, he was clearly relieved to get them out of his office. Utah had authorised him to pass them on.

PROLOGUE

With a nervous glance across the adjacent tables of jolly country folk enjoying a boozy lunch, he explained that some of the enclosed documents were the statements he had prepared to enable his client to seek indemnity from Australia's peak crime-fighting body, the Australian Crime Commission. The crimes they detailed were, he explained, so horrific that he had not wanted his office staff to know anything about them because he feared the risk to them if they did: 'I don't want my name associated with this fellow at all. I've checked him out as best I can. He's the real deal. I think he did what he says he did. And I warn you, he has been involved with some very dangerous people.'

He is a decent man and, as we shook hands on the street, he told us he felt Utah's case raised major concerns in relation to just how serious police agencies are about combating the organised crime menace in outlaw motor-cycle gangs. He had seen it before and it would happen again, he warned, if nothing was done to change the system that handles the 'crims who turn'.

We'd driven back to Brisbane and then boarded a plane to Sydney, with the documents burning a hole in the briefcase, too wary of peeks from fellow plane passengers to attempt to read them on the crowded plane. When we did finally read them, what they detailed was chilling. But even more disturbing were the alleged failures by police agencies. The evidence suggested that Utah had been one of Australia's most important moles inside the bikie gangs—and that his usefulness to police had been squandered because of personality clashes, police distrust, petty bickering and stupid turf wars.

Which was why today, in the sticky heat of the Glasshouse Mountains hinterlands, we were looking for a corpse somewhere around this cemetery. We had it on good authority that, despite Stevan Utah giving the same information to police about Hombre Jonker dumping a body somewhere around this graveyard, the police had never done a search. After three months of investigating Utah's claims, we had learned very fast to take them seriously. We knew from the documents, and from talking to police sources, that the last time Utah told sceptical police he knew where a body was, it had taken three searches, but they finally found another murder victim exactly where he said they would.

To the Bandidos and other gangs in clubhouses along Australia's east coast, from Queensland down to Geelong in Victoria, Utah was a trusted hang-around, a novitiate to the strange and violent hierarchical world of the patch-clad biker gangs. Rat-cunning and extremely intelligent, Utah was drawn to the camaraderie, mateship and discipline of the outlaw motorcycle gangs; and in his chameleon-like way, he became a key player in many of their often publicly denied extensive criminal enterprises.

Except for what he describes as a police blunder, Utah might today have been inside the Bandidos, still passing the covertly recorded conversations on miniature digital audio recorders to his police handlers at luggage lockers in Brisbane city buildings. Instead, Utah is now a man on the run. Wanted by police and hunted by his vengeful former bikie blood brothers, he admits he is a marked man—a 'dead man running', to use his own words. In hiding overseas, Utah is anxious to prove the value of the information he passed on to police—tips which, he says, have all too often been ignored by our major crime-fighting agencies.

The story of the breakdown in his relationship with his police handlers is what has brought us here to this lonely graveyard. If they had not fallen out with each other, there is a good chance Utah would, like many witnesses who have worked for police on the inside of an organised crime network, never have told his story. He would probably be living under a new name on the other side of the world, maybe running a pet shop trading in his beloved tropical animals—and his customers would be none the wiser. Instead, Stevan Utah is a haunted man, constantly looking over his shoulder—waiting for a bullet, a knife, a bomb, or the cruel beating which will finally signal that his bikie colleagues have found him.

That police blunder, Utah claims, almost cost him his life. His former bikie brothers tried to kill him because they suspected—correctly as it turned out—that he was a police informer. The way Utah tells it, he was dumped by his police handlers once his informant role was compromised. He says he was forced to flee overseas, painting Queensland police efforts to return him to Australia on criminal charges as an attempt by that force to silence him from revealing what he knows.

Whatever the truth of his protestations of innocence, Stevan Utah knows a lot. And with the same discipline with which he set about informing on the crimes of his bikie brothers, he now intends making things as difficult as possible for his former Bandido associates. He intends to get even with the men who tried to kill him by revealing what he knows—to anyone prepared to listen. And that includes helping find the corpses of some of the people he saw them murder:

> I know this is going to sound glib and self-serving but I don't give a shit what anyone thinks. I am sorry for what I did and I want those families to get some closure. And if I get fucking knocked in the process, I'll be glad to have done so with all the best intentions. Coppers will scoff but I truly want to put this all behind me. I want people to know just how fucking dangerous these people are . . . because for a few years I was one of them.

There is a movie Utah loves called *Donnie Brasco*, an American gangster flick about a young undercover cop who penetrates a mafia gang and becomes a witness to the ugly world of killings, extortion and intimidation enforced by the strict mafia code of silence. Utah is full of admiration for how close that film comes to describing the world he witnessed for years inside the outlaw motorcycle gangs. There is a phrase he quotes from the mouth of the young undercover cop, who realises that being inside the mafia is changing him: 'All my life I've tried to be the good guy, the guy in the white fucking hat. And for what? For nothing. I'm not becoming like them; I am them.' Stevan Utah admits that for a time he became what they are. And the window he offers onto the violent criminal world of outlaw motorcycle gangs is what this book is all about.

Back up in Beerwah, where we're gently stepping through the knee-deep scrub surrounding the grassy graveyard with its neatly ordered tombstones and crosses, it is easy to understand why, if Bandido bikie boss Joseph Hombre Jonker did dump a body here, he chose this spot. On a Google satellite photo this is a rare, quiet, place close to the crowded tourist and retiree strips along the beaches just ten kilometres or so to the east. We are barely half an hour's drive from the clubhouse where, according to Utah's account, the victim was shot years ago. This tiny speck of green lawn and red dirt is surrounded by a dark swathe of green—the Beerburrum State Forest—on a map otherwise dotted with retirement villages, resorts and tourist parks. For a bikie boss carrying a corpse in the back of his car, Beerwah cemetery is just the place to dump it.

Left out in the open in a tropical climate like this, insects alone can turn a fully fleshed corpse to bare bones in just a couple of weeks. Counterintuitively, the tropical air decomposes a body in the open eight times faster than if it is buried. There is a small chance the murderer just dumped his victim here on the ground—some distance from the nearby tombstones of Beerwah cemetery's more legitimate residents. Maybe Hombre took the gamble that no-one would ever be game to venture out into the long grass and scrub under the pine trees. It concentrates the mind wonderfully to know that this region is home to one of the world's deadliest snakes—the Coastal Taipan. Every time we kick a clump in the undergrowth to see if it's a boot or a bone, we expect to see a flash of golden olive scales and feel the sickening pain of snake fangs in the leg.

Out here too, there are wild animals, including pigs and dogs, that might disturb a corpse lying in the open. Chances are the victim was buried. From the other side of the world, Stevan Utah is adamant: 'Hombre would have buried him, but not too deep. Probably no more than a couple of feet. He wouldn't be standing on ceremony. No fucking six feet under. Too much effort. I remember though he giggled 'cos he'd given him a proper send-off at a cemetery.'

Sadly, human nature dictates that even the most beautiful spots in the world must have an underbelly and this part of south-east Queensland is no exception. It is possible to holiday here in the Glasshouse Mountains, enjoying the hippy mountain markets around Flaxton and Maleny and the cooling waters at Kondalilla Falls, and experience a tranquil excursion into a gentler part of Australia. It is a favourite playground for Brisbane city-dwellers looking for a cooler alternative to the brassy, plastic tourist strips running from Noosa down to the Gold Coast.

And that is pretty much the same with outlaw motor-cycle gangs around much of Australia. They operate, deliberately, just under the radar, keeping a low profile and occasionally promoting a charity event to get some positive spin in the evening news. Most citizens go about their normal lives oblivious to the numerous unsolved murders and the growing casualties of gun violence and illicit drugs—all of them victims of now systematic bikie organised crime.

For us, that trip to Beerwah cemetery was just the beginning of a trip to a seamy side of Australia we never knew existed.

1

ENTER THE ONE-PERCENTERS

*The trouble was caused by the one percent deviant
that tarnished the public image of both motorcycles
and motorcyclists.*
American Motorcyclist Association

The two wheels hit the road in 1885 in Stuttgart,
Germany, when Gottlieb Daimler fired up the world's
first petrol-engined motorcycle. Just like the four-wheel
car designed by fellow German Karl Benz, the concept
took off. Motorcycles were the natural successor to the
horse, offering low-cost transport, freedom and mobility.

In 1903, the year the Wright Brothers took to
the sky in North Carolina's Kill Devil Hills, the Ford
Motor Company was incorporated, and William Harley
and brothers Arthur and Walter Davidson formed the
Harley-Davidson Motor Cycle Company in Milwaukee,
Wisconsin, the Federation of American Cyclists was born.
The club first met in Brooklyn, New York. The club lasted
only until 1924, when it was replaced by the American
Motorcyclist Association (AMA). From its earliest days

the association was committed to fostering what these days we'd call a 'positive image' of motorcyclists.

One feature of the federation that made its way into the activities of the American Motorcycle Association was the 'gypsy' tours. In its issue of 19 March 1925, *Motorcycle & Bicycle* reported on the rapidly growing popularity of the tours. It said, 'the Gypsy Tour idea originated eight or nine years ago, the object being to set a certain date for an outing where riders, dealers and everyone interested in motorcycles would tour to some convenient spot for a day's sport and a real old fashioned good time.'

On the fourth of July weekend of 1947, the second fourth of July America celebrated in the peace following World War II, around four thousand bike enthusiasts and gypsy tourists gathered in Hollister, California. The positive public image of motorcyclists got a terrible battering that weekend. The 'real old fashioned good time' was reminiscent not of a picnic, but of a saloon brawl from a B-grade Hollywood western. Lots of boozing, reckless driving and brawling put the quiet seat of San Benito County on the national map. Chief instigators of the problem came from a group of bikers known as the 'Boozefighters', who found their entertainment by hurling empty liquor bottles at anyone within range. They were joined in the mayhem by the equally stylishly named 'Pissed Off Bastards'. Thanks to *Life* magazine, the town that was previously best known for straddling a branch of the notorious San Andreas Fault was now known around the United States as the scene of the 'Hollister Riot'.

By the end of that weekend the toll was three people seriously hurt, sixty suffering various scrapes, bruises and breaks, and fifty arrested. One local sheriff described it as simply 'a hell of a mess'. On the cover of *Life* was a member of the Boozefighters. The gentleman was seated astride his bike, which was mounted on a pile of shattered bottles. A bottle of booze was in each of his outflung fists. The good public relations of the American Motorcyclist Association was in tatters.

They were horrified, and quickly held a press conference. Their spokesman tried to quell the story, noting, 'The trouble was caused by the one percent deviant that tarnished the public image of both motorcycles and motorcyclists'. Many years later, the AMA would try again, saying, 'We condemn them. They'd be condemned if they rode horses, mules, surfboards, bicycles or skateboards. Regretfully, they picked motorcycles.' The bike gangs that were soon to make their impact on the scene rather liked the notion of being a 'one-percenter' and clutched it to their leather-clad bosoms. Marlon Brando's swaggering, leather-jacketed, Triumph Thunderbird-riding bikie in the 1953 classic *The Wild One*, based on the riot, added to the mystique of the one-percenters.

The picture in *Life* magazine, and Mr Brando's starring role as a free spirit, caught the mood of many young

Americans. Most had lived through the Depression only to find themselves drawn into the brutality of World War II. Many had come back to America only to be saddled with mundane jobs. The adrenalin rush found in war was gone. The rush to conformity in the vacuum that followed war, and the looming Cold War, became oppressive. A little touch of freedom was what they wanted. The timing was perfect because war surplus motorbikes were both cheap and plentiful. The iron horse replaced the horse and it was time for a more modern reprise of the old West.

One of the first major bike gangs to emerge in the Hollister aftermath, and still the dominant gang in the world today, was the Hells Angels. There are a few tales of how the name came about. Various Hells Angels members have disagreed with the origins over the years; however, all the tales offer a glimpse of adventure and life on the edge. Some reckon it hails from the US army's elite World War II troops of the 11th Airborne Division. These men were paratroopers who parachuted themselves behind enemy lines in France, apparently with twenty pounds of TNT strapped to each leg, and bent on mayhem. They took the nickname 'Hells Angels' from their descent.

Others prefer the story that the name was borrowed from the 'Hells Angels', the US Air Force 303rd Bombardment Group that bombed occupied Europe from their base in Molesworth, England. The lads from the 303rd had in turn borrowed the name from the 1930 Howard

Hughes film *Hell's Angels* about pilots from World War I. There's a fair chance that the fighting men of either group weren't deeply impressed at having their war exploits associated with a bike gang.

The Hells Angels club began in 1948 in a town called Fontana, California. Fontana is in San Bernardino County and lies on the outer edge of modern Los Angeles. It rose quickly from obscurity in the 1940s thanks to the arrival of the San Bernardino Freeway and the Kaiser steel mill, which supplied steel to build World War II's famous Liberty ships. For men coming back from the war it was a place where they could find work and live cheaply. It was also, in 1948, the site of the first McDonald's fast food restaurant.

The formation of the gang was the outcome of on-going tensions between the Boozefighters and the Pissed Off Bastards. It all got too much for old Bastard Otto Friedl. He formed a splinter group and created the Hells Angels. Over the next decade the irreverent or just plain antisocial behaviour of the Angels saw their fellow southern Californians grow less tolerant.

By 1956 the more tolerant locals of the San Francisco area saw the Oakland chapter of the Hells Angels become the club's de facto US head-quarters. Among the Oakland ranks was one Ralph 'Sonny' Barger, who had just come out of a hitch in the US army. Barger reckoned he had a choice of either becoming a beatnik or a motorcycle rider, and chose the latter. Despite his lack of imagination at the time, he would eventually become the public face and spinmeister of the gang. He'd also end up as an author and media tart, and be self-described as 'An American Legend'.

Like many of those who followed, Barger was the product of a lousy childhood. Born in 1938 in California, his mother left him with his alcoholic father and an older sister when he was only four months old. While at school he found a taste and talent for fighting, but unfortunately had a habit of assaulting his teachers. Suspensions from school were not infrequent.

It was Barger who was the driving force behind the gang's codes of conduct, laws, colours and the like. Thanks to his skill with public relations, the myth of the Hells Angels grew. This gang became the model for the gangs that would follow. Birney Jarvis, an early member of the Hells Angels who later became a police reporter for the *San Francisco Chronicle*, captured the true nature of the bike gangs when he commented, 'Some of the guys are pure animals. They'd be animals in any society. These guys are outlaw types who should have been born 100 years ago—then they would have been gun-fighters.' Barger took a somewhat softer line, describing his organisation as 'definitely a men's club. It's a group of motorcyclists who like to ride around the country. Having fun and doing it with their friends.'

Things were moving along quite nicely in the myth department until the Labor Day weekend in 1964 when the bikers once again found themselves the focus of the nation. Some of their friends didn't like the idea of 'doing it' with them it seemed. The scene was a weekend run to Monterey, California, until that stage better known for its glorious ocean-front location and John Steinbeck. It was a weekend that the 'pure animal' of some members came to the fore. Of that weekend, *True, The Man's Magazine*, noted in August 1965 with remarkable accuracy, 'They call themselves the Hell's Angels. They ride, they rape and raid like marauding cavalry—and they boast no police force can break up their criminal motorcycle fraternity.'

Bikers converged on the coast around Monterey. The motivation for the gathering was, local police believed, to collect funds to send the remains of Hells Angels San Bernardino chapter vice president, Kenneth Beamer, back to his mother in North Carolina. Beamer's demise had been caused on the road near San Diego when he found that bike versus truck is an unfair match. Hunter S. Thompson, who would later make his name chronicling the Angels, noted that Beamer 'had died in the best outlaw tradition: homeless, stone broke, and owning nothing in this world but the clothes on his back and a big bright Harley'.

The lads gathered at a bar called Nick's that Saturday night, and as the night and the booze wore on, moved down to a bonfire on the beach. That's when things got completely out of control. A deputy sheriff summoned to the scene stated he 'arrived at the beach and saw a huge bonfire surrounded by cyclists of both sexes. Then two sobbing, near-hysterical girls staggered out of the darkness, begging for help. One was completely nude and the other had on only a torn sweater.' The two teenage girls were both locals, and had come with some friends to gawk at the gathering both at Nick's and later on the beach. As Hunter S. Thompson commented:

> Not even Senator Murphy [a former tap dancer turned senator] could expect them to gather together in a drunken mass for any such elevated pastimes as ping pong, shuffleboard and whist. Their picnics have long been noted for certain beastly forms of entertainment, and any young girl who shows up at a Hell's Angels bonfire camp at two o'clock in the morning is presumed, by the outlaws, to be in a condition of heat. So it was only natural that the two girls attracted more attention when they arrived at the beach than they had earlier in the convivial bedlam at Nick's.

The local police didn't share the same caring view of the lads. They promptly arrested four Hells Angels and charged them with rape. One of the arrested was a guy who could readily be described as the definitive bikie. His name was Terry the Tramp. Six feet two inches tall, two hundred and ten pounds, massive arms, full beard, shoulder-length black hair and, as Thompson described, with 'a wild jabbering demeanour not calculated to soothe the soul of any personnel specialist. Beyond that, in his twenty-seven years he

ENTER THE ONE-PERCENTERS

had piled up a tall and ugly police record: a multitude of arrests from petty theft and battery to rape, narcotics offenses and public cunnilingus.' The poster boy for bike gangs.

Though Hunter S. Thompson made his name thanks to his sympathetic writings on the gangs, his relationship came to a somewhat ironic end when his subjects turned on him, delivering a very significant kicking. Sonny Barger was no fan of Thompson. Something of a cultural clash, it seemed. He commented:

> I don't like Hunter S. Thompson as a person. He's probably the greatest writer in the world. When he was with us on a run, we was going to fight the cops one day and he locked himself in the trunk of his car. That guy ain't my friend. He's not going to help me; he's going to run and leave me there when he's supposed to help us. He also didn't take care of what he was supposed to do. All we told him was buy us a keg of beer and he didn't do it. He's offered to do it later but we don't want it now. He didn't do it when he was supposed to. He got beat up by us, but he set that up. After the book was all done he come around us and said can I go on a run with ya. He got in an argument with a guy, he caused a fight, he got beat up and the cover of the book said 'I met, I lived with and I was almost killed by . . .' what a guy.

One of the intriguing quirks of the criminal justice system of most western countries is that a major source of a lawyer's revenue is directly derived from the proceeds

9

of the crimes committed by the people they're defending. A twist on money laundering perhaps, and rather like the US military policy of 'don't ask, don't tell'. It was the need to secure decent legal representation for alleged rapist Terry the Tramp and his three alleged cohorts that, as historians now believe, turned the Hells Angels on to crime as their primary source of cash flow. The crime they turned to was a perfect fit for the mood of California at the birth of the flower power era. Drugs, and in particular marijuana and the community's rapidly developing taste for amphetamines. Risks were low, profits high and police either weren't overly interested or just a bit slow to catch on to the trade. Bikies, of course, were none too talkative about their exploits either, so information was tightly held. One quaint gang motto of the time was 'three can keep a secret if two are dead'. The code of silence was firmly embraced.

The case against the four was very high profile. Thompson wrote, 'their blood, booze and semen-flecked image would be familiar to readers of the *New York Times*, *Newsweek*, *The Nation*, *Time*, *Esquire* and the *Saturday Evening Post*'. The light-footed Senator Murphy didn't miss the chance to up the ante, telling the media, 'they're built low to the ground so it's easier for them to stoop'. In an interesting defence to the bad publicity, one Angel told *Newsweek*: 'We're bastards to the world and they're bastards to us. When you walk into a place where people can see you, you want to look as repulsive and repugnant as possible. We're complete social outcasts—outsiders against society.' The media loved it.

Despite their national notoriety, all four were freed when a grand jury found insufficient evidence to proceed. There were some serious reservations about the stories of the two girls.

While their defence may have been costly, it was obviously money well spent. However, the success didn't bring an end to the criminal activities. With cash pouring in hand over fist, the gang just kept on marketing their wares. Why give up a good thing? And it was certainly better than working nine to five. As Barger said, summarising the Hells Angels' history for the *Los Angeles Times* (17 May 2001): 'In the '60s, we started gettin' in trouble. The '70s, we got into a little bit of crime and stuff. And by the '80s, we were all in prison.'

Barger made it to California's notorious Folsom Prison near Sacramento following his arrest in 1973 for selling thirty-seven grams of heroin. He commented that his breaking of the law may have had something to do with his exuberant use of cocaine. The judge wasn't that sympathetic and gaoled him for ten years to life. He joined the alumni that included Charles Manson, not Johnny Cash (despite the songs) and Timothy 'turn on, tune in and drop out' Leary, the pop-king of the acid counterculture. Leary and Barger were there at the same time, with Barger commenting that Leary was an informant. 'I don't like informants any more than I like policemen,' he later said. Barger was released in 1977.

The mystique and notoriety of the Hells Angels for that 'little bit of crime and stuff' continued to grow, and by the late 1970s the US government was gravely concerned about their criminal activities. To try and come to grips with the gang, they dusted off some racketeering legislation originally developed for use against the mafia. Unfortunately for the hapless government prosecutors, the case failed dismally. The prosecution cost around $15 million. Prosecutors screamed it was a miscarriage of justice, and Sonny Barger, by then head honcho of the gang, was reported to have thrown a party for the jurors. Angels 1, Government 0.

Federal prosecutors did have a brief stroke of luck in the mid 1980s when Barger and others were arrested for conspiring to violate federal law to commit murder. The murder in question involved plans to bomb the Chicago clubhouse of the Outlaws motorcycle gang. The Hells Angels had been asked to assist and had agreed. What they didn't know was that the FBI (Federal Bureau of Investigation) had a highly placed informant in the gangs, Anthony Tait, who had set up the plot as a type of 'sting' operation and who later gave key evidence. After a lengthy trial, Barger was again behind bars, this time in Arizona. He was released in 1992.

If nothing else, these prosecutions stirred the growth of the Hells Angels. By the end of the twentieth century there were thousands of members in chapters spread around the globe. The FBI considered them a 'criminal organization'. Canada agreed, with a supreme court judge finding, in 2005, that 'the Hells Angels Motorcycle Club as it existed in Canada was a criminal organization.' They are a wealthy global business with many legitimate fronts. However, law enforcement is on the record as stating they're also deeply involved in drug trafficking, weapons trafficking, extortion, murder and fraud. According to an FBI agent, they operate in a similar manner to 'network' marketing organisations, with each member having '9 to 30 criminal minions out there working for him all the time'. The Amway of crime perhaps?

Barger, not surprisingly, took a slightly more romantic view, stating, 'The story of the Hell's Angels Motorcycle Club is the story of a very select brotherhood of man who will fight and die for each other, no matter what the cause.'

2

THE BANDIDOS SADDLE UP

*Fuck the world. We are the people our parents
warned us about.*
motto of the Bandidos

Inspired, for want of a better term, by the Hells Angels'
activities in California reported nationally, and by Hunter
S. Thompson's 1966 book *Hell's Angels: The Strange and
Terrible Saga of the Outlaw Motor Cycle Gangs*, a rival gang
was formed. These were men who were drawn to what
Thompson described as 'a world most of us would never
dare encounter'.

The rival gang was the one with which young Stevan
Utah would later become enmeshed: the Bandidos. They
were formed in March 1966 in Galveston, Texas, by one
Donald Eugene Chambers. Chambers, like many before
and many who would follow, was ex-military. He had been
a marine and was then working on the docks. The name
came from the Mexican bandits of the late nineteenth
and early twentieth centuries, men who 'refused to live by
anyone's rules but their own'.

An early recruit, Royce Showalter, recalled that Chambers and some cronies had read Thompson's book. He said, 'all of us read it to get some ideas on what we should be doing, and then we looked at one another and said "hell, we can do a lot better than these guys".' Chambers recruited members from other biker gangs and bars around the waterfront. He was not a particularly civilised man. His daughter, with obviously misplaced reverence, said of him: 'When daddy started downing shots of Canadian Whiskey, people learned real quick that he was not someone to mess with. God, daddy was famous for the way he could throw a punch. And if that didn't work, he'd pull out his knife and start swinging that around too!'

According to Showalter, Chambers 'wanted as many badass bikers who cared about nothing except riding full time on their Harley-Davidsons. He wanted bikers who lived only for the open road. No rules, no bullshit, just the open road.' The Bandido motto was 'Fuck the world. We are the people our parents warned us about.' Just like the Hells Angels years before, many members came from the military, and brought with them planning skills, camaraderie and discipline. They also had a quaint initiation rite. Bikers always rode wearing the club vest. New members were told to put their vest on the ground and then his fellow members would urinate, defecate and vomit on it. The new member would then put the now moist vest back on, hop on his bike, and go motoring until the vest had dried.

Despite this charming rite, the Bandidos grew quickly. Unfortunately for Chambers, he wasn't around too long to enjoy the success of his new baby. While he didn't have much in the way of rules, the State of Texas did. Though the Hells Angels talked up their misguided yet vaguely honourable lifestyle, it was pretty obvious from day one that Bandidos were bad through and through, and Chambers had a very hands-on approach to their criminal enterprises.

In 1972 he and two colleagues were arrested for fatally shooting two drug dealers in El Paso. It wasn't rough frontier justice; it was just a drug deal that had gone horribly wrong. Prior to shooting them, Chambers made them dig their own graves. He also set fire to the bodies before burying them. The State of Texas sent him to prison on two consecutive life sentences. Local police hoped this would create a void that would see the gang disband. They were out of luck.

Into the vacant space at the top stepped Chambers' right-hand man, Ronnie Hodge. Like Chambers he was a tough man, a former marine and recruited from the docks. Hodge was built like a bear and held a similar view on life to that of Chambers. Under his guidance the gang rapidly developed both its criminal enterprises and its presence in the United States, Canada, Australia and Europe. Like Chambers, his reign would be brought to an abrupt end by a hefty prison term in 1988. In Hodge's case it was for bombing the home of a member of a rival gang.

THE BANDIDOS SADDLE UP

In January 1982 the FBI was reported to be 'investigating an international mafia style network allegedly involving
Australian bike gangs and their counterparts in the US',
for links with 'dangerous drugs, prostitution, extortion
and contract killings'. As one wit noted, 'a sort of Cosa
Nostra on wheels'. One of their prime targets in this
investigation was the Bandidos. The FBI noted that the
gangs were 'well-organised, sophisticated, with a regular
organization structure'. Other contemporary reports said the
gangs had 'built up a highly sophisticated crime network,
amassing tax shelters, high priced lawyers and an arsenal
of weapons including machine guns'.

A US Department of Justice report in October 2002
noted the corporatised Bandidos boasted 'elected and
appointed leaders at the international, national and local
levels. A president, vice-president, secretary and sergeant at
arms represent each level. The leaders establish and enforce
Bandidos rules, settle disputes, appoint new officers and
often co-ordinate criminal activities.' More worryingly, it
noted: 'earning membership is a lengthy, phased process
designed to measure a potential member's commitment
to the outlaw motorcycle gang' and they are 'recruiting
aggressively in an attempt to boost the membership'. The
Bandidos also have 'recently begun recruiting members
who have business and computer skills'. Membership also
meant being able to wear the coveted Bandido 'patch'.

In Australia, the Bandidos fired up their bikes in
August 1983. Their first clubhouse was a stately pile on

the waterfront on Long Nose Point in Louisa Road, Birchgrove, an elegant Sydney suburb favoured by lawyers and the wealthy end of the media and arts community. The Bandidos enjoyed a superb view of Sydney Harbour from their five-bedroomed, two-bathroomed Federation-style clubhouse. However, their interior renovations weren't in keeping with the architecture or the neighbourhood. The genteel pastel-painted dining room was redecorated in yellow, black and red colours, murals of blokes on bikes adorned many walls, and the living room was converted into a 'discotheque', even though disco was in its dying days. On one wall was the sign, 'If it's white sniff it, if it's female or it moves fuck it, if it narks kill it'.

Not surprisingly, the neighbours weren't too pleased and complained bitterly to anyone who would listen. Court action to have the bikies tossed out for 'disturbing the peace' didn't proceed. The bikies continued to enjoy their harbour views.

The original members of the gang had previously been members of the Comancheros. Police believed the founding Bandidos had fallen out with their former mates over drugs. The Bandidos took a loftier view, saying, 'the split from the Comanchero MC was caused by an ongoing rift between chapters and resulted in a total loss of respect for the mother club especially the founder and club president'.

The Comanchero view of the motivations for the split was a little different. Their president and founder was one William George Ross, born in Glasgow, known as 'Jock' and carrying the self-styled title of 'Supreme Commander'. Ross was a former soldier in the British army's royal engineers. His father had been in the army and his grandfather had survived the battles of World War I only to die on the beaches of Dunkirk in World War II. Ross immigrated to Australia in the 1960s. In 1973, while watching John Wayne strut his stuff in a Western called *The Comancheros*, a light clicked on above Ross's head. What a great name for a bike gang, he thought. By 1983 Ross had forty full members in his gang, and two chapters in Sydney. He'd also grown to be rather imperious and more militaristic. One gang member noted, 'If I wanted to march around the fuckin' backyard, I would have joined the fuckin' army'.

Ross blamed new members of the Comancheros for the split. By his rules, adultery was not on, drugs were not on, and drinking exuberantly on a Saturday night was pretty normal. He observed: 'Then new men came into the club with new ideas and new ways to make money. I just wanted to go away. I told them I just didn't want to be there. They wanted to deal in drugs and they were taking each other's women. They were breaking the rules I had running.'

The founder of the Bandidos in Australia was the former head of the Comancheros' city chapter, Anthony Mark Spencer, known as 'Snotgrass'. Like many of his compatriots in the United States, he was the product of a childhood spent in homeless children's institutions and boys' homes. He'd also had a brief stint in the navy. Spencer's woes had been around for a while and early in 1983 he and some cohorts travelled to the United States where they'd 'met Bandido members and were greatly impressed by their brotherhood and hospitality'. Spencer was also doing some shopping for Harley-Davidson parts which were still a bit scarce in Australia at the time. To form the Australian chapter, Spencer dealt directly with the then US Bandido chief Ronnie Hodge. The two met in Albuquerque, New Mexico. 'By giving us a charter in Australia, Ronnie Hodge paved the way for Bandidos International', the Australian Bandidos proudly boasted.

The FBI held a rather different view. They thought the Bandidos' new Australian chapter had been established, as one newspaper article noted, 'to give the gang access to Australian chemicals, banned in the US, that could be used in the production of amphetamines'. Snotgrass wasn't at all fazed about the FBI's view of things, or their investigations into allegations that the Bandidos were responsible for the murder of a US federal judge and an assistant US attorney in San Antonio, Texas. Nor was he concerned about investigations into allegations that the Bandidos were gun-running into Lebanon, which was then being torn apart by war.

According to William Marsden and Julian Sher in *Angels of Death*:

What interested him was that the Bandidos specialized in exporting stolen and used bike parts and were eager to open a supply line to Australia. They had also started secret laboratories for manufacturing speed. Hodge suggested that the Comancheros patch over [or merge in] to the Bandidos and supply the US club with base chemicals, primarily methylamine P2P, just as the Angels were doing. In return, the Bandidos would teach their Aussie brethren how to cook crank [a form of methamphetamine that is usually snorted].

The reference to the Angels harked back to the work of the Melbourne-based 'Speed King', Peter John Hill. Hill was one of the original members of the Melbourne chapter of the Hells Angels, joining in 1972. Tattooed on his arm was his quirky version of Psalm 23: 'Yea though I walk through the valley of the shadow of death I fear no evil because I am the evilist motherfucker who ever walked through the Valley.' Peter must have a rather long arm. He also had a large slice of business acumen, and saw drugs as a very nice little earner, particularly if he controlled both manufacture and supply. In the late 1970s he pioneered the trade in Australia by heading to California and meeting up with the Hells Angels in Oakland. A former Shell Oil chemist, Kenny 'Old Man' Maxwell was a dab hand at amphetamine manufacture and had passed his skills on to other club members who had become expert cooks. The star chefs included Jim

Brandes, who would eventually find himself in a spot of bother in Australia, Sergei 'Sir Gay' Walton and Kenny 'KO' Owen.

When Hill made his visit, Sonny Barger, Walton, Brandes and Owen were up on RICO (racketeer influenced corrupt organizations) charges. The charges would later collapse. Walton was also in prison on weapons charges. The Angels needed cash to fund their defence, and Hill was nicely positioned to help. He visited Walton in prison and Walton handed over the family recipe. In return Hill shipped the vital ingredient P2P, then illegal in the United States but legal in Australia, to the boys in Oakland. In a display of patriotism the Australians shipped the P2P in three-litre cans of a national icon, Golden Circle pineapple juice. They simply drained the cans by making two small holes in the side, and refilled them with the chemical. An estimated three hundred litres were shipped by surface mail between 1980 and 1982. It was enough chemical to make about US$50 million worth of speed. In both the United States and Australia, the Bandidos saw this as a pretty good model for a profitable business. A few little extras among the bike parts stood a good chance of going unnoticed by the prying eyes of Australian Customs.

But the Bandidos' start in Australia would soon become a bloodbath, even by Bandido standards. On 9 August 1984, with tensions running high between both gangs, three Comancheros were severely beaten by about fifty

Bandidos at the Bull and Bush Hotel in Baulkham Hills in Sydney's leafy north-west bible belt. Unfortunately for the Comancheros, the pub was a favourite of the Bandidos, and they didn't take too kindly to the visit. Two days later, peace in our time was shattered by a declaration of war between the two gangs. Ground rules were laid down during a conversation between the rival presidents, including no approaches or assaults at the homes of gang members or in public places. War being war, these ground rules were completely and violently ignored by all, including the presidents.

Ross, arrogantly and in hindsight very foolishly, believed the Bandidos were scared of him. In an interview he observed:

> They were on speed and speed brings paranoia. They had tried to flex their muscles in the Cross but they couldn't make it so they were forced out west, where I was. They thought if they could destroy us, the other clubs would back away and they could take over. I went to the police but they didn't want to know. They told me I was on my own. That is why we were armed; Bandidos were out to kill me.

Paranoia may not have been confined to the Bandidos.

On Sunday 2 September 1984, Father's Day, both gangs headed towards the Viking Tavern in Milperra in Sydney's working class south-west. Both gangs were armed to the teeth with shotguns, pistols and bats. It wasn't going to be a genteel gypsy tour. Instead, it was going to be the seminal day in the history of bike gangs in Australia, and an event that would bring world focus on this country. That day the hotel was to host a swap meet held by the British Motor Cycle Club. It was usually a pretty quiet place, a low-rise building with a large car park; as one local noted, 'the most likely cause of a fight around these parts is if you tell a group of St George [rugby league team] that you're for Canterbury'.

When the warring gangs converged on the car park, where about five hundred men, women and children were engaged in the swap meet, it was, as the *Daily Telegraph* aptly headlined, 'The day Mad Max came to a quiet suburb'. One eyewitness, who had been enjoying a cold beer in the hotel, said:

> I saw the bikies arriving with shotguns and baseball bats on the motorcycles. Something told me there would be big trouble but I didn't move. Then it happened: a shotgun blast echoed through the place and people screamed. I couldn't believe it—dozens of people were jumping off their cycles, raising guns and blasting away at each other. And groups of men were smashing the brains out of others at their mercy. I dived for cover under a long table and lay there with shotgun pellets singing through the air. The only sounds were people screaming in fear and agony and those awful gunshots.

By the time the police arrived and put an end to the battle, seven people were dead and many others injured. Two of the dead were Bandidos, four were Comancheros, and one was a fifteen-year-old girl, Leanne Walters, not associated with gangs but just someone who tragically happened to be in the wrong place at the wrong time. Jock Ross, a tough bugger by all accounts, ended up surviving a bullet in his brain and shrapnel in his chest. Murder charges were laid against fifteen Comancheros and twenty-seven Bandidos. Thirty-one would eventually be convicted of either murder or manslaughter in what would be, at the time, the longest and most expensive criminal trial in Australia's history. Snotgrass committed suicide in prison. Some of the participants would go on to see their children join the gangs and rise to prominence over the next decades.

Inevitably there was a rattling of sabres from the politicians. The New South Wales premier, Neville Wran QC, had a press release out the door for the next morning's media. The community was stunned by the magnitude and ferocity of the Father's Day fracas. A 'three pronged attack aimed at curbing and eradicating this type of totally unacceptable behaviour' was proposed. Gun laws would be tightened, police powers reviewed, and police patrols increased to deal with the 'elements' involved in the disaster. As with most of these fairly waffly 'initiatives' very little changed for the better, unless you were a Bandido, in which case you prospered.

By 1990 the NSW Police Tactical Intelligence Section had gone public with their worries. 'The similarity (of bike gangs) in their illicit (drug related) operations, their hierarchical organisation and their ruthless use of violent standover tactics has led to comparisons being drawn with the Mafia' they reported in the *Police News*. What they also thought was that the bikie gangs were decidedly nastier when it came to intimidating their enemies or anyone who might have a potentially adverse effect on the rivers of gold that drugs brought. They also kept their houses clean by preventing infiltration by 'getting the wood' on new members, as the police report said, 'throwing them into situations where they would have to commit offences which would land them in gaol—rape, armed robbery, serious assault and even murder'.

If all that wasn't disturbing enough, what really startled police was that the gangs had managed to set up a very slick counterintelligence operation, with the wives of gang members or gang sympathisers allegedly in key roles in bodies like the Roads and Traffic Authority, telecommunications providers, and the tax office. What police were loathe to admit at the time, but later evidence would prove, was that their own force was also a leaky old ship.

In 1993 the *Sunday Telegraph* quoted from a police intelligence report that stated 'the gangs are evolving along the same lines as the American and Canadian gangs did 20 years ago. Bike gangs are now rated as one of the major criminal problems in both countries.' The report went on to say, 'there has been a steady increase in biker related homicides in New South Wales, a gradual infiltration of cocaine as a popular drug among bike gangs, the biker movement organising itself into political lobby groups, the exploitation and use of propaganda'. Bike gangs in Australia were evolving on what FBI and other experts described as a five-stage descent from lifestyle rebels to serious criminals. Detective Sergeant Mark Loves, a specialist in bike gangs, reported:

> drug distribution (previously individually operated) starts to have a more prominent place in the bike gangs' activities. The club starts to show its wealth and flex its power. Gang wars (including murder) break out over disputed territories . . . they become involved in basic money-laundering businesses such as bike repair shops and tattoo parlours. Anti-social behaviour continues, but to a lesser extent.

The police were also more than a little worried that the gangs were playing hard ball by targeting police, something of a first in Australian policing. In the good old days crooks gave police a very wide berth, unless of course they were acting together, as in the not-so-good old days epitomised by Sergeant Roger Rogerson and the 'green light' to commit mayhem that he gave career crook Neddy Smith. Of the bike gangs' activities, the police commented, 'Experience in New South Wales is that the larger gangs regularly carry out surveillance of police premises and they always monitor police radio frequencies'. This just wasn't cricket, chaps. Ominously, and with considerable foresight, the police commented, 'there will be an increase in American biker gang members visiting Australia' and that Australian bike gangs 'have strong links with US groups'.

By 1997 the National Crime Authority, the forerunner of the Australian Crime Commission, in their investigation into motorcycle gangs reported that gangs were up to their armpits in 'the manufacture and distribution of amphetamines . . . cultivation of cannabis, counterfeiting, importation of firearms, tax evasion, money laundering and serious assault'. So much for the success of Neville Wran's three-pronged plan.

Into this nicely developing little business empire stepped Stevan Utah.

3

NOT QUITE A FLYING START

Promise me you'll be good.
Stevan Utah's mother

Seymour in Victoria is a pleasant little town at the base of the Tallarook Mountains, an easy hour's drive from Melbourne, north along the Hume Highway. Back in the nineteenth century it was a popular spot for bushrangers to drop by for a bit of rest and recreation, or robbery, depending on their mood. It is also a town with a place in Australia's military history. It was the home of the 7th Light Horse, and even the famed Kitchener of Khartoum popped in.

For a generation of Australian men finishing their schooling in the mid to late 1960s through to the arrival of the Whitlam Government in 1972, it was where they had their first, and often unwilling, taste of military life. Puckapunyal army base, just out of Seymour, was where many of the conscripts were sent for basic training before being shipped off to a war stimulated by the dated or just plain wrong notion of the yellow peril, reds under the bed, and the good old domino theory: Vietnam.

In the midst of this conflict, and more precisely on the first of July 1968, William John Hovey was born in Seymour. Almost two decades later he'd change his name to Stevan Utah, thus giving him forty-nine other states to dicker with if fluctuating fortunes dictated the need for another name change. We'll keep calling him Stevan Utah to keep things a little less tricky. Not surprisingly, his father was a career army man at the nearby base. His parents' marriage didn't last, and by the time young Stevan arrived, his father was off the scene. For Stevan, a peaceful and rather ordered life in rural Victoria was now swapped for the less certain environments of inner-city Melbourne, and then the hardworking city fringe hubs of Geelong on the western side of Port Phillip Bay, then Frankston on the eastern side.

At this point in its history Melbourne was enjoying the reputation as Australia's crime capital, which may not really have been deserved. Crime in Sydney was booming, as it had for many years. However, the dazzling combination of the gloriously corrupt New South Wales Premier Sir Robert Askin, and what coppers humorously referred to as 'the best police force money can buy', kept the bad smell well away from the public's nose. Melbourne, just like it has in more recent times, had all manner of unpleasantness happening publicly.

The notorious and soon to be aurally challenged Mark 'Chopper' Read was shooting and thumping his way into a long stretch at the infamous Pentridge Prison. Italian gangs were doing great business in all manner of mafia-like enterprises. Some members of the Painters and Dockers Union—once described by Frank Costigan QC in his investigation into their activities as having 'attracted to its ranks large numbers of men who have been convicted of and who continue to commit serious crimes . . . violence is the means by which they control the members of their group. They do not hesitate to kill'—were busily involved in turf wars, drug-running and the occasional assassination.

In loftier quarters, eminent lawyer Barry Beech and his inquiry had come to the conclusion that the Victorian police had a real problem with corruption. Hector Crawford and his pioneering TV production company weren't helping Melbourne's reputation as the crime capital either, turning out a supply of cop shows featuring stern pork-pie hat wearing detectives chasing louts and other ne'er-do-wells around the tram tracks of the southern capital. Oh, and Carl Williams, who would grow to be the plump face of Melbourne's gangland in the new century, was taking his first steps. He spent his formative years in the working-class suburb of Broadmeadows, home also to Ford Australia and Victoria's favourite son, Eddie McGuire, game show host, football fan and one-time chief executive of the Nine Network.

For those keen on psychology, Utah's early days are a feast. In hindsight it is a minor miracle that he made it to his majority. His first significant memory is being told, at the age of four, about the death of his grandmother, who he visited in Melbourne's now fashionable inner-city suburb of Richmond. Back in the early 1970s it was anything but fashionable. He vividly remembers their house and their kindness, which sounds very much like the memories of a child for whom kindness wasn't regularly on the menu. He remembers sitting at the kitchen table in Frankston with his mother saying to him, 'Billy, now Grandma is gone, promise me you'll be good'. Grandma died of natural causes. While he doesn't remember his response, he recalls, 'The question my mum asked upset me, it has haunted me all my life. Not a week goes by without me reflecting on it.' In one of those quirks of memory, like the way baby boomers can remember where they were at the time they heard of the assassination of J.F. Kennedy, Utah remembers he'd been watching 'Bulldog' Brower in *World Championship Wrestling* on a flickering black and white television set when the bad news about his grandmother was delivered.

The family, which included his mother, brother and sister but minus his natural father, would live in the Frankston area for most of Utah's childhood and adolescence. Despite its pleasant bayside location some forty kilometres south of Melbourne, and its status as the gateway to the more prestigious playground of the Mornington Peninsula,

Frankston worked hard, and had some rough edges. Many local kids had brushes with petty crime and knew how and when to fight. Pampered city kids they were not.

Utah's father was an explosives expert in his army career, and Utah obviously inherited some talents from his father, particularly manual skills and an affinity with chemistry. Especially things that explode. At around the age of eight, Utah made his first bomb. While most kids just toy with a bit of petrol scavenged from their father's lawnmower, Utah took a creative step further. He found that if he added the petrol to chlorine, a gas was produced. The more fuel, the quicker the appearance of the gas. His first lesson in how things could go wrong was when he significantly increased the volumes and found himself gasping for breath. As he noted, 'Fuck me, I almost killed myself a couple of times'.

The brush with potentially deadly gas didn't quell his inquisitive mind. He soon moved on to creating 'cannons' using a 44-gallon drum, compacted newspaper and rather a lot of motor mower fuel. The trick was to get the paper so saturated that when combustion occurred the contents of the drum would be hurled into the air. With fiery newspapers keeping the lawn in check, the need for mowing was probably reduced.

Aside from dickering with explosives, Utah's eighth year gave him his first taste of violence, and an example of the interesting morality he'd show for the rest of his life. He would always be a fan of the underdog, and a bloke with a strong protective streak. That year, Utah alleges his older brother, in a curious display of family loyalty, encouraged a fellow student to beat him up. Not an unusual occurrence in the schoolyard, but Utah recalled, 'I was like an animal, I was so damn dirty about the fight, I kicked him in the balls and jumped on him'. Unfortunately for Utah, the tables soon turned and he ended up with a serious beating, much to his brother's amusement.

What his brother didn't understand was that something had kicked over in Utah's brain. Retribution for the brawl was swift and brutal, with Utah cutting off the head of his brother's pet mouse and placing the remnants in his brother's school bag. Very *Godfather* part 1. Retribution for the retribution came two days later. The hot water service at their home was arthritic, so the bath was first filled with very hot water, and then cold water was added before you jumped in. Utah had just finished the first part of the operation when, he alleges, his brother crept up behind him and shoved him into the bath full of scalding water. He recalls his mother's reaction was to start belting his brother while her second husband scooped him out of the bath, covered him in a sheet and rushed him to the hospital. It was months before the burns had healed sufficiently for Utah to walk again. Mother wisely decided that young Stevan would benefit from a brief respite, so he was dispatched to his father for a few months. At least it took some of the heat out of the anger he had directed at his brother, however the brother is still absent from Utah's Christmas card list.

His mother's second marriage didn't survive either. Though Utah was fond of the new father in his life, things took an unexpected turn when he found his stepfather 'cuddling' a close male friend. His mother later found the cuddling was a little more intimate than young Utah had observed and so father mark 2 was given his marching orders. Father mark 3 would arrive a short time later. His mother was not a woman who wasted time, it would seem. Utah also grew accustomed to regular surname changes.

With his burns finally healed, physically at least, Utah added sport to his pastimes. He took to athletics, and particularly cross-country running, with a vengeance. Australian Rules football was also on the menu, with him joining the local Karingal club coached by Paul Brereton, brother of the famous player Dermott. Almost a brush with fame.

His physical pursuits unfortunately seemed to have little effect on the speed of his temper and fists. At the age of ten he had his first run-in with the police. Fortunately for Utah, the copper was an old-style man who firmly believed that a decent clip around the ear or a kick in the trousers would sort out most erring kids. The target of Utah's anger on this occasion was a boy who was 'the baddest bastard in the school'. The bastard's crime was to attempt to sexually molest the sister of one of Utah's friends. She was a 'wonderful girl, innocent, defenceless, sweet', and a girl who, along with her sister, was terrified of her violent father. When Utah saw what was going on, he 'watched for thirty seconds, and it felt like a whole day in my memory. I don't know why but I kicked him in the face and he was holding his mouth.'

The girl escaped, but Utah pressed on: 'I kept kicking him and stomping on his face. It was easily the most savage beat down I have ever given anyone and it went on for a quite a few minutes. I remember kneeling down next to him and punching him in the nose, it was bleeding, and rubbing dirt in his eyes and leaving him there.' The police collected him from his home later that night and administered a bit of old-style summary justice.

It didn't work. Two days later and back at school, the victim of the beating, who was sitting a few desks away in the classroom, told Utah he was 'fucked'. Bad mistake. Utah responded immediately. He said: 'So I jumped him in class and kept smashing his head off the wooden desk. The other kids were running out of the room etc. I was out of control.' The classroom emptied, and a teacher pulled Utah off the boy and chucked him out of the way, breaking Utah's wrist in the process. More unheeded lessons from the police followed.

Retribution again popped up, though this time a little less violently. Utah crept into the garden shed at the boy's home, doused his much loved mini-bike with petrol and lit a match. A quirky sidebar to the story is that ten years later, the girl to whose rescue Utah raced became his lover for a short period.

Utah's dismal childhood did not improve when he began high school. Ballam Park Technical School was suited to practical matters rather than educating the intellectual elite. Utah was a bright kid who inclined more to the woodwork, graphic design and engineering opportunities offered by the school. But in his first year there he rushed to the aid of a schoolboy being set upon by a local gang, 'the bowling alley boys'. A disagreement with a teacher led, almost inevitably, to the teacher finding his pride and joy, an MG sports car, with a brick through the window and scratched paint. Being on Utah's bad side was not a healthy occupation. It was rather curious, however, that when his sister was molested by a neighbour during a vacation with their grandmother in Geelong, nothing happened. Utah still loathes the man, but the man and his property remained intact.

Even though poised on the brink of puberty, Utah was one of those poor kids who still wet the bed. His mother, not the most sympathetic of creatures, told him he 'wasn't normal' and carted him off to a psychiatrist. The treatment did little for his self-esteem, and even less for his notion of 'normal'. His mother was given a plastic sheet to put on his bed, and the sheet was wired up so that at the first hint of moisture, young Stevan would be given a mild electric shock.

Utah's head was also wired up with electrodes. The doctor then put him through a series of tests. Utah remembers the experience vividly: 'They made me do this test, I don't know what it is to this day, but they had all the electrode things on my head and then made me keep breathing in and out as hard as I could. I remember getting angry and the doctor asking me to do it harder and harder, and the more I started to feel like I was going to faint, my eyes were open but everything was black.' Mother didn't help the traumatised son much either, forbidding Utah's friends from staying over because she was embarrassed by his bed-wetting. Unsurprisingly, the treatments didn't work, and Utah simply grew out of the problem by the age of sixteen.

It comes as no surprise that the school soon worked out that young Utah was in need of a bit of help. He was deemed a 'special needs student' and given a mentor. He wasn't a truant, but issues of self-control were significant. What the school rather sensibly thought that Utah needed was a strong and reliable male role model in his life. Though he bonded with one of his mentors, it was a little too late. At the age of thirteen he was running with a group of local kids who at best could be described as wild. Some would go on to notable criminal careers. Their stock in trade was burglary, car theft and the occasional sale of fairly mundane drugs like marijuana. Crimes of opportunity rather than planning. In a pattern that would be repeated in his later life with the Bandidos, Utah ran with the gang but didn't get too involved in their criminal adventures.

Everyone's first sexual encounter tends to be memorable for good reasons or bad. Utah's maiden outing was with a school-mate, one Roberta Mircieca. Like Utah's, her life had been a rough one. Her father, a truck driver, had been burned to death in an accident when she was eight months old. She was one of eight children whose mother had poor taste in the common law husbands who came after the death of her husband. At the age of eight, she was a kid who roamed the Frankston streets, and at eleven she was made a ward of the state. At seventeen she was married and a mother.

The fling with Utah was a brief one. Utah is a little old-fashioned in his reticence to elaborate, but he did comment that he didn't try the experience again for a while. 'If my heart's not in it, my cock's not in it'—crude, he admits, but accurate. He later observed, 'I like friends and going shopping with girls and knowing I can be me'.

Roberta Mircieca's luck went from bad to worse when her marriage failed in 1995, leaving her with the children. She soon found herself in the arms of the former Broadmeadows supermarket shelf stacker, Carl Williams. By that stage Carl had had his first brush with the law, being imprisoned in 1994 for conspiracy to manufacture amphetamines. On appeal, the judges gave Carl the benefit of the doubt and reduced his ten-month sentence to six months, noting, 'there are grounds appearing from the material before us to suggest that he has excellent prospects of rehabilitation'. What the judges didn't know was that Carl's father was an active drug dealer. In January 2001 Roberta married Carl and, within the twinkling of an eye, the boy described by his mother as 'very well mannered, always did what he was told and never answered back to his parents' would be the most feared man in Melbourne gangland, and eventually in prison for murder. One of the most sensible decisions Utah ever made was to avoid Carl and his 'Carlton Crew'—too mad, he reckoned.

Things really hit the fan for Utah when he was told he had to repeat year ten at school. He was fifteen and the special needs program wasn't working. After football practice one day he'd stopped for three beers with his mates before wandering home. It was the last straw for his mother. She took her problems to the child welfare authorities and Stevan was declared 'uncontrollable'. This was a popular course of action at the time, and had been so for many years. It was the fate that befell teenagers involved on the edge of crime who didn't want to mend their ways, children who refused parental guidance and discipline, and sometimes a convenient way for parents to abrogate their responsibilities. All too often, it was a combination of all three.

Utah's first move was not into some type of foster care. Instead it was a nine-week stint at Turana Youth Training Centre in Parkville in the centre of Melbourne and a long haul from Frankston. The centre has now closed, but in its declining days Bernie Geary of Jesuit Social Services said of it, 'Conditions are absolutely archaic, dangerous, dirty and unhealthy'. It certainly wasn't an appropriate place for people who Geary described as the 'most troubled kids in the state'.

It wasn't Utah's first experience of life under lock and key either. Throughout his childhood he'd been a regular visitor at prisons in Victoria, dragged along by his mother and grandmother to see his Uncle Andrew, a convicted rapist. One of the unlovely venues the child was taken to was Melbourne's Pentridge Prison, a chilling example of prison culture more in line with the times of Queen Victoria than modern Australia. Pentridge was also the site of the country's last lawful execution, that of Ronald Ryan in 1967. Inside the walls was the notorious H—'hell'—Division, temporary home to some of the worst criminals. It was known as Victoria's darkest secret, and a place where solitary confinement was a welcome respite from social interaction with Her Majesty's other guests.

According to Utah, his uncle spent three years, three months and thirty days in Pentridge, some of it in H Division. Among those doing time with Uncle Andrew was Kevin Taylor, who was on a lengthy stretch for manslaughter. His victim, gunned down outside the Druids Hotel in South Melbourne in 1973, was Pat Shannon, member of the justly infamous Painters and Dockers Union. The demise of Shannon was apparently the upshot of a factional dispute. On the other side of the argument was union heavy Billy 'the Texan' Longley, who paid Taylor $6000 to bump off Shannon. Longley would end up in the dock with Taylor.

Taylor would later gain notoriety as the man who trimmed the ears off celebrity gangster and fellow H Division inmate Chopper Read. Contrary to his tough guy image, Taylor reckoned Chopper, during the trimming, 'screamed and cried like a little bitch'. Some decades later, Taylor would also spend a bit of time in a cell with Stevan Utah. Utah would leave with his ears intact.

Though Turana was a harsh place, one officer showed Utah some compassion, telling him he thought the punishment certainly didn't fit the crime. He also saw in Utah someone with a spark of humanity worth saving. Instead of slinging Utah in with some of the hard cases, he put him in with a young man who was a victim of child abuse. Apparently the young man's parents had taken turns in beating him, at one point tying him by the neck to his bed. Utah commented: 'I recall all the bruises on him. They were all over him, his neck marks are still sketched in my mind. He was so submissive and pathetic in his own way.' Utah soon became his rather vigorous self-appointed protector, recalling: 'He was scared of his own shadow, scared to shower, just scared. I didn't know what post-traumatic stress was then; I was rather fearless in many ways as a kid.'

One evening at dinner Utah showed his mettle, and rather fierce temper:

There was this big kid that came to pick on him during dinner one night. I stabbed him in the hand, sick shit really. I should have cut his throat for trying to be a tough ass and picking on him. The dude was just trying to eat, like fuck he was hungry and was trying to eat, he was in there because his parents always tried to kill him. I'll never be able to get that out of my head. He put his hand on the table to stand over him. I remember watching him come over trying to stare me out as he came over. I just kept eating, didn't say a word, I just put my knife through his hand.

Of his ward he said:

I think this kid went through enough, like seriously I felt for him, sympathy and compassion, it was bad at the time. I had issues comprehending how this could happen to an innocent child. This wannabe tough guy was not going to fuck with this kid. I deterred his aggression, end of story. Coincidentally, I found out a few months later [the child] was returned to his parents by child services and the father beat him to death.

After nine weeks of poor food, communal showers, cells without toilets and a fairly undesirable peer group, Utah was sent back to the Frankston area, but not to his school or his mother. He was collected by his remaining grandmother, who wasn't too happy. As Utah put it tactfully, he'd 'never seen her that pissed, she was like a dog with rabies. I remember looking at her, I felt so guilty. I let her down, I cried that night. I was thinking of my Uncle Andrew.'

A condition of his release from Turana was that he lived at the Bayside Hostel in Frankston. It was a place for kids aged between twelve and eighteen described as having 'multiple complex issues', which was a pretty accurate description of Stevan Utah. The day after arriving there he found work in a timber mill a twenty-kilometre daily pushbike ride away. For Utah, the stint behind bars had the effect of focusing him on a chance for a decent future. He said:

I was so determined, I remember it was hard to find work but I did the following day in a timber mill. Same day I had my first cigarette too. I was working for a company called Pre Cut Timbers in Japaddy Street, Mordialloc. My boss was a guy called Doug Fortune, he owned the place. He treated me well; he knew I was a kid with somewhat special needs. My immediate supervisor was a guy named Barry Cash and he lived in Noble Park. He used to take me to the Sandown Greyhound races with him. You know what? For all I was involved with back then and what occurred, I was still a kid and an innocent kid.

He kept up his interest in football and, as he put it, 'I was like a man possessed. I have never played so hard. So much rage, it was my vent, and yes, in hindsight sport was my vent.' He worked hard, played sports hard and looked toward a future. A local policeman who had kept a paternal eye on him asked him what he'd do when he turned seventeen. Utah told him he was going to move interstate. He wanted to put his past behind him and become a soldier. The policeman responded, 'Well, give it your best shot and don't let them beat you'.

Not long after, he very sensibly declined an offer made by two mates. The lads had broken out of the Turana facility and were keen to flee the Melbourne scene and go interstate to start new lives. Unfortunately their mode of transport was a stolen car and, even more unfortunately, on the way they encountered the police. The ensuing high-speed car chase saw innocent bystanders killed as the stolen vehicle ploughed into a shopping centre. When he was released from prison one of the lads, Utah's best friend from his school days, promptly decided to improve his cash flow by pulling a stocking over his head, arming himself with a screwdriver and trying his hand at robbery. Not a good criminal, just a busy one and one that landed straight back in prison. Utah commented, 'Turana was a place where you met people. It was all he knew.'

Utah reflected that if it hadn't been for some education, a job, football and a desire to make something of his life, there could easily have been a third person in that car. At last for Stevan Utah, the discipline and routine of his time under formal control had worked . . . for a while anyway.

4

THE ARMY WILL MAKE A MAN OF YOU

*If you can't exercise some self-discipline we'll give
you some force discipline.*
Australian Army saying

The disaster of his friend's attempt to escape the life
rattled Stevan. Though he freely admitted to being
immature and lacking in wisdom, he also knew that
it might just be time to move on. His destination was
Albury, a few hours further along the Hume Highway from
Seymour. Albury is a major regional city with an army base
on its outskirts. Utah's estranged father, now a twenty-year
veteran of the regular army, was stationed there.

With a good work record at his prior employment
Utah immediately found full-time work at a local mill. He
got to know his father, and his father's army mates. After
helping the daughter of one his father's friends with her
reading, the friend suggested Utah come to work for the
army as a civilian contractor. His task consisted of clerical
work and inspections relating to stored ammunition and

explosives at the 3-11 Supply Company, an ammunition dump just on the edge of Albury. This suited his affinity with explosives: 'I got a lot of hands-on stuff, fusing grenades, inspecting rapier missiles and charge bags on 105 rounds, small arms ammunition. Yes, it was good shit!' Fortunately for Utah and his colleagues, he was a little more careful this time than he had been as a child.

Six months later, in 1985, Utah joined the Australian Army as a soldier. The troubled young man took to army life quickly and responded, at least in the first few years, to the responsibilities and discipline. As Utah eloquently put it, 'The army had a saying back then—if you can't exercise some self-discipline we'll give you some force discipline. I didn't have too much self-discipline, but I found it pretty quick.'

Originally he worked in the ordnance corps as a clerk, but the army spotted his knack for mathematics and wanted to make him a pay clerk. Utah had other ideas. He wanted to follow in his father's footsteps: 'I wanted to be an ammunition technician, blow shit up, and the only way I could do that was as a minimum rank corporal.' Utah sat through a battery of psychological tests and evaluations and topped them. Former Lance Corporal Utah reckoned he was the youngest ranked person in the force at that time to get through the tough tests.

He became an expert in emerging military computer technology, all manner of explosives, and weapons from a simple handgun through to rocket launchers. One of the tasks of these experts was the destruction of weapons that had passed their use-by date. In December 1989 he was at Townsville's Lavarack Barracks, one of the largest military bases in Australia and home to the Ready Deployment Force and Utah's 3rd Combat Engineer Regiment. It was also where Utah became friendly with a fellow munitions expert, Shane Della-Vedova. Della-Vedova's name would come to national infamy in April 2007 when he was arrested and charged with twenty-one offences relating to the theft and sale of ten M72 anti-tank weapons. These handy little armour-piercing rocket launchers are a popular item with terrorists. At his bail hearing the prosecution alleged that only one had been recovered.

During this time Utah made one other friend who would give him some interesting introductions in the years to come. That man was an army cook we will call 'Cleaver'. He was involved with the Bandidos and his brother, whom we will dub 'Brutus', was one of the club's leading lights in south-eastern Queensland. It was a friendship that would take Utah to some of the highs, including chemical highs, and lows of his life.

In Townsville, Utah looked up to, and was on fairly close terms with, the commanding officer of his unit, Colonel Ken Gillespie—at the time of writing, Lieutenant General Ken Gillespie AO DSC CSM and Vice Chief of the Defence Forces. Of Gillespie and their relationship Utah said: '[he] was the sort of person that if you walked past him and you felt his aura you would give the man respect. Not because he was a colonel but because he was a man who deserved it. Soldier first, gentleman second . . . always treated me with respect.' Respect was a little something that had been missing in Utah's life and something he'd craved and would go on, quite reasonably, craving. Perhaps it was a major motivator in what was to come years later too. Utah would subsequently comment that Gillespie was the most memorable male influence in his life.

Sadly for Utah, it was in Townsville that he started to unravel emotionally. He suffered bouts of depression—not a handy situation for someone handling explosives. In 1990 he was accused of rape by a female soldier of lower rank. Though the allegation was proven to be false and swiftly dismissed, it had a dreadful effect on the already emotionally and mentally taxed soldier. The army doctors, not unlike his childhood psychiatrist, didn't bother to get to the root of the problem. They responded by trying to smooth the rough edges with drugs, in particular two old favourites: Valium and Mogadon. They also tried a brief and unsuccessful bout of hospitalisation. As Utah said: 'In the early nineties people didn't understand mental illness. I was simply burnt out from working too hard, I was so anal as a soldier. They gave me a medical certificate and told me to go home and masturbate.' Utah ended up, as he put it, 'a pill head'.

His problems grew in September 1992 when he and a fellow soldier went motoring. Utah was asleep in the back of the car when his mate decided to play with a gun they'd brought along. He opened fire on a defenceless paddock in the countryside outside Townsville. The bad news was that a cow was in the way. Utah and his mate were arrested for killing the cow, and stealing and possessing a weapon without a licence. Utah knew that it was only a matter of time before his condition made him a hazard to both himself and those he worked with.

At his wits' end and contemplating suicide, he turned to his commanding officer, Ken Gillespie, and asked him to demote him and approve his discharge. Gillespie saw the mess Utah was in and allowed him to leave the army of his own free will. Gillespie's only request of Utah was that he seek treatment from a local doctor in Townsville in whom Gillespie had faith.

In the dying days of his army career Utah travelled back to Melbourne and was discharged at the District Support Unit, Watsonia, on 10 November 1992. He didn't linger in Melbourne, instead headed back to Townsville. Luckily for him, he soon found the local general practitioner recommended by Gillespie was just the right fit for him. He credits the doctor with saving him from going completely around the twist. Both the doctor and Utah recognised that suicide was a distinct possibility. They talked at length, and it was painfully obvious that Utah's reliance on pills was a large part of the problem. The doctor's treatment was a little unconventional. He gave Utah a prescription for 'Valium or diazepam—the little would say I bought them off a guy at the pub and there was nothing they could do about it. They would say you need permits and I would say I don't. I was getting $2200 per scrub python and they were sold for $4500 in Victoria.'

'You have to understand I rationalised this in a particular way and you may not agree or like it but that's the way I was. Driving on the road in Queensland I would come across huge pythons on the road. They were going to get killed on the road. I'd collect them and take them to the southern states', Utah says.

More money could be made if a reptile was pregnant. An animal like a tiny pink tongue skink would sell for $300 each in a southern state but if that animal was pregnant, because Utah got a cut of its offspring, he could make as much as $3000 from each animal. The common Queensland green tree frog could be collected a thousand at a time. Once Utah got them into Victoria and South Australia he got between $20 and $30 on the domestic market. Overseas customers back then would pay as much as $120 for one frog, and even today they sell for around $60 to $80. There is no room in this illegal trade for the morally squeamish.

Utah is contemptuous of the more ruthless criminal dealers who he claimed would often destroy habitats to get just a few valuable birds or eggs. One notorious Queensland crime family would chainsaw down entire trees to get the eggs or the lucrative foxtail palm seeds, much sought after overseas.

Another group making their way into this lucrative business in the mid 1980s were the outlaw motorcycle gangs, including the Bandidos. Two of those bikie players in tropical Far North Queensland at this time were James 'Bingey' Douglas and the gang's national president, Michael 'MKK' Kulakowski. Their paths were soon to cross with Utah's. 'MKK was a high-end dealer', Utah recalls. 'He often got insanely valuable items from me and they went all over the world. Back in those days a black-headed python fetched US$50 000. A gravid animal was an easy 200 to 250K.'

MKK had first popped up on the radar in the late 1980s and early '90s when New South Wales wildlife officials were tracking the smuggling of the superb parrot in Young on the state's south-western slopes. MKK was never caught because he always seemed to be one step ahead of the rangers. 'He was named by an informant as being a player in the Young smuggling but we never got near him. He was very clever and very hard to track. And there were obviously people helping him with information from inside our investigations', one now retired New South Wales National Parks and Wildlife officer recalled.

Utah tells a story that illustrates just how internationally connected Kulakowski had become in the wildlife smuggling trade. He told the Bandidos president how he wanted a pet spitting cobra—a snake indigenous to the Indian subcontinent, and not available anywhere in Australia:

yellow fuckers!' Along with the prescription came good advice: 'When you crave you have to fight, they will only last a few minutes, but fight as hard as you can.'

The advice worked. Utah commented:

> Well, it was only a couple of years ago that I threw that full packet of diazepam out. Yep, I kept it all those years like a trophy. I beat the bitch, I went back, played football for Townsville, went running eight kilometres every day. It was a horrible experience, I lost everyone's respect, my friends, my dignity, everything. When I think back I find it strange seeing myself lying in the foetal position for hours at a time, couldn't get out of bed and crying all the time. It was horrid, I feel stupid now.

On 16 December 1992, he fronted the Townsville Magistrates Court to answer the charges arising from the dead cow incident. His good service in the army kept him out of serious trouble and he was fined and put on probation. No conviction was recorded. Just as well, as Utah had been toying with joining the Victoria Police. With his military record, he would have been a shoo-in. There goes that need for strong male role models again. However Utah had another plan in mind.

What neither the court nor Gillespie knew was that Utah, aside from fighting his own demons, had been developing a nice little earner in the wildlife smuggling trade. This is a trade that rates third in profitability after trafficking in drugs and weapons.

5

FROLICKING WITH THE FAUNA

He was very clever and very hard to track. And there were obviously people helping him with information from inside.
Retired New South Wales National Parks and Wildlife officer

When Vincent 'Vinnie' Teresa waddled down the steps of a flight from the United States to Sydney in 1977, he was incapable of making an unobtrusive entry. Few onlookers could have doubted his mob credentials, for he was an incongruous sight in 1970s Australia. Fat Vinnie was the mafia don from central casting. Endowed with the corpulent jowls of a hearty pasta eater and the greasy pores of a man who devoured salami and provolone by the kilo, he hailed from the Boston branch of the Patriarca crime family, and was a former number three in the New England Mafia.

He was also a rat-cunning and devious con-man who boasted that he used loaded dice on his high-value casino customers. He also had an eye for an opportunity. The history of his foray into industrial-scale Australian native wildlife smuggling is instructive to tell in some detail here because Steve Utah warns that the same failures Fat Vinnie exploited thirty years ago are still making Australia's efforts to combat wildlife smuggling an international laughing-stock.

Thirty years ago, as Fat Vinnie explored criminal opportunities in Australia, Steve Utah was a schoolboy in Frankston, Victoria. In between selling golf balls back to the local golfers for $1 each, Utah and his school friend Matt Ryan were catching snakes for fun. Utah did not know it at the time but that skill was to propel him into his first flirtation with organised crime, for Utah was to follow in Fat Vinnie's footsteps years later; and he confirms that outlaw bikie gangs are heavily involved in the illegal trade, a fact that has gone unacknowledged until now.

How Fat Vinnie Teresa got to Sydney alive back in 1977 is anyone's guess, because there was a prudent, self-preserving reason for him to be looking for a business opportunity far from New England. Four years earlier, Fat Vinnie had given very dangerous evidence against the notorious 'chairman of the board of [American] organized crime', Meyer Lansky. Lansky enjoyed the formidable reputation of being possibly the most dangerous criminal mastermind in the United States, notorious also for his claim, alleged to have been recorded on an FBI bug, that the crime syndicate he masterminded was more powerful than US Steel (a boast later borrowed by the scriptwriters of *The Godfather Part II* movie).

Fat Vinnie's evidence against Lansky had been a debacle for the FBI. Vincent testified that he assisted Lansky in a massive tax fraud, organising gambling junkets from the United States across to London casinos. He told Lansky's trial jury that the huge cash skims off those profitable forays went straight to Lansky, and tax was not paid. For the feds this was a classic Al Capone tax fraud, to be able to pin such a minor tax matter on a don like Lansky. But Lansky was not stupid. His wife credibly testified that on the occasions when Fat Vinnie said Lansky had met with him, her husband was in fact in hospital being treated for a double hernia. The case crumbled—and, not surprisingly, Fat Vinnie was looking for somewhere far away from Lansky's New England operations to make a quick profit. Australia beckoned.

He was in Sydney using a passport in his new FBI protected witness identity of Charles Cantino. Since he had testified against fifty mafiosi across America, the feds seemed to have naively assumed that Fat Vinnie would go into quiet retirement under a new name, living on the US west coast. But old habits die hard and Teresa was playing his protectors for fools, looking overseas to diversify his criminal gains.

Incredibly, in light of his notoriety as a former organised crime figure, Teresa had actually been invited to Sydney in 1977 to give evidence to a citizen's committee fighting drugs and the illegal gambling industry. But it was an act of appalling naivety by the good burghers of that town, for Fat Vinnie's greedy eyes quickly saw the potential for a big profit opportunity Down Under. He probably gave up on casinos when he saw just how much of a green light the illegal gaming joints across the city already got from then corrupt senior police and politicians.

The obvious alternative market was for heroin, to feed the growing demand among local addicts who washed up in the wake of the cashed-up American soldiers hooked on heroin who had visited Sydney on R & R from the Vietnam War days. It also didn't take Vinnie long to hear from his Sydney gangster buddies—people like standover thug Lennie McPherson—about the huge potential in wildlife smuggling. Fat Vinnie fell into the incredibly lucrative world of Australian native wildlife smuggling in much the same way that Stevan Utah would do nearly a decade later. There was just so much easy money to be made.

There was a short-term problem, though. As celebrated crime reporter Bob Bottom revealed in 1985, when Australian federal police found out about the presence in Australia of Fat Vinnie, aka Charles Cantino, they moved to deport him very quickly for not disclosing his criminal record. But this was not before Vinnie had linked up with someone he just happened to know: well-known restaurant and nightclub owner Alfred Ferdinham Franz Schmid, who had migrated to Australia in 1955 and was refused Australian citizenship twelve years later on criminal and security grounds. Schmid became Fat Vinnie's

Aussie connection in the wildlife smuggling racket and it probably helped that his popular restaurant, Freddie's Weiner Wald in Sydney's Kings Cross red-light strip, was a favourite haunt of detectives from the New South Wales police's Criminal Investigation Branch. As they wolfed down their schnitzel, not one of them noticed a thing.

US laws at the time did not ban imports of Australian native birds, even though Australian laws banned their export. A cockatoo or galah bought in Australia for a dollar each could be sold in the United States for $3500 each. Private zoos in Japan and South-East Asia were paying up to $2 million for a pair of breeding koalas. Rare peregrine falcons were reportedly being smuggled to the Middle East for the pleasure of Arab sheiks who were prepared to pay $60 000 each.

Under the blind eyes of corrupt police, quarantine staff and airport workers, Fat Vinnie thrived. It was a cruel trade, but Vinnie's syndicate was not motivated by ecological concerns. Native birds were drugged with Valium then packed, sardine-like, into wood and wire mesh cages measuring less than a metre square. The cages, each containing at least thirty birds, were then trucked to Cairns in containers marked 'computer parts'. From there they were freighted in a light plane to the United States via South-East Asia. In August of 1979 alone, a consignment of nine hundred birds worth more than $2.2 million was seized—a rare bust that was to be Fat Vinnie's undoing.

At the same time there were also allegations that employees at the secret US base at Pine Gap, near Alice Springs, were smuggling birds out in the giant USAF Starlifter transport planes, which were not subject to Australian Customs clearance. Everyone was in on the game, including—it seems—some politicians. In 1979, the Queensland parliament heard allegations that four politicians appeared on police narcotics bureau files, in cases linked to drugs and native wildlife smuggling; and that a convicted Sydney heroin trafficker had named the then Queensland justice minister as being in the trade.

The Queensland parliament was told how planes smuggled drugs into Australia and took native birds out. In a delicious touch of irony, the charter plane company implicated was also chartering its aircraft to Australian Customs to provide aerial surveillance. Locals reported seeing a DC3 aircraft flying into isolated airstrips in northern Queensland. It allegedly brought in drugs, picked up a load of birds, flew to Jakarta to get a clearance and then flew to San Francisco.

Despite an initial flurry of excitement from the parliamentary allegations and promises from police and politicians to crack down on the illegal trade, nothing much happened to stop what was for all an increasingly profitable enterprise. The idiocy of the weaknesses in the laws was obvious. Two Americans were caught cutting down a tree in a Western Australian country district to get the birds and the eggs of a black-tailed cockatoo. They were also caught red-handed with twenty-nine galah eggs, three long-billed corella eggs and two from a red-tailed black cockatoo. They stood to make US$175 000 if they raised all the young birds to adulthood. They were fined just $1200, plus costs.

One of the tricks of the trade was for the wildlife thieves to don wetsuit pants and rubber boots to help them climb the high trees. A climber could earn big money—$50 000 per week during the nesting season around Cooktown, in Far North Queensland, from August to October. Eclectus parrots, glossy black and palm cockatoo chicks were taken from nests as high as eighty metres up a tree. By June 1990, the *Australian Magazine* reported that the eclectus parrot population in that state's Iron Range region had dropped by 80 per cent since smuggling began in the early seventies.

One of the great scams was for crews on visiting foreign cargo boats docking at ports like Cairns in Queensland to switch Australian native birds for birds which customs had listed as being on board on the boat's arrival in Australia. Customs would write down that there were a dozen birds and they would be switched for valuable ones while the boat was in port. If a dozen birds were eventually checked out of the country, no-one noticed the switch. The 'switcheroo' was an easy way to move $100 000 worth of birds out of the country. In those days the customs service launch was based in Cairns, and it was the only sea patrol in Far North Queensland. The only other regular patrol consisted of coastal surveillance aircraft but they did not liaise with state fauna and wildlife police.

Another scam was for smugglers to load suitcases onto commercial aircraft flying overseas with the help of corrupt intermediaries in the baggage handling area. The smugglers were also using forged ticket tags to get the suitcases, loaded with birds, onto the planes. It emerged that the syndicate had access to the secure baggage area and they would just walk in and put the luggage on the belt. It was no coincidence that more than a few bikie gang members were—and still are—baggage handlers at major Australian airports. Being a member of a bikie gang does not bar a person from gaining the vital security clearance to work in a secure airport area.

Things were getting so blatant two years into Fat Vinnie Teresa's Australian operations that his getting busted was only a matter of time; and it was his schnitzel-cooking Kings Cross sidekick, Alfred Schmid, who was his undoing. In June 1979 Schmid pressed a $100 bribe into the palm of an airport clerk at Sydney's Mascot airport. But that clerk, young David Stewert, was an honest kid and he chose not to ignore the twittering noises coming from a container marked as computer parts and addressed to Oregon, USA. The crates inside were broken open to reveal seventy-seven sulphur-crested cockatoos and ten galahs. Purchased on the black market for about $9 each, they would have fetched nearly half a million dollars in the United States. Confronted with this evidence, even police began investigating.

Then in August that year, an alert motel owner provided the incriminating link between Schmid and Fat Vinnie. The motelier was suspicious enough of one of his guests to listen in on a call to a Seattle address, which turned out to be a number used by Fat Vinnie for his bird importation business. Vinnie, aka Charles Cantino, was busted.

In 1979, he rolled to the FBI once again, admitting his role as the head of a massive international drug and bird smuggling ring linked to Australia. One of the Sydney men charged was a customs officer and a former member of the federal police's Narcotics Bureau. But even with Fat Vinnie's conviction in December 1984, not a lot changed on the wildlife smuggling front.

6

A NICE LITTLE EARNER

The things that man got away with were just incredible.
Stevan Utah

By 1989 Stevan Utah found himself in the middle of the honey pot. He was by then based at Lavarack Barracks in Townsville, with the Australian Army. Extremely physically fit from his army training, Utah loved getting out into the tropical rainforest in Far North Queensland on training exercises; and his growing love of the native wildlife he spotted on patrol burgeoned from a collector's interest to an eventual illicit career on the side.

At that time the country's wildlife laws were a hodge-podge mess. Hundreds of thousands of Australians held permits to sell, breed and raise local wildlife, but it was illegal under the wildlife protection laws to export for commercial purposes any native animals (apart from fish). Exceptions existed for the legitimate transfer of wildlife between zoos. It meant that any Australian wildlife found overseas had to have been bred from stock exported prior to 1982, or else it was deemed to have been smuggled out of the country illegally.

Utah soon realised, on his trips back to visit family in Victoria, that the black and white letter of the law was not exactly being heeded by many wildlife dealers in New South Wales and Victoria. Moral and legal concerns aside, as long as he could get whatever they wanted out of Queensland, there was money to be made. Free trade guarantees in the Australian constitution also meant it was a bit of a grey area whether anyone selling native wildlife could be prosecuted unless it could be proven they had actually done the smuggling over the border, no matter what state wildlife and fauna protection laws said. 'We would argue that you don't need permits to possess native wildlife once they're out of Queensland where you could be busted, and the police and wildlife officers in other states would more often than not back off', Utah recalls.

For that reason Utah made a specialty of dealing in native animals that were indigenous to an area outside the states where he sold them. For example, scrub pythons, Australia's largest snakes, are rarely found outside a three-hundred square-kilometre area in Queensland and Utah faced serious criminal charges if he was ever caught taking them from the tropical jungles of that state. Absurdly, once he got them across the border it was hard to touch him. 'Once I got them out of there I was fine. Possession of a snake was not evidence that I had stolen them out of Queensland. We would say I bought them off a guy at the pub and there was nothing they could do about it. They would say you need permits and I would say I don't. I was getting $2200 per scrub python and they were sold for $4500 in Victoria.'

'You have to understand I rationalised this in a particular way and you may not agree or like it but that's the way I was. Driving on the road in Queensland I would come across huge pythons on the road. They were going to get killed on the road. I'd collect them and take them to the southern states', Utah says.

More money could be made if a reptile was pregnant. An animal like a tiny pink tongue skink would sell for $300 each in a southern state but if that animal was pregnant, because Utah got a cut of its offspring, he could make as much as $3000 from each animal. The common Queensland green tree frog could be collected a thousand at a time. Once Utah got them into Victoria and South Australia he got between $20 and $30 on the domestic market. Overseas customers back then would pay as much as $120 for one frog, and even today they sell for around $60 to $80. There is no room in this illegal trade for the morally squeamish.

Utah is contemptuous of the more ruthless criminal dealers who he claimed would often destroy habitats to get just a few valuable birds or eggs. One notorious Queensland crime family would chainsaw down entire trees to get the eggs or the lucrative foxtail palm seeds, much sought after overseas.

Another group making their way into this lucrative business in the mid 1980s were the outlaw motorcycle gangs, including the Bandidos. Two of those bikie players in tropical Far North Queensland at this time were James 'Bingey' Douglas and the gang's national president, Michael 'MKK' Kulakowski. Their paths were soon to cross with Utah's. 'MKK was a high-end dealer', Utah recalls. 'He often got insanely valuable items from me and they went all over the world. Back in those days a black-headed python fetched US$50 000. A gravid animal was an easy 200 to 250K.'

MKK had first popped up on the radar in the late 1980s and early '90s when New South Wales wildlife officials were tracking the smuggling of the superb parrot in Young on the state's south-western slopes. MKK was never caught because he always seemed to be one step ahead of the rangers. 'He was named by an informant as being a player in the Young smuggling but we never got near him. He was very clever and very hard to track. And there were obviously people helping him with information from inside our investigations', one now retired New South Wales National Parks and Wildlife officer recalled.

Utah tells a story that illustrates just how internationally connected Kulakowski had become in the wildlife smuggling trade. He told the Bandidos president how he wanted a pet spitting cobra—a snake indigenous to the Indian subcontinent, and not available anywhere in Australia:

I had a taipan and death adders but I wanted an Indian cobra. I told him and he took just two days to get me one. When he came back with it, he let the fucking thing go in my lounge room. It just sat up making this stupid fucking noise. They are scary things because they spit their venom which blinds and disables their prey. I had it for twelve months and I was getting scared I would be busted with it. I called him Charlie the Cobra. I also had Terry the Taipan. I loved them.

Utah learned not to ask too many questions about how Kulakowski and other high-end dealers got their animals out of the country undetected, but he remains in awe of how MKK got away with it: 'MKK was the master of camouflage. That cunt. The things that man got away with were just incredible', Utah said.

It is clear that Utah knows a lot more about the illegal international trade in wildlife smuggling than he is prepared to admit even now. He claims, for example, that members of a US mafia crime family were involved in one huge transaction in which sixteen koalas were smuggled out of the country to an overseas zoo. Utah names the Australian end of that criminal operation as a dealer we will just call 'Jim', who used to live near him. Jim, ironically, was a trusted Queensland prison officer and he still has a taxidermy business on the side, which has no doubt provided great cover for his illicit smuggling activities. 'He was a big-time mafia-linked, international wildlife smuggler. He got smacked [arrested] once in his life and got away with it for years,' Utah recalls.

By the time he quit the military in 1992 and moved into wildlife trafficking full time, Utah had become something of an expert on the bugs that were killing too many of his and other dealers' animals. He is a cited author in the scientific publication *Herpetofauna*, produced by the Melbourne Zoo. He also befriended another wildlife aficionado who was to become one of the world's most loved and, sadly as things would turn out, much mourned TV nature show hosts, Steve Irwin—the original Crocodile Hunter.

Steve Irwin and Joe Bredl, the older brother of Rob Bredl, nicknamed the Barefoot Bushman who owned a wildlife park at Queensland's Airlie Beach, were having trouble breeding the popular huge diamond pythons that many tourists flocked to see. It was Stevan Utah who figured out how to breed these sensitive reptiles in captivity. 'A lot of people say they have done it but they've just got them from the wild. I did it', Utah explains:

> They are very hard to breed. The temperature and humidity are linked to ovulation. I know this is going to sound weird but I watched them for six weeks. I just kept changing the temperature slightly, and the humidity. Not that snakes turn me on but she was looking like a sexy bitch. When a female is ripe to have a baby they are looking great. It's so obvious

when a woman is ready to breed. That's what I do. I watch things.

By 1990, he claims, he had one of the most extensive private collections held outside of any zoo or wildlife park in the country, allowing him to make his money by breeding animals in captivity rather than stealing them from the wild. And that brought him squarely into the sights of the Queensland government rangers, who had started microchipping and DNA testing animals as a way of stopping the illicit trade. They, not surprisingly, were suspicious about where Utah had got his breeding stock from in the first place. Utah says he did not 'do' birds because of the cruelty and high death rates that resulted from sealing them inside containers for transport interstate and overseas. But his huge collection of reptiles, in particular, was making him a prime suspect for the wildlife and fauna investigators and—as it turned out—undercover investigators from the United States who were secretly monitoring the illicit trade in North Queensland.

It was in 1993 that Utah was approached by two Americans in a Townsville watering hole called the Toucan Bar in the popular Criterion Hotel. It is a classic, sprawling old Queensland colonial hotel with four-metre-wide verandahs looking out over the city's Strand Esplanade and with breathtaking views across the shimmering blue bay to Magnetic Island and the Coral Sea. One of the Americans was a police agent from the US Federal Bureau of Investigation, and the other an officer of the Drug Enforcement Agency (DEA). The US investigation was prompted by the realisation that vast amounts of illicit drugs were flowing into America along the same illegal pipelines as the stolen wildlife. Utah was friendly with one of their targets, a Florida-based dealer called Tom Crutchfield.

Crutchfield was one of the biggest breeders of rare and endangered wildlife in the world and he had already been charged with trafficking protected Fijian iguanas when the two US officers spoke to Utah in Townsville in 1993. That case, though, was to fall apart within months. It turned out the US prosecutor who was running the case was a rival herpetologist and a former customer of Crutchfield's company. The court found his gross misconduct in running the case against Crutchfield was serious enough to warrant throwing the charges out. The reason the FBI and DEA were back in Townsville was to shut Crutchfield down once and for all.

The money that could be made from smuggling native wildlife and fauna was huge. In 1995, Australia's largest parrot, the palm cockatoo, was being sold in the US for as much as $100 000 a pair according to the Australian Nature Conservation Agency. The birds have a distinctive curved beak and brilliant red and black feathers and grow to more than half a metre long. They are also listed on CITES—the Convention on International Trade in Endangered Species of Wild Flora and Fauna—as being in danger of extinction. In 1995 there were only about five hundred of them in the United States and, because they are extremely difficult to breed in captivity, authorities believed that birds and eggs were being smuggled from Australia. Galahs could fetch up to $15000 a pair, red-tailed black cockatoos up to $20000 and sulphur-crested and Major Mitchell cockatoos up to $10000. Shingleback lizards sold for $1000 each and diamond pythons for up to $10000. Goannas were $4000 a pair. Prices like these were being openly quoted in US catalogues and at wildlife fairs, including Australian tiger snakes at US$675 each. Quite why someone would want one of the world's deadliest snakes in their living room is difficult to understand but the market did not exist in a vacuum. People wanted to buy these creatures, and they were not too worried about the legalities of procuring them.

The American authorities needed someone to make an example of and Crutchfield's prominence as a reptile breeder and dealer made him ideal. That's why, over a cold XXXX beer on the verandah of the Criterion Hotel, they were now putting the squeeze on Utah, who explains:

Nobody knew where I was getting these things. They knew I was in the middle of a circle and I wasn't directly involved in international smuggling. They knew I was involved in it in Australia and, once it was moved interstate, some of it was then going overseas. They didn't know that part. Their investigation was around breaches of the international CITES convention on wildlife trafficking. Back then, wildlife smuggling around Australia wasn't seen as such a bad thing.

The Americans wanted Utah to tell them who all the local dealers were. And to Utah's shock and surprise, it was clear they had been watching him very closely indeed. To show him how much they knew, they put a series of photographs down on the bar table. They showed Utah on the job in the bush, stealing wildlife:

They had been doing surveillance on me for months. They had one photograph of me in the bush with my knapsack carrying two pillowcases out of Tully Gorge. I can remember what I was doing that day and it's funny. I had been hired on a special request to get four native scrub pythons. The requirement was that they had to be a minimum of fifteen feet long each. They got a photograph of me, I've got this fucking snake under my feet. I didn't know I was being photographed. When you are wrestling pythons on the edge of a croc-infested waterway you don't worry about whether you are being photographed. They had been watching me for almost twelve months. They could name things about me that only I knew.

One of the problems the Americans faced was that there were clearly corrupt elements inside the Australian government agencies that were meant to be prosecuting the wildlife smugglers. In 1997, *Sun Herald* newspaper journalist Fia Cumming reported allegations linking federal and state government officials with wildlife smuggling and at least four mysterious deaths of people suspected of involvement in the illicit trade. A former policeman, Bill Zingelmann, and rainforest nursery owner Adrian Walker made detailed claims about smuggling and murders in North Queensland to the senate inquiry into commercial utilisation of native wildlife. They warned that wildlife smuggling was a huge racket linked to the drug trade. They also alleged that a number of unsolved deaths were linked to this racket.

Whatever one thinks of Utah's flouting of native wildlife laws, anyone who knows him from that time speaks highly of his care for the reptiles he bred and sold. He began complaining to Queensland's anti-corruption agency, the Crime and Misconduct Commission, about the activities of one of the state's environment and heritage wildlife officials in North Queensland. This official was keeping large numbers of rare and endangered reptiles at his private home, and Utah complained that, in breach of wildlife protection laws, the official had illegally given two highly sought-after black-headed pythons to dealers. It was cheeky of Utah to cause grief for such a powerful alleged rival, whom Utah claims was misusing his official status to harass Utah out of the profitable trade.

As wildlife expert Ray Hoser revealed in his book *Smuggled 2*, an investigation into corruption in Australian National

Parks and Wildlife services, there was more than a whiff to this official's harassment of Utah that indicated he wanted the clever young reptile breeder and dealer's rival operation shut down. One scientific project, backed by a number of institutions, including the curator of the Queensland Museum, asked the Queensland Environment and Heritage Department to issue Utah with a scientific permit to collect and study blue-nosed monitor lizards on Cape York because he had an extraordinary knowledge of just where to find them. But the permit was vetoed by the official.

Then things began to get very nasty. Utah came home one day to find his house broken into and his much loved American pit-bull terrier dead in the backyard. It had been beaten to death, and his computer, books, documents and disks stolen. To this day he believes it was corrupt individuals within the Queensland national parks service who were responsible. Weeks later he was charged with possession of stolen snakes—a charge that was to fail when the two Crown witnesses flown to Townsville from Victoria refused to give evidence or answer questions on the grounds it might incriminate them. As Ray Hoser's *Smuggled 2* records, a wildlife official from Victoria, Tony Zidarich, told the court that he had seized the snakes on the basis that they were stolen. He admitted: 'I now know that not to be the case.'

Then, on 13 January 1994, Utah came home one night to find a man waiting in the darkness under the stilts of his Queensland house. As he approached, the man fired at him with a pistol and then fled. Utah was grazed by the ricocheting bullet but otherwise unharmed. His photograph and the story of the attack were splashed across the front page of a Townsville newspaper—publicity which dried up the support he had long enjoyed from many reputable universities and scientific institutions: 'No-one in academia wanted to know me after that. They were scared off by the home invasion and they heard the FBI was sniffing around me.'

At the time he suggested publicly to a Townsville newspaper that it was a warning to him to back off because he had complained about corrupt government officials to the Queensland anti-corruption watchdog. But he says now that he believes the real reason was because some of those officials and illegal wildlife dealers knew he had spoken in secret to the American DEA and FBI officials investigating Crutchfield and other big international buyers of their stolen animals. 'It was to shut me up, for talking to the Americans', Utah claims:

> I am sure that home invasion I got shot in was to silence me. I remember speaking with another high-profile drug dealer and smuggler back in those days, he came up and stayed for a weekend. He laughed so hard, he said someone put a hit on you and you bashed him. I never found out who he was, but a few people made some very cautious remarks about how he won't bother you again.

What the Americans discovered, and Utah confirmed, was that government wildlife officials were often improperly seizing snakes off of licensed dealers on false pretexts, and claiming the reptiles had died. Ray Hoser alleges many corrupt officials were then shipping the same seized creatures overseas for a profit—but deliberately sterilising them with x-rays as they left the country to ensure no breeding stock could be raised overseas. There was also a curious and concerning pattern to a series of unexplained thefts at the private homes of snake owners who held the necessary permits with the local government agency. The suspicion was that corrupt wildlife officials were misusing their knowledge of those addresses to steal the reptiles for profitable export overseas.

While there is no doubt that what dealers like Utah were doing was illegal, the official hypocrisy on wildlife protection was also appalling. Utah heard how a then Queensland member of state parliament, who was also a mango grower around the town of Ingham in Far North Queensland, was seeking a permit to shoot four million rainbow lorikeets that were threatening his mango crop. A study showed he would have to use twelve million shotgun pellets to kill so many birds, and that amount of lead in the environment would be a serious contamination issue. At the time the state government charged a fauna royalty on exporting lorikeets of $12 a bird to licenced bird catchers. Utah says he had a contact in the United States who was prepared to buy

100 000 of these birds: 'I was prepared to pay the state royalty and get these birds sold overseas rather than kill them. The shoot went ahead. Those birds were fucking killed', he complains. 'Rainbow lorikeets, to this day, are rare in North America. There are none in Canada. It's encouraging the illicit trade. There's still huge money in it. Crims do things for a reason—revenge or greed. The best way to shut down the illegal trafficking is to legalise an export industry, but that's against the interests of a lot of people.'

Even today, in the country where Utah is now in hiding from those who want him dead, he regularly sees Australian native animals on sale illegally: 'Black-head pythons are pulling $3000 each on the black market. If I had ten Woma pythons today I would have $10 000 an animal overnight, no trouble here.' The huge irony is that what was Utah's undoing was his decision to go straight as a breeder rather than continue illegal trafficking. 'The second I became legit [as a breeder of native wildlife] I got squashed.'

In 1997 the World Wildlife Fund commissioned a report on the issue by intelligence analyst Don McDowell. He argued then that the only way to end the illicit trade was to manipulate the market by controlled commercial breeding which met proper standards, thus broadening the genetic pool and eliminating criminals. As Utah told writer Ray Hoser about the Queensland situation back in 1994: 'Up here, you can't get a snake unless you have a licence. You can't have a licence unless you have a snake. You can't get an import permit unless you have an export permit, and you can't get an export permit unless you've got an import permit. So, how's the system meant to fucking run?'

Tom Crutchfield eventually did a deal with the US authorities, pleading guilty to one count of smuggling. Sentenced on 19 April 1995, he was fined US$3050 and gaoled for five months. The sentence was deliberately agreed by both parties to commence after 15 August that year in order to allow Crutchfield to attend the International Reptile Breeders' Expo in Orlando, Florida.

As if to prove Utah's point, that prosecution did nothing to deter Crutchfield or other big-time international dealers. In 1999 Crutchfield was sentenced to thirty months in prison after he pleaded guilty to seven counts of wildlife trafficking. He was caught up in a massive operation against wildlife smuggling which targetted a Malaysian known as 'King Rat', Anson Wong, who ran what the BBC's *Panorama* programme described as the biggest global animal smuggling operation that has ever been broken. Anson ran a private zoo in Malaysia and he had used Crutchfield and other contacts to smuggle the almost extinct komodo dragons from their one remaining island in Indonesia. He had ruthlessly targetted the most endangered and rare of animals and shipped them around the globe. Almost a decade on, the illegal trafficking continues—and thrives.

A NICE LITTLE EARNER

At the tail end of his smuggling career, Utah would have a job with the federal government's Australian Quarantine and Inspection Service (AQIS) but it would not be a government job for life. He was soon to move on to other criminal enterprises, vastly more dangerous than wildlife smuggling.

7

FROM CONTROL TO KAOS

*They have achieved in forty years what the Cosa
Nostra took eighty years to achieve.*
Canadian Criminal Intelligence

Many people, and particularly those who choose to
lead their lives dabbling on the fringe, will encounter
someone who will change the course of their life, and
not necessarily for the better. For Stevan Utah, then a
disenfranchised ex-soldier and noted fauna fancier, one of
those moments happened on the New England Highway
in northern New South Wales. It would take him into the
heart of the Bandidos.

It was 1995 and Utah was heading south to Melbourne
with the ute well stocked with reptiles destined for the
export market. As sometimes happens on that stretch of
road, the weather changed dramatically and the rain came
down in buckets. Visibility dropped and Utah was dog
tired, so sheltering for a while seemed like a very good
idea. The prospect of ploughing on through the murk,
combined with a full and pressing bladder, persuaded

Utah to find a safe spot on the roadside for a bit of 'stop, revive, survive'. Having an accident with a ute full of unhappy and occasionally poisonous passengers might also be a little more problematic than usual.

In what was a quirk of fate, Utah pulled to the side of the road where two lads on motorbikes were sheltering. They'd been having trouble with the conditions, so Utah gave one his pair of sunglasses to help shield his eyes from the rain. Utah commented:

> They were standing under a lean-to sheltering from the rain. Harley helmets don't give any protection for the eyes in the rain and he couldn't see it was so strong. So I gave him my sunnies to get him down to the roadhouse where we could get a feed . . . I wasn't scared of him which probably impressed him. We had a really clicky relationship from the start. He probably thought this little prick isn't scared of me for starters.

They pressed on again and met up at a roadhouse a little further down the highway. A friendship developed from that single act of kindness. One of the bike-riding gentlemen was Ricky de Stoop, a former competitive body builder and sometime male stripper. The other, and recipient of Utah's sunglasses, was 'MK Kaos'—a reference to the *Get Smart* TV series. His real name was Michael Kulakowski, and he was the president of the Bandidos in Australia and a wildlife smuggler. He and Utah would soon discover their mutual interests.

For someone like Utah, Kulakowski could have been the strong role model type from central casting. Their relationship would give Utah the credibility to gain access to the inner sanctum of the exclusive club that was the Bandidos. Utah was very taken with Kulakowski from the word go. He was a bloke that, while looking the part of the tough bikie, had an aura of strength, ability and leadership. A man very different to the Bandidos founder in Australia, Anthony 'Snotgrass' Spencer, and a much classier and more dangerous type of human to the first Bandido, Donald Chambers. Kulakowski was no white trash, disgruntled ex-military man.

Kulakowski was the son of Robert Kulakowski, a former Australian Army officer and a crack pistol shot who, when he left the military, moved to the western fringes of Sydney and became a very successful businessman. His military career followed a family tradition, with forebears as commissioned officers, including a general, in the Polish and Russian armies. His rebellious son grew up on the family's dairy farm near Penrith on the western fringe of Sydney. Michael's passion for horses saw him mustering cattle in Queensland and Tasmania.

It was almost inevitable that young Michael would follow in the family tradition. He joined the Australian Army and was trained at the Kapooka Recruitment Training Battalion, graduating at the top of his class. Service in artillery units around the Sydney area followed. The problem the younger Kulakowski found with army life in peace time was that it was boring. This was a man born to fight. He lasted just twelve months. Leaving the army he kicked around, joining his father's business and rubbing shoulders with corporate Australia. Boredom quickly set in again and he enjoyed a brief career as a champion bull rider in rural rodeos. By the time he'd reached his mid twenties the bucking bull had been swapped for a throbbing Harley-Davidson and the camaraderie of a bike gang. A different sort of army, and one not necessarily at peace.

In 1984, the year of the Milperra Massacre, Kulakowski joined his first bike gang, the Nomads. He'd soon move to the Bandidos. Robert Kulakowski caught the spirit of many bikies when he said of his son, 'Our family is quite a close one, but he was looking for something outside. He was seeking more independence and the routine of running a business was not really his cup of tea. But it was not the motorcycles—it was the association, the camaraderie, that sense of belonging he was looking for.' In an interview with the *Sunday Telegraph*'s Warren Owens, Robert Kulakowski observed: 'Michael was not an ordinary bikie. He can't claim an underprivileged family background for a start. Basically he was an adventurer, bored with society. And a leader—not a redneck. He had great leadership qualities.'

His father was pretty much on the mark. Kulakowski and his abilities were credited with taking the Bandidos from the fairly undesirable gang of thugs that came to prominence because of the Milperra Massacre to what police claimed in 1994 to be one of six bikie leaders involved in 'a pact to take control of criminal money spinners like drug distribution and violence for hire crime at the expense of the lesser gangs as necessary'. Not surprisingly this eminence was denied by the gang leaders, as well as Kulakowski's father, who noted that his son 'should have been rich if he was involved with that'.

Kulakowski did live with little in the way of the trappings of the wealthy. His house was in Cranebrook in Sydney's hardworking far west, he had a Mercedes and a bike on lease, and a hefty mortgage. A man of some charm, he also had a few children here and there for which he paid maintenance. He reckoned he traded second-hand cars for a living. Unkind people might think that a supply of second-hand cars registered to other people might also be handy to keep police surveillance on its toes. He was also a truly hard man. Utah commented:

> MKK was a migraine sufferer and could really lose the plot when he had a migraine. He was tough, the toughest fucker I have ever met in my life. I remember when Bull came into the Bandido clubhouse saying 'fucking Bandidos' and 'I will kill all you cunts!' Bull was at Milperra and his brother Shadow was shot and killed there. Bull was one big boy. Kaos walks up to him casually as Bull has ten Bandidos hanging off his arms and says, 'I have a gun, cunt, do you? Now

get out of my fucking clubhouse!' Kaos didn't flinch,
Bull's eyes showed fear!

You know though, I don't think MKK would
have hesitated to shoot him for a second. It was like
fucking business. Bull pissed his pants and left. I'm
standing six feet away during this thinking this dude
is about to die. MKK had like this aura. It was like
fucking business.

Police reckon that Kulakowski was the driving force that
gave the Bandidos a stranglehold on the rapidly expanding,
and very popular, amphetamine market, along with a
healthy sideline in marijuana growing and distribution.
Under his leadership, the Bandidos added to their strength
by taking over some of the small clubs, acquiring members
with charming nicknames like Fess, Hombre, Crab, Fats
and Bingey, all of whom would come to play significant
parts in the life of Stevan Utah. The acquisition of hard
men, and the expanding drug market, meant Kaos was in
the perfect place at the right time to take his band into the
exploding market for drugs like ecstasy that were sweeping
through the club scene. What also wasn't known at the
time Utah and Kaos met and developed their friendship
was that Kaos had forged strong bonds with Bandidos in
the United States and Europe.

In August 1989, the Bandidos had set up shop in
Marseilles, France, selling Harley-Davidsons to the like-
minded. As happened in Australia, the Harleys were

exported to France by Bandido-operated enterprises
in the United States. It was good business for the
clubs because the bikes would sell for around twice
their US value. A nice little earner, and the cynical
might wonder what was stashed in the bikes' numerous
cavities, like tyres and fuel tanks. The French Hells
Angels didn't take kindly to the Bandidos' arrival. They
shot the club vice president dead, and wounded two
other members. Things escalated, with the Bandidos
launching a massive recruitment campaign to support
its battle for territories. The campaign drew to it all
the old favourites like Neo-Nazis, soccer hooligans,
skinheads, members of smaller gangs and the usual mob
of disaffected young men.

With life getting very tricky for all, an accord was
called for. The gang leaders met in Paris in 1993 in what
William Marsden and Julian Sher in their book, *Angels of
Death*, called 'the motorcycle gang version of Munich',
and the authors quoted Churchill's insightful comment,
'Europe had peace now; it would get war later'. Chillingly
accurate. Peace lasted until December 1993, when the
Bandidos tried to expand into Denmark. It triggered what
Marsden and Sher called 'The Great Nordic War'. Their
leader, Jim Tinndahn, according to one Hells Angel, 'filled
his club with dirt. Tinndahn recruited all that garbage, and
such a sick mixture produces more sick things.' Of course,
no-one gave much credit to the Hells Angels' attempt to
scale the high moral ground.

The first death of the war came in a hail of bullets fired by Hells Angels on 13 February 1994 in Helsinborg, Denmark. The Bandidos, to arm themselves for the war, took to raiding military depots and ended up with a cache of pistols, rifles, grenades and shoulder-fired anti-tank weapons. The Bandidos weren't subtle in their choice of weapons. The battle was on.

Over the next three years, around four hundred violent incidents would occur. There would be eleven murders, seventy-four attempted murders, and numerous people just gone missing. The stupidity and futility of the battle drew their American counterparts into the fight. The US leaders of both gangs set to the task of striking a lasting peace. One of the key people involved in this task was Australian Michael Kulakowski. He flew to the United States in July 1997 and was pivotal in brokering the peace that ended the Great Nordic War. Peace was declared on 25 September 1997, when Danish Hells Angels president Bent 'Blondie' Nielsen shook hands, on Danish national television, with Tinndahn. Of course both gentlemen were dressed in full bikie regalia for the event.

Both Marsden and Sher assert that the peace Kulakowski had been instrumental in forging was not merely an end to fighting. They neatly summed it up as 'the two clubs got down to the business of making money. What police didn't realise at the time was that this was more than a peace accord. This was a precursor to a Versailles Treaty, where the two gangs carved up Scandinavia and eventually all of Europe.'

Some later reports also suggested there was a second purpose to Kulakowski's visit. That year the Victorian police had managed something of a coup. They'd got two 'wingclippers', a colloquial name for police investigating bike gangs, into the Ballarat chapter of the Bandidos. Their brief but effective sortie led to information that saw raids in four states, with twenty gang members and their associates arrested. The head honchos in the United States were very keen to chat about that breach of their internal security.

Kulakowski didn't have much time to bask in the warm glow of his success. On 9 November 1997, he and Ricky De Stoop, along with Sasha Milenkovic, the Bandidos sergeant-at-arms, and fellow Bandido Robin David went for an evening's entertainment at a nightclub called Blackmarket in the seedy inner Sydney suburb of Chippendale. The club, in what had once been an elegant and substantial Victorian-era building, had opened in the 1980s as an upmarket place called Saffrons, named after Abe Saffron, 'the King of the Cross' and perhaps the most colourful of all of Sydney's colourful identities. It was named after Abe by its owner, the rather cheeky and less colourful Eric Jury. Abe didn't find the joke amusing. On the outside, the club was painted a drab black. It looked old, scruffy and rundown. When business sagged, the club chased the downmarket drug-enthused dance crowd and held once a week an S & M venture called Hellfire, which provided cheap thrills for the well-heeled. Unfortunately, they also ended up with the Bandidos and their hangers-on.

On that November evening, Kulakowski, Milenkovic and De Stoop went to the basement of the nightclub to meet with Rebels members Constantine Georgiou, an unemployed lad from beachside Bondi, and the Taylor Square (then the heart of Sydney's gay community) tattooist Bruce Malcolm Harrison. The story the Supreme Court would later hear was that the meeting was to discuss control of the nightclub's door. Control of the door was the key to controlling the drug trade in the club. When Georgiou and Harrison arrived, they spoke with a Mr Culshaw, a Rebel member and off-duty Blackmarket doorman. Culshaw got a key for the club's basement and gave it to the lads.

A little later they had a word with Milenkovic, and they all arranged to meet shortly afterwards in the basement. Around 1 am witnesses saw the men variously depart toward that dank and dusty basement. About five minutes later, even above the din of the nightclub, shots were heard. Witnesses saw Georgiou run from the basement door followed by Harrison, who was waving a gun. Both men took to the street, with one witness noting that Harrison, who was looking a little like the assassin from central casting in his long black overcoat, which was a bit unseasonable for Sydney in November, had his hand down the front of his trousers 'as if concealing something'. The witness avoided the joke, but it is fair to say it was not a friendly weapon. Georgiou hopped into the driver's side of his silver Porsche, not a bad car for someone described as 'unemployed', and Harrison slid into the passenger seat. The Porsche took off at speed.

Unluckily for our assassins, someone called the police on the 000 emergency line around 1.15 am and they were quickly on the scene. In a stroke of bad luck a police car had been passing in any case and took off after the fleeing Porsche. Sensibly the police decided that chasing a Porsche in a police car through the inner-city streets wasn't too clever an idea, so they backed off and followed at a safe distance.

When the Porsche got to Crown Street in Surry Hills, just a couple of kilometres from the scene of the crime, the vehicle slowed and 'a metal object' was thrown from the passenger side window. The police didn't miss it, later finding a Smith and Wesson pistol and, nearby, a Beretta pistol. Just around the corner they found the Porsche dumped in Hutchinson Lane, a quiet little street surrounded by light industry and a smattering of upmarket apartments just moments from the glare and bustle of Taylor Square. Georgiou wasn't anywhere to be seen, but Harrison was. When he tried to break free of the police he was deftly handcuffed and carted off for questioning. Police also found a pair of bloodstained gloves on the front seat of the Porsche.

In a recorded interview on 10 November Harrison did not bother with the truth. He told police that he was drunk when he and Georgiou arrived at the club. He'd headed off to the toilet and then to the cloakroom when his hand was hit violently. He saw it was bleeding. He went back into the body of the club where his mate Georgiou noticed the problem, took him by the elbow, and bustled him out of the club and into the nearby Porsche. Harrison reckoned his mate was taking him to hospital, which was odd considering the nearest hospital was less than a five-minute drive in the opposite direction to the one which they were travelling.

When asked about the guns lobbed out of the passenger side window, Harrison denied knowing anything about them. His denials lacked merit, particularly when police found his DNA on a .25 calibre spent bullet in the basement, and de Stoop's DNA on Harrison's shoes. Hopefully Bruce's skills as a tattooist were of a higher order than his skills as an assassin.

The court would later be told that the three Bandidos were shot 'execution style' in the head at close range. Kulakowski, gravely injured with the head wound, lingered in hospital for about twenty-six hours before dying. Robin David was wounded in the shooting. Rather than hang around, he walked out of the club and calmly hailed a taxi which took him to nearby Royal Prince Alfred Hospital where he was treated for wounds to the neck and hand.

Georgiou fared a little better after escaping the Porsche and the police. He'd kept his head down since the murder, which was just as well because police were very keen to arrest him for multiple murder, and he'd also failed to appear in court in November 1997 to answer charges of supplying seventy grams of cocaine, a pile of amphetamines, and several 'banned' weapons.

Thanks to a call from some wisely suspicious customs and immigration officers, the police slipped down to Port Botany on 3 February 1998 and boarded a cargo ship, the *Arafura*, which was soon to leave Australia bound for Yokohama, Japan. The gentleman causing their suspicions was Georgiou. When police searched his cabin, they found $10000 in cash, a fake British passport in the name of Jonnifer Mario Ross, and two fake New South Wales drivers' licences in the same name. Georgiou was arrested and escorted off the ship. When police repaired to his beachside address in Bondi, they found a treasure trove, including a Smith and Wesson pistol that had been given to Georgiou in 1990. They also found pictures of the swaggering Georgiou showing off with both the Smith and Wesson and a Beretta, the same style as used in the killings. They searched the premises where the photos had been taken and recovered cartridges fired from both weapons. Some of the cartridges were matched to evidence from the murder scene and, in a somewhat grisly twist, from the body of the late Michael Kulakowski. Georgiou's subsequent attempt at an alibi failed miserably.

Theories about the murders were quite predictable. The Rebels were suspect number one and in the first days after the killings the then leader Alex Vella was named in the media in connection with the case. He later sued several newspapers and television stations for defamation, alleging they had falsely implied that he and the Rebels were responsible for the deaths. Other lines of inquiry quickly took over and the focus moved away from Vella. But he was still having a fairly bad time back then, with the New South Wales Crime Commission recently having frozen about $3 million of his assets.

On paper, Vella was a migrant success story. He was one of eleven children of a Maltese family who took up the genteel pursuit of strawberry farming in the market gardens of Sydney's west. By 1993, when seeking a loan, he quoted his assets as including a Newtown office block (with the New South Wales Department of Community Services as one of the tenants—nothing like the security of government tenants), a Horsley Park home on acreage, industrial land at Campbelltown in Sydney's rapidly expanding south-west, and cars and jewellery worth about $1 million. He later noted that the cars and jewellery included two Rolls Royces, up to about seventy motorcycles, mainly Harleys, two Chevrolet Corvettes and a Bentley. Alex protested that his assets were the result of 'the profits of motorcycle sales, more than $200 000 in accident compensation payments and some shrewd property investment'. As reported in the *Sunday Telegraph*, the Crime Commission, under the Drug

Trafficking (Civil Proceedings) Act, took a different view, alleging Vella's wealth was the 'bounty of criminal activity'. Vella later settled his dispute with the Crime Commission, and reports suggested that most of the property was returned to him.

The National Crime Authority had also launched Operation Panzer against the bike gangs, which had added to Alex's disquiet. Panzer was focused on the gang's alleged links to the trade in amphetamines and cannabis, counterfeiting, importing firearms, tax evasion and money laundering. The crime manager handling the early inquiries, Superintendent Dave Perrin, commented that police were unsure whether the murders were part of a turf war over the designer drug trade, or possibly delayed payback for Milperra, or just simply, like many murders, an argument or fight gone bad—and in this case very bad. But a murder inquiry is a quirky thing, and as the evidence swiftly rolls in, the focus can move very very quickly and in interesting directions.

Most murders tend to involve close family and friends, which is why when one partner dies, the other partner usually makes for a pretty good suspect early on. What the investigating police soon found in the Blackmarket case was that rather than being a crime simply motivated by greed, the murder of the three Bandidos may have had a goodly chunk of sex and passion rolled in. A few days after the murders, police conceded that the dispute may have come to a head over a girl. Of the notion of a crime of passion—well, at least a bit of passion—a police source told the media, 'that seems to be coming through quite strongly at the moment'. Kaos' father, Robert Kulakowski, also offered some insight into the murders and, inadvertently, into the relationship between two formidable gangs: 'Michael was very close to Alex Vella. Whenever Michael spoke about Alex it was with regard and friendship. Whoever the perpetrator was, he was not acting with the Rebel club's approval. It must have been personal.' He later added, 'I don't think there's going to be any drama emanating from this'.

He was on the money. Police later arrested a woman for her complicity in the murder plot. According to Utah, the woman was 'the sister of a girl that Mick was shagging. Her father was part of the NZ group the Mongrel Mob [a notorious bike gang].' Utah reckons she finally returned to New Zealand and is now listed as a missing person, possibly murdered.

While the murder of the three Bandidos was the most significant violent event since Milperra, the funeral of Michael Kulakowski was the largest gathering, but this time they were all unarmed and the outcome was peace and unity. Some five hundred bikies from around the globe came to St Thomas Anglican Church in Mulgoa, not too far from the Kulakowski family farm. Represented were Bandidos from around Australia, France, Sweden, Denmark and the United States, all flying their home country flags. The honour guard, about one hundred and eighty strong, included men from the Bandidos, Outlaws, Black Uhlans, Highway 61, Finks, Life and Death, Outcasts, Nomads and the God Squad.

On his coffin was a poster bearing his club rank and colours, and the words, 'God forgives—Bandidos don't'. He was described as a 'man of steel' and 'a force to be reckoned with'. Overseas Bandidos pledged their love, loyalty and respect. Bandido Porky delivered a passionate eulogy, describing his late leader as 'a man who commanded respect. He was cool, tough, the kind of man every man wanted to be and loves. He was always there to be our therapist, our mentor, our bank manager, our brother. He was a man every man wants to be and every woman loves.'

He was also Utah's VIP ticket into the gang world. Utah was in the throng of mourners. 'Mate, I don't have words for what I saw. Ever seen two hundred of the toughest fuckers you have ever met be speechless? Ever seen some seriously tough dudes cry? It was one of those things I simply will never forget.' He later recalled his dead mate, saying he was 'one of the last of the true one-percenters' who 'genuinely believed in the brotherhood and leadership. He would give his own in a fight, he was fearless but he was a great bloke with his friends and brothers. Anyone else ... don't get into a fight with the cunt, he was fucking ruthless.' The perfect leader for a group about which Canadian police would later note, 'They have achieved in 40 years what the Cosa Nostra took 80 years to achieve'.

The unity and strength of the amassed mourners at the Kulakowski funeral should have chilled the police, who had been keeping a close eye on proceedings. Neville Wran's three-pronged attack born of the Milperra Massacre obviously hadn't worked.

At the trial of Georgiou and Harrison in August 1999, the jury of six men and six women took merely two days to find both men guilty. Justice Dowd called the murder of the three men a 'callous, senseless and cold blooded killing'. He gave the murderers a minimum of twenty-eight years' hard labour. Both Georgiou and Harrison had a brief stroke of luck on 21 November 2001 when the Court of Criminal Appeal granted them a retrial. Their luck didn't last though, because on 19 December 2003, Justice Greg James found them both guilty again. He noted:

> There was very little of what they said which was exculpatory or mitigatory that I would be minded to accept. About all that I am prepared to accept is that they embarked on this exercise of going to the Black Market Café with heavy calibre weapons as part of some exercise involved in the same way with the motor cycle club of which they were members and influenced to some extent by one of the senior members of the club. Although I am not prepared to conclude they were influenced to the extent that they went reluctantly.

He gave them thirty-three years' hard labour with a non-parole period of twenty-eight years. Back to square one.

For police it was the end of one chapter only. Of the potential for reprisals, Utah noted: 'War was never "undeclared" after Rick, Sasha and Kaos were murdered in Sydney ten years ago. Things were simply put on the "back burner" whilst other issues were attended to.' Those issues were primarily to make sure it was business as usual. Why let a few murders stand in the way of a tidy profit?

A few months before Kulakowski was murdered, the Australian Federal Police were on edge with the arrival of a large shipment of a Chinese 'new age' drug. Four and a half kilograms of 'pink ice' was seized in Melbourne. That seizure was followed by seizures of ice in Sydney. While it was early days, police described the drug as a 'potential threat'. By the middle of the first decade of the new century, that potential threat was a harsh reality. The bike gangs were driving the production and distribution and the profits were simply extraordinary.

8

YET ANOTHER LIFE-CHANGING EXPERIENCE

It's the biggest mind-fuck you can go through to be put in there. It's counter-productive.
Stevan Utah

On 10 June 1995, William John Hovey, thanks to a change of name by deed poll in Victoria, formally became Stevan Utah. Utah cited 'irreconcilable family differences', which was probably substantially correct, but being chased around Townsville by an armed man may also have had an impact. Whatever his reasoning, Stevan was definitely due for a change of lifestyle.

Unfortunately, that change came his way on 20 November 1996. The scene was the Magistrates Court in Redcliffe, Queensland, a city perched on the edge of Moreton Bay about forty minutes from Brisbane and a quick cross-country run from Caboolture, where Utah had been keeping out of the limelight. His problem that November morning was the small matter of a fraud allegedly perpetrated on his recent employer, the Australian

Quarantine and Inspection Service. Utah's timing was not great as it came at the height of allegations flying about politicians' rorting their travel claims. Examples had to be made. Utah's alleged crime was a travel rort to the tune of $3128 on a claim he'd made earlier that year. Utah's view was: 'I signed a declaration in my tired state and received $3128.00 in travel benefits for a New South Wales trip. The neglectful part on my side was I was told the day before the trip was off. The following day I paid back the full amount to the receiver of public monies. However, my employment was terminated and a subsequent search on my residence by the AFP [Australian Federal Police] produced a shotgun for which I was unlicenced.'

Utah reckoned his tiredness was the result of working 'for AQIS by day and worked stacking shelves at Woolworths by night. I was tired. I had recently moved to Brisbane from Townsville. I had stopped taking medications prescribed to me. I was getting on with my life.' He went on, 'I recall the Redcliffe magistrate asking me why I had the shotgun. I stated, "to kill myself with". He asked me if I needed help. I had actually also kept it because every time I look at it, it was the object of encouragement to try harder and be better than average.'

While the magistrate appeared sympathetic, it was the age-old case of a velvet glove masking an iron fist. Utah's convictions for minor weapons offences earlier that year, and another minor travel rort fraud back in 1995, didn't do him any favours either. The magistrate gave him eight months behind bars, and indicated he could be released after two months if he entered into a bond to be of good behaviour for two years. Utah headed to the cells that day rather than home. Of his day in court Utah said, 'I accepted my sentence on the grounds of my personal stupidity, negligence and personal exhaustion. Not on my criminality.' Sensibly, he didn't share that view with the magistrate.

Utah's brief time in prison was made a little easier owing to his established contact with members of bike gangs. The connections gave him some credibility and protection from some of the more avaricious prisoners. His relationship with the gangs dated back to the late eighties and early nineties thanks to his association with Brutus and his army brother Cleaver, and Hombre Jonker. When talking of his early acquaintances in the gangs Utah says: 'During the early to mid 1990s I became a close acquaintance of many members of the [name omitted] Motor Cycle Club mainly through ex-military members and some people I met in North Queensland during my military service. During this time I saw many drug deals, often sat in a room whilst people discussed murders, strippers and prostitutes, police tip-offs, bashings, drug dealing, drug production.' One notable he met during this learning curve was a bikie 'well known for his ability to not only cook large amounts of amphetamine, but to source it immediately. I call a large amount anything higher than one kilogram of pure. He has often tried to sell it to me for $3000 cash an ounce or $80 000 a kilogram. There wasn't anything I wasn't exposed to,' Utah asserted.

Utah was also in the room when, he alleges, a Victorian police officer handed over photocopies from a restricted Victorian Police Service Manual that included all the frequencies and call signs of all senior police in Melbourne and all other Victorian areas. He also alleges there was a list of names and addresses of all senior police in Victoria. Utah recognised one name as someone he knew. The information was correct. Utah reckoned he later tried to pass on the information to the police officer as he was 'scared for him'.

Not surprisingly, Utah did not have any rosy-hued view of what the bike gangs were about. He says the first moment he became aware of just how involved the Bandidos were in criminal activity was difficult to pin down, but 'I always knew they were and ah . . . I haven't known anything else. I can walk into a room and tell you who you should be careful of. I have known nothing else but violence. And I'm not a violent person, but I've been around a lot of violent people.'

Among those on the periphery of the gangs and their criminal endeavours was a gentleman called Earl Mooring. Earl was a friend and occasional lover of Utah's mother, who had also been acquainted with a few bike enthusiasts over the years, and a member of a chapter of the Ulysses Motorcycle Club, which derived its name from a poem by Tennyson. If gangs like the Bandidos were considered

'Wild Ones', then Ulysses members would be more accurately described as 'Mild Ones'. The club focuses on riders who are comfortably middle aged, and more likely to be accountants, solicitors and business owners rather than tattooed hell-raisers. Stevan Utah claims that unlike his fellow members, Mooring had some associates on the dark side of the bike world.

At this juncture it is apt to quote Mark Twain, who once wrote that 'The very ink with which all history is written is merely fluid prejudice'. Earl Mooring, as you will soon see, is no longer around to defend himself. He met a rather nasty and brutal end and, of what little even Stevan Utah is prepared to admit, Utah played an unwilling role as an accomplice after the fact in Earl's demise. It is inevitable that Utah will be accused of talking up Mooring's criminal connections to mitigate his own. So since the victor—or in Utah's case the 'survivor'— writes the history books, it should be noted here that Earl Mooring's ghost has had no say in what his family and no doubt Victorian police will see as Utah's self-serving account of their relationship.

Mooring and Utah met in 1994 at Utah's mother's home in Geelong. Though she and Utah weren't on the friendliest of terms, they did keep in touch. Neither seemed capable of finally discarding the other. Utah reckoned Mooring was a 'very meticulous, careful, safety conscious character. He was controlled and paranoid about things in general.' Mooring was also a fairly unattractive man with a shape like a collection of poorly assembled parts and a face not unlike a squashed pie. Utah called Mooring an acquaintance rather than a friend. Their relationship was maintained through Utah's mother. Mooring was involved in a local security business, and was a sometime security person on the *Abel Tasman/Spirit of Tasmania* service that sailed from Melbourne to Tasmania.

For a man who was a bit on the paranoid side, Mooring quickly found himself trusting Utah. There may also have been a fair amount of braggadocio in Mooring. Utah, for all his experiences, was a man who needed recognition and always responded to strong figures, something that Mooring had sensed. A few months into their 'acquaintanceship' Utah was in Geelong visiting his mother. He says he'd also visited Mooring, who took him into the kitchen and, knowing Utah's expertise, pulled two handguns from the kitchen drawer. Utah commented: 'From that point onwards I felt I had gained his trust because anything that was said in the presence of the people that I had met through him remained confidential and I never spoke of such dealings with anyone.' Not unlike the bikies' habit of involving new members in crime to compromise them into silence.

The benefit, and a benefit of dubious merit, was that Mooring rapidly drew Utah into his highly illegal dealings. Utah said: 'Such dealings included buying and selling guns, drugs and dealing in significant amounts of money, sometimes up to hundreds of thousands of dollars.

I was often a party to these dealings and had first-hand knowledge of them.' Utah estimated that in the course of his mixing with Earl Mooring he would have seen about '$800 000 worth of cash and an endless supply of drugs including amphetamines, acid, marijuana, etc and hand guns and firearms etc'. Utah claims he kept himself at arm's length from these dealings, watching from the edge of the game. He added: 'Our relationship was such that I knew that if I ever required money or anything, all I had to do was ask Earl and it would be given to me. I never did, however, as I knew that a favour would eventually be required in return.' One very sensible choice by Utah. Silent, but not in debt.

On Utah's account, in the midst of Mooring's criminal colleagues were some members of the Bandidos. One regular deal that Utah alleges was the acquiring of materials for drug manufacture in Tasmania. Utah reckons that Mooring, while working security on the run to Tasmania, 'would often source large amounts of pseudoephedrine, a drug commonly known as the main ingredient in the production of amphetamine'. Mooring would often brag how easy it was to slip on the ship after hours after the port officials had left and walk straight through and pass it on. He would give it to a member of the Bandidos Motor Cycle Club and the drug production and sale process went on from there. Both Utah and Mooring, thanks to the intervention of the Bandidos some six years later, would both come to grief.

Meanwhile back in Queensland, Utah went straight from the courtroom to the Redcliffe watchhouse. Shortly thereafter his first port of call in the euphemistically titled 'corrections' system was the privately operated Arthur Gorrie Correctional Centre. This was the first stop for many people found guilty and sentenced to incarceration in the Brisbane and south-eastern Queensland region. Utah spent two weeks at Arthur Gorrie in something called 'the fishbowl', a glass-walled cell with its meagre furnishings screwed to the floor. It was the place they put prisoners they believed to be at high risk of committing suicide. Utah was not a great fan of the fishbowl, declaring later, 'It's the biggest mind-fuck you can go through to be put in there. It's counter-productive.'

He survived his time there and, after classification, it was off to a masterpiece of 1950s prison architecture, Her Majesty's Prison Wacol, merely moments from Arthur Gorrie. At least for Utah there was a little more privacy in the two-man cell he ended up sharing. His cellmate was an experienced resident, just chalking up his seventeenth year in prison after being caught mid crime by a security guard. As Utah rather drolly put it, his newfound friend had been locked up 'after a bit of a shoot-out'.

At Wacol, Utah had a reunion with his Bandido mate and fellow wildlife smuggler 'Bingey' Douglas. The two had met a few years earlier in Far North Queensland. Bingey's given name was actually James, but the nickname came from his exuberant use of drugs and alcohol. He was a former member of the tastefully named Sadists, who had been 'patched over'—the bike gangs' term for merger and acquisition—by the Bandidos. According to Utah, Bingey had a long history of involvement with drugs and assaults, along with a few run-ins with police, hence this prison time. Bingey was aware that Utah was acquainted with a local heavy in the Bandidos, Hombre Jonker.

Utah's credibility in prison got a major lift one day thanks to the soon to be 'late' Kulakowski. Utah was being visited by a female friend, and Bingey was also receiving guests that day—in particular, 'Packles', more formally known Mick Reed, then the president of the Sunshine Coast chapter of the Bandidos, and none other than Michael Kulakowski. Kulakowski recognised his mate and fellow fauna fancier. Of that confluence of bikers and biker fanciers, Utah said: 'I remember that visit, MKK saying to Bingey as I was walking away to give them some private time to have a chat, "Make sure nothing happens to that little cunt". Over the next few weeks Bingey would not sit next to me or anything but he would make sure that people knew not to touch me or annoy me. I could see this was going on and I did nothing about it.'

Utah managed to endear himself further when Bingey was looking for a little relief from the boredom of prison. Utah remembered:

> Bingey one day was complaining 'I can't find any fucking joints in this fucking prison'. I don't smoke

dope but my price for a lot of things is a fucking joint. He was there with his cellmate. He said, 'I would give anything for another joint'. He said he would give a packet of Ox [tobacco] for every joint I could get. I pulled the other two out of my pocket. He said, 'You are a smooth little cunt . . . I would never have known'. I said, 'That's what it's all about, isn't it, not to be detected?'

An intriguing foretaste of what would become a key aspect of Utah's future, the knack of not being detected.

When Utah left the prison in January 1997, he left as a man with the reputation of being a model prisoner. He also reckons that by that stage he was 'known to the national presidents of the Rebels, the national and all chapter presidents of the Bandidos, armed robbers, drug dealers, and smugglers'. The first two associations came courtesy of Michael Kulakowski; the rest, according to Utah, can be attributed to Earl Mooring and the great networking environment of prison. However Utah, at least at that point, had a very clear view of his future: 'But no, again I didn't want to be a criminal.' Despite his best intentions, Utah's past wouldn't take too long to catch up with him.

On his release, he very quickly found work in a security firm in Brisbane, just a stone's throw from the CBD. It was a profitable little business, providing alarms and other security measures for a range of domestic and commercial clients. Included in the mix, Utah reckoned, was the Queensland Police Service and the ever security conscious Bandidos, who needed some good quality electronic security for their clubhouses. Utah had met the principal of the business, a person we'll call 'Mr Linus', about six months before he started working for him. They'd met socially and had developed a friendship to the point where Mr Linus, finding a sympathetic ear in Utah, talked of his business problems. Utah, ever practical, made some useful suggestions. The offer of work soon followed.

Initially he was paid $35 000 per year, plus expenses, to get about and entertain clients. Mr Linus would occasionally give him some cash, around $200 or $300, 'for a drink at the casino'. Utah was many things, but casino habitué was not amongst them. Utah's primary task was to use his knack for maths as an accounts clerk, making sure the cash flow was in the black, maintaining the ledgers and, as he put it, 'clearing up the problems'—a troubleshooter. He also found time, both his and the company's, to dabble in hands-on installation work. He managed to keep himself at arm's length from temptation, and buried himself in his work. The only hiccup in those early years was a bit of a setback to the business when, on 13 October 1998, a wild storm hit inner-city Brisbane, ripping part of the roof off the office and warehouse.

During his time at the security firm he still kept in close contact with the Bandidos and, in particular, his ex-prison mate Bingey Douglas—not involving himself in their activities at that stage, just enjoying the rub-off from their exploits. Utah revelled in the knowledge of what they were up to without getting himself too embroiled. What he hadn't anticipated was that the time would come when the bikies would demand he either 'shit or get off the pot'. You can only be a voyeur in that line of business for so long.

In May 1998, life got a little complicated when Utah married. The marriage was not destined to last. The complication came courtesy of Earl Mooring. On the guest list was Earl Mooring accompanying Utah's mother, and Bingey Douglas. *Dimboola* with drugs. The way Utah tells it, the day prior to the wedding Earl asked Utah to drive with him to Lutwyche, an inner-city Brisbane suburb. Earl sweetened the request with an offer to pay Utah for his company. When he slid into the seat beside Mooring he found he wasn't the only other occupant. Mooring had brought five kilograms of amphetamines with him, and he proudly asserted the product was pure. Utah, still on his bond to be of good behaviour and looking toward a slightly less dodgy future, wasn't too impressed. He got out of the car and told Earl the drive was off. Earl was none too pleased, and spent the next few days abusing Utah's mother for her son's lapse into good judgement.

At the wedding, Earl was seated next to that other stellar guest, Bingey Douglas. Utah noted they 'were as thick as thieves'. It was also a pretty fair guess where the five kilograms of amphetamines had gone. His relationship with Mooring was not enhanced by what he had observed at the wedding, and Utah claims his mother continued to cop the brunt of Mooring's annoyance to the point where Utah interceded to protect her. The conversation wasn't too pleasant, with Mooring allegedly telling Utah to pull his head in or he would slip his mother a deal (plant drugs on her). With Mooring's connections Utah reckoned his mother might find the police on her doorstep with a search warrant, and find some drugs that had been planted in her house. A pillar of the community was Earl—or was he?

When Victorian police began digging into Earl's background a year or two later, they had nothing on the mild-mannered gentleman bikie to suggest he was as implicated in criminal activity as Utah alleges. If Earl was moving drug base around the country in league with outlaw motorcycle gang members including the Bandidos, then it was unknown to law enforcement. That would not be a first. But Utah is indeed wide open to the accusation that he is talking up Mooring's criminal links to mitigate the awful events that were to unfold. What was definitely the case was that Earl Mooring had somehow accumulated a large amount of cash. The fact that its existence became known to some of Utah's bikie associates was to be Earl's undoing.

Despite the fickle nature of their relationship, Mooring and Utah's mother still had an occasional fling, and Utah and Mooring maintained a somewhat strained truce. One of the upshots of that truce was Mooring's offer of a nice little bit of cash to Utah. It was Christmas 1999 and Utah had driven to Geelong to see his mother. At a family gathering with the cast including Utah's mother, his sister, his wife, former Pentridge resident Uncle Andrew, and Mooring, Utah noticed more disquiet than he'd expected. When his mother was quite drunk, Utah started asking questions and claims he found that Earl had been stalking her, and possibly monitoring her phone calls. Earl, it seemed, was getting rather paranoid about being 'ripped off' and didn't trust Stevan's mother, or his own children, and other family members as well. Oddly enough, he seemed to trust Utah, and a few days later, on New Year's Eve, Utah and his wife, and Mooring and Utah's mother, went to a ball. During the evening, Mooring took Utah aside and, on Utah's account, offered him $5000 to bash a local bloke in the toilets at the ball. The proposed victim was Utah's mother's previous boyfriend. Utah politely declined, but he was getting rather unnerved by Earl's increasingly erratic behaviour.

Thanks to Bingey Douglas, Utah said that his involvement with the Bandidos 'just steamrolled along'. Having Kulakowski, the national president, as a mate and occasional business associate didn't do him any harm at all. Doors were opened and Utah had a seat at the table. That seat at the table quickly gave Utah a few interesting experiences.

Though he was not too keen to elaborate on the details, he was on site in New South Wales where Bandidos went to play with some of their new toys. The toy was a '66 rocket launcher', and the target was a 'tractor or a bulldozer'. This popular little piece of military hardware was not the sort thing you'd like to see in the hands of a bike gang. They also had a stash of hand grenades. While obviously Utah was in awe of the bikies, his expertise with weapons made him a highly desirable acquisition for them. And a bit like your mother or grandmother handing over the family recipes to the child with a passion for cooking, the bikies found that in Utah they also had a dab hand at the cooking of amphetamines. The old family recipes fell into his hands.

On the other side of the argument, law enforcement was certainly making loud noises about the ascent of the gangs. In New South Wales police had taken army bomb disposal and explosives experts, like Utah had recently been, on raids around the western suburbs. They'd come away with a nice selection of drugs, firearms and other bits and pieces, but only four men had been charged.

Up in Queensland, the state was still feeling quite righteous about cleaning up its act after the Fitzgerald Commission had torn the heart out of police and political corruption. In 1995 the local broadsheet, the *Courier Mail*, threw a spanner in the works in a piece called 'The Vile Ones', in which they reported police as saying:

As many as 10 outlaw motorcycle gangs are operating within Queensland in the illegal methyl amphetamine drug trafficking trade. Crime fighters say the bikie gangs are transporting the mostly powdered form of the narcotic, commonly known as speed, up and down the eastern seaboard of Australia. Law enforcement agencies believe Brisbane has become Australia's main producer of the drug with illicit laboratories dotted throughout the city.

Police were very concerned, saying 'the outlaw motorcycle gang's members are thought to be taking huge quantities of amphetamine interstate and returning with large sums of cash'. In a clever twist the gangs were also thought to be using cannabis, which grew superbly in the warmth of the Queensland sun, to buy the raw materials for the amphetamine production. Well-armed bikies kept the operations nice and secure.

Police had a surprise that was both pleasant and unpleasant. They successfully raided a Brisbane drug operation in February 1996. That was the good part. They found one hundred and forty kilograms of amphetamine, which quite reasonably scared them. At least briefly, the supply of the drug dried up, probably causing a few less befuddled revellers at the Sydney Gay and Lesbian Mardi Gras a few weeks later. The police's Operation Marlin had made a small dent in the bikies' business, and their methods. Inspector Bauer of the Queensland police commented:

YET ANOTHER LIFE-CHANGING EXPERIENCE

Many of the outlaw motorcycle gang's members have legitimate jobs or businesses. However some of the businesses we say shield other activities. They launder their money through these legitimate businesses. The people involved in the amphetamine trade use every means available to them. Places where motorcycles are repaired, which are frequently visited by outlaw motorcycle gang members known to be involved in the amphetamine industry, present an ideal opportunity for them to distribute while going about their lawful business. They make their contacts within those types of premises and it is suspected that many more premises of this type are used in a similar manner.

The trick, as police knew only too well, was to get behind the façade of these operations. The gangs were experienced and clever. Getting past the literally and metaphorically large and ugly men at the door to the inner sanctum was almost impossible. What they needed was to get information from someone already in that inner sanctum.

9

SOME MINOR DOMESTICS

*When we all unite, maybe then we will be
unstoppable.*
An unnamed Bandido

In the bikie world things were getting a little tense. In 1999, three bikies, all Bandidos, were shot to death in Adelaide. A rather chilling obituary in a local paper began by asking for something that initially sounded civilised: 'We ask for peace, not war.' Good start, but the kicker was: 'When we all unite, maybe then we will be unstoppable.'

The then Federal Justice Minister Amanda Vanstone had a clear view on the future of the bikies. She said there was a national commitment to curb escalating violence between rival gangs, noting that over the last eighteen months there had been at least five murders and more than twenty bombings, arson and machine-gun attacks on clubhouses around the country. Her estimates were a bit conservative. She commented, 'the States have agreed to upgrade the collection and sharing of intelligence and that sure shows a strong support from the States to improve law enforcement efforts against motorcycle gangs.' That was the theory anyway; the reality, as Utah would observe in the coming years, was totally different, and not for the better.

Alex 'The Maltese Falcon' Vella, boss of the Rebels, had a crack at some positive public relations on behalf of the gangs. Unfortunately, Alex lacked the deft touch of legendary Hells Angel and prince of public relations, Californian Sonny Barger. Rather than getting some positive spin, Alex got a headline in the *Sydney Morning Herald* on 10 August 1999: 'Gang warfare? No, we're just having domestics.' Vella was quoted as saying the incidents around Australia were just 'all minor domestics'. Minor for some, but unlikely to be minor for those killed or their families. He told journalists, 'Some of them involved disputes over women, others were minor things. It has nothing to do with the clubs, my friend.' They published a nice photo of Alex outside the former nudist camp in south-western Sydney's Horsley Park, which was now the Rebels' clubhouse.

Things went south for Alex when the article noted police and criminal sources suggesting the fight was over the massive recruitment efforts by the Rebels and Bandidos, and the 'lucrative amphetamines trade'. They also noted 'both gangs have increased their membership base and are fighting it out "toe to toe" for the control of drug markets, suburban prostitution, and other side rackets such as the control of the tow truck industry'. Alex was very unhappy. His best laid public relations plans were in tatters. His attempt to mitigate the bad press was a disaster, and so he decided to litigate, suing the *Sydney Morning Herald* newspaper for defamation. Seven imputations went to the jury to consider. The jury chucked out each and every one of them. He became even more unhappy when ordered to pay costs.

The *Courier Mail* in Brisbane added to the tension in the air when it reported on 11 August 1999: 'Fears of interstate warfare between rival bike gangs has spilled into Queensland after a suspected firebombing of a bikie owned tattoo parlour yesterday.' The tattoo parlour, Ink Attack, in suburban Capalaba, went bang around 4 am. The ensuing fire took care of what was left. Police declined to comment on whether the attack was linked to problems in other states. They were not forthcoming on the accuracy of the *Mail*'s reporting, prevaricating on whether the explosion was an accident or the result of the Molotov cocktail found nearby. State Crime Operations Assistant Commissioner Graham Williams said police were in constant contact with their interstate counterparts and were aware of the violent rivalry that existed between gangs. He also warned that the violence witnessed in the southern states would not be tolerated in Queensland. In hindsight, the assistant commissioner was dreadfully wrong. Misinformed perhaps, or over-exposed to the warmth of the Queensland sun.

Notwithstanding the assertions of the assistant commissioner, the local Bandidos undertook a security upgrade of their East Brisbane clubhouse, investing quite a few thousand dollars in it. The upgrade was triggered by a drive-by shooting. Up in Caloundra, the gateway to Queensland's Sunshine Coast holiday playground, just a pleasant hour and a quarter's drive from Brisbane, the local chapter of the Bandidos decided a bit of extra security wouldn't be a bad idea either. For a tasty little wad of cash, Joseph Hombre Jonker had his mate, Stevan Utah, upgrade the club's security.

Hombre was a former president of the Sadists, who had moved across to the Bandidos, and ended up as president of their Sunshine Coast chapter in 1999. The Bandidos clubhouse is not situated in a scenic part of pretty Caloundra. Instead, it's in a light industrial area off the road into the town, tucked discreetly behind a service station and surrounded by car repair businesses. The clubhouse is in a factory-type building and is distinguished from its neighbours by the sprinkling of surveillance cameras and a sign saying 'Bandidos'. In the evenings and on weekends the area is deathly quiet. The locals don't like to talk about their scary neighbour.

After Utah had done his security upgrade, including the installation of security cameras so the Bandidos could see who was snooping about outside, or tapping on their front door, he found himself drawn even closer into the inner circle. He spent much of his spare time at the clubhouse. This did little for his marriage. The proximity of his relationship with the Bandidos was confirmed by

Hombre with a seminal act. It was clearly designed to show Utah the strength of the club, and to make sure he was so implicated that ratting on the club and its members would be most unlikely. Standard Bandido operating procedure.

Hombre was revered among his fellow bikers. According to Utah he also enjoyed very close ties with Bandidos in both Canada and Europe, taking over their affections after the demise of his mate Michael Kulakowski. Utah both feared and respected Hombre, saying: 'Whilst Hombre was a good man he was a very nasty calculating criminal without remorse or boundaries. You messed with this man and he would simply shoot you. I actually had Fess [Harris] say this to me once. For Fess to fear him, he was definitely a dangerous individual.'

The lead up to Hombre Jonker's act was the arrest of a mate, Dallas Devine, the gang's sergeant-at-arms. He ended up pleading guilty to trafficking, twelve counts of supplying dangerous drugs and three counts of receiving stolen goods. He was sentenced to five years by the Queensland Supreme Court in March 2001. The court was told that in 1998 and 1999 he'd made the mistake of selling speed, cocaine, hash and LSD to an undercover police officer known as Gary Barlow. Barlow had also bought two handguns and four stolen guitars, adding an unusually musical touch to the crimes. Devine had also generously offered to sell stolen motorcycles, pure amphetamine and explosives.

Jonker reckoned that Devine's problems could be

traced back to a spy in the Bandidos' midst. The spy was either another undercover police officer or an informer. It didn't really matter to Jonker, and he had a fair idea who that person might be. The Bandidos he represented were not fans of proof beyond reasonable doubt, the presumption of innocence, or imprisonment as a penalty. Summary justice and a swift execution was more the Jonker style. Utah, visiting the Caloundra clubhouse one evening in mid 2000, takes up the story:

> I was sitting there having a drink with [Jonker]. And there was a girl in there at the time. She was, you know, there to do some favours for Hombre. He looked up at the security monitor and went out and fucking shot [the alleged informant/undercover cop]. He came back in and asked me to stay in the clubhouse for an hour and I looked at him and said, 'What was that about?' I didn't want to get involved but you know someone just got shot in front of me, I want to know a little bit of what's going on. And he said to me, 'That's the dog that gave up Dallas'.

Utah thought, '*Fuck, you shot a copper!*' He recalled that Jonker then walked to the bleeding and moaning man on the ground and dispassionately shot him again. Utah was able to watch the entire event unfold on the security monitor, and the report of both gunshots was easily heard within the clubhouse.

When the murder happened the only people in the clubhouse were Jonker, Utah and the woman. Utah didn't know her name. He said of her: 'All she wanted to do was show me her tits.' When the murder actually took place, the woman, bizarrely, was still 'trying to show me her tits'. Not only did Utah not know the woman's name, he still to this day doesn't know the identity of the dead man. That he didn't know the man didn't faze him—Bandidos, it would seem, weren't fans of Dale Carnegie style networking. He observed: 'You can be in a room with ten people and know two of them. Just because you are there doesn't mean you know the names of these people.'

Utah, even after his eventful life, was shocked by the horrific and cold-blooded act. He was also smart enough to know that he'd reached a very interesting point in his affair with the Bandidos. Of the event he said: 'Well of course you're shocked but you got to ah . . . how do I word this? With these sorts of people, if you display a fear, a panic, anything they would consider adverse to their own personal security, you make yourself a target. And that's just not related to the Bandidos, that's any criminal element.'

The next test of Stevan Utah's fidelity was the tricky matter of disposing of the evidence and, in particular, the deceased alleged informant. Jonker took on the role of funeral director all on his own. Utah did as he was told and stayed in the clubhouse. He didn't see either Jonker or his cargo depart as they were very shortly out of the coverage of the cameras. Utah waited, and Jonker was back in about an hour or so. On his return he bragged to Utah—it was all a bit of a joke for Jonker, it would seem. Utah recalled, 'He laughed, he giggled and he said to me, "I'm a good guy, I put him in the cemetery at Beerwah".' The destination gelled perfectly with the length of Jonker's absence.

Utah kept his mouth shut and didn't discuss it ever again with Jonker. It was back to business as usual. As Utah said, 'You don't have subsequent conversations with people like that'. However, he conceded that the event did wonders for his standing in the eyes of the Bandidos. He says, 'Well, there's been people all over the country that for years have seen me as a person who won't talk.'

What this incident did prove in Utah's mind was the utter ruthlessness of the gangs. Jonker didn't even bat an eyelid about murdering another human being. He had completely disregarded the repercussions of murdering someone who might have been a policeman, an event that brings on a scorched earth investigation by the police. He just didn't give a damn. In hindsight, it's pretty fair to assume, judging by the absolute-zero reaction from the authorities either then or in later years, that the dead man was an informant and not an undercover cop. Informants by their very nature are fairly low down the police's list of people they need to care about.

The law didn't catch up with Jonker either, though some may unkindly suggest he was sentenced by a higher power. Where the police failed, cancer didn't. In January 2004 he was dead. In the hatched, matched and dispatched section of the local Caloundra paper there was a funeral notice: 'JONKER—Joseph (Hombre) of Noosaville. Life Member of Bandidos Motorcycle Club Nomad Hombre. Family, friends and members are invited to attend the funeral service for Joseph to be held in Our Lady of the Rosary Catholic Church, Edmund St, Caloundra on Friday 30th January 2004 at 2.00pm. NO FLOWERS BY REQUEST. In lieu of flowers donations to the Qld Cancer Fund would be appreciated.'

Unlike its effect on Jonker, the impact of the murder on Utah was massive. He'd enjoyed his vicarious thrills; he hadn't been too troubled about the dealing in drugs and weapons, that was just business, but murder, no. It rocked a man who despite his bravado was still a guy with a lousy past and a propensity for depression and self-destruction. He needed to make a break. The problem confronting him, of course, was that he was now 'accepted' into the inner circle, and in real terms was an accessory to murder, in addition to a few lesser matters. Ratting out the bikies was not an option. He'd seen what happened when you did that. Hanging around the Caloundra clubhouse wasn't a great idea either.

Utah took the plunge, telling his associates in the gangs he'd be moving to a quieter life in the country—wife, a possible impending family, all the usual reasonable excuses. He hadn't been faring all that well at the security firm so the decision to leave his stable job wasn't too hard either. The failure of this relationship, according to Utah, was simply a matter of respect. He'd proved himself invaluable to the business, and as he'd been there a few years, he requested an increase in pay to $40 000 per year. Mr Linus's response had been along the lines of 'yeah, yeah' and hadn't progressed any further than that. A few months, and rather stressful ones for Utah, had passed.

Utah finally had a decent dose of the shits and resigned. Mr Linus promptly offered him the pay increase. Utah said, 'If he had respected me he would have given it to me when I asked the first time. In any event he did not convince me to stay on.' He gave notice on 15 May 2000, but things deteriorated and he was gone within the week. In the twinkling of an eye he and his wife were living in rural Dalby, Queensland, a quiet, well-established farming town of 11 000 people, some two and a half hours' drive inland from Brisbane, and a little longer from the Caloundra clubhouse of the Bandidos. As an acknowledgement of the respect in which the Bandidos held him, Utah was marked as 'do not touch' by the gang. Utah later commented that those vouching for him were Bandidos royalty and included Peter 'Fess' Harris, Mick 'Packles' Reed, a man we will call 'Gronk', Ivan Glavas, Lance 'Kid Rotten' Purdie (of Milperra Massacre repute), Danny Purdie and Sava Cvetkovic, president of the Bandidos Gold Coast chapter. In their eyes, Utah was now 'a man of honour and his word', he reckoned.

He and his wife bought a house on acreage, and he began a nine-to-five existence as the administration manager of a local business, and by night returned to his old profession of supermarket shelf-stacker. Being a natural networker, and good with his hands, Utah quickly established himself as a useful member of the Dalby community. Sometimes he could even be spotted having a quick cup of tea and a chat with the lads in the kitchen of the local police station. But trouble, which seemed to stalk Utah all his life, would soon come his way yet again.

10

IF I HAD A HAMMER . . .

He just pulled it out and went fucking bang.
Stevan Utah

Stevan Utah may not have much liked his mother's boyfriend, Earl Mooring, but there was one thing they had in common—according to Utah, they were both criminal chameleons. They had the knack of always hovering on the periphery of things stinky and dodgy while rarely being noticed or detected. Maybe that is what drew them together.

Earl Mooring had his public image—as a gentleman bikie member of the Ulysses Motorcycle Club in Geelong, not one of the so-called one-percenters, and as a law-abiding security guard on the trans-Tasman ferries between Tasmania and Melbourne. Put Earl in a business suit and, with his metal-rimmed reading glasses and receding hair, he could easily have passed for a suburban accountant or bank clerk. The only hint that he wasn't was the tiny stud in his left ear. And that is pretty much what Victorian police concluded. Steven Utah, though, tells a vastly different story about this mild-mannered Geelong father.

Utah claims that Earl was up to his eyebrows in all sorts of crime. Whether it was guns, drugs, you name it—although he never got caught for it—Earl was allegedly into it. At least that's how Utah explains things now. By his account, in early 2000 Utah was worried that while he was, momentarily, trying hard to go straight, his mother still had Earl as her boyfriend. The son was finding that looking after Mummy was becoming something of a headache. When allegations of Earl's infidelities with other women surfaced, Utah's mother told her son she had dumped him. Utah later told police his mother believed Earl was stalking her because neighbours had seen him outside her house with what looked like a radio frequency scanner, and a repairman had found a bug in her television set. She also allegedly told Utah how she suspected that Earl was coming into the house when she was not around. Earl, Utah claims, did not know when to take no for an answer.

But it would be fair to say that Earl's family and even some in Victorian police suspect Utah and his mother are now speaking ill of Mooring all too secure in the knowledge that he cannot defend himself. The Mooring family doubts the claims that Earl was harassing Utah's mother and believes he was in fact trying to dump her. That all the dirt being poured on Earl is aimed at deflecting Utah's and his mother's culpability for what happened next.

IF I HAD A HAMMER . . .

We may never know who is right, but we do know that what happened was horrific; and the people who did it still walk free. Victorian police are still extremely sceptical of the accounts that both Utah and his mother gave about what would later happen to Earl Mooring in October 2000. There are contradictory accounts of who knew what and when. Suffice to say, what happened was nasty and bloody . . . and not everyone can be telling the truth.

In July that year Mooring had often telephoned Utah up in Queensland where Utah, still rattled by the fresh memory of a bullet-riddled corpse at Caloundra, was supposedly trying to put the bikies behind him. But the way Utah tells it today, the one thing he needed at the time was money. So when Mooring offered him $2500 for what sounded like a victimless crime in July 2000, he agreed to meet Earl at a pizza shop in Geelong. Utah's efforts to go straight were about to come horribly undone. Utah says Earl wanted him to burgle his Geelong home in a curious ploy to win sympathy from Utah's mother. Earl's problem, he adds, was that while he wanted the theft to look convincing, he needed to ensure that two handguns and at least $160 000 in cash were not stolen from the back shed at his home. Why Utah agreed to do this is something he is still asking himself, because he acknowledges it was 'quite possibly the silliest thing I had ever done because he was using it as a way of getting back with my mother. I told my mother not to do so as I knew the robbery was a set-up to in effect gain her sympathy.'

The sham break-in went ahead and, according to Utah, he drove all the way from his home in Queensland to Victoria to supervise the 'theft' to ensure that Mooring's hidden stash was not stolen. Not surprisingly the Victorian police found this explanation for what took place to be curious to say the least. The inevitable alternative suspicion is that the break-in was an attempt by Utah and his mother to steal off her ex-boyfriend. Utah's claims about this burglary were also undermined by his own later admissions to police that he burgled Earl's house in league with a particularly aggressive member of the Queensland Bandidos—the man we dubbed 'Brutus'—and that this burglary was done on behalf of his mother. According to that version of events, Earl Mooring knew nothing about the burglary at all.

The idea of a homicidal thug like Brutus coming all the way down from Queensland to assist his little mate Stevan with his mother's love life does strain credibility. What Brutus and his accomplices in the Bandidos would have wanted was the money; and they turned Earl's house upside down looking for it, ripping apart furniture and smashing door jambs in the search. Oddly enough they didn't find it—police later confirmed the huge bundle of cash had stayed secreted under a floorboard. Earl Mooring returned later to find his house had been trashed and that those who did it had gone.

While there the burglars had made no secret of their contempt for Earl's beloved leather jacket which was covered with the patches of the Ulysses motorcycle club. Police suspect it was Brutus who methodically pulled each Ulysses patch off the jacket and tossed them into the family home's combustion heater.

Even if the break-in was a crime of passion as Utah claims, for Mooring to win back Mum's heart, it failed. Mum did not run back to Earl. Earl, not without good reason, got very scared and paranoid. Then, a few weeks later, Utah says he got a call from his mother telling him that Earl had tried to commit suicide. Utah admits he dismissed this as another attention-seeking gesture by Mooring and he was angry with Mooring for hassling his mother. The two men had a fight over the phone. Clearly Earl was a troubled and tormented man, for more than a few reasons, and Utah and his mother were the focus of his upset. What was to happen next, then, was all the more concerning for Utah.

Somewhere along the way, word of Earl Mooring's substantial stash of illicit cash had clearly got back to several other members of the Queensland Bandidos, 2000 kilometres north of Geelong. Utah flatly denies it was him who told them about the money, or that he was involved in conceiving the original plot to steal it. But he admits that he was an after-the-fact new accessory in what happened next, to his eternal shame and regret. His mother later told police a different story.

We know the Bandidos believed Earl was making big money out of selling amphetamines, because, as Utah claims, he had sold the five kilograms of speed to Bandidos like Bingey Douglas. But stories began circulating around the Queensland chapters that there was as much as $360 000 locked up in Earl's home. It was a tantalising prospect and a group of the Sunshine State's Bandidos decided to travel from Queensland to Geelong to relieve him of his ill-gotten gains. Already horribly compromised by Hombre's callous murder of the anonymous informant at the Caloundra clubhouse, Utah was about to get sucked into the vortex even further.

The second weekend of October 2000 began reasonably well for Utah in his new guise as a gentleman farmer. He wasn't exactly smoking a pipe and wearing tweed but Stevan was in Sydney, taking in the Rosehill races near Parramatta, and checking out his latest idea to earn an honest quid on his Dalby property: fish farming. Utah later admitted to police that on that weekend he also dropped in on a Sydney Bandido whom we will call 'Steed'. Steed was then and still is a big-time dealer in drugs and guns and, in keeping with that curious flirtation that Stevan Utah has always had with the dark side, he could not help but call on his bikie mate.

Utah also told police that while at Steed's house he saw a weapon in a toilet bag in his bathroom—possibly a Glock semi-automatic pistol. Steed's house was a place where Stevan Utah admits he had previously seen frequent drug dealing and bundles of tens of thousands of dollars in cash, bulletproof vests, and even fake police IDs. He was not seized with an urgent need to immediately alert Her Majesty's New South Wales Police to this fact, which, in retrospect, would have been a much better idea. If ever Utah had a chance to walk away and put it all behind him, that was the moment.

On the afternoon of Sunday 8 October, Utah says he got a message on his mobile from his mother that turned his weekend into a bad trip in every sense of the word. Utah's recollections put Mum right in it, suggesting that her message said: 'We are going to get him tonight, fix his little red wagon.' He says he unsuccessfully called his mother about ten times and that he then tried to find Brutus, whom he thought was in Sydney but he admits he did know that by now Brutus was actually on his way to Earl Mooring's house in Geelong to knock off his cash. When Utah could not find Brutus in Sydney, he claims he then decided to drive alone overnight to his mother's house in Whittington, near Geelong.

If by this stage you are wrinkling your brow and thinking Utah's account so far is a little lacking in logic, then you are not the only one. It is not unreasonable to think the Victorian police also believed that aspects of Utah's explanation for how he came to be driving to Melbourne that night required further investigation. His mother later told police that Utah was in on the robbery from the start and that it was he who had told the Queensland Bandidos about Mooring's stash of cash. Utah admits that he found out the day before his mother's call that a robbery was planned but he suggests it was his mother who tipped off the Queensland bikies about the bounty they could find at Chez Mooring and that it was she who lured Earl Mooring to her house: 'I found out about it two days beforehand . . . and I made . . . Well, the police have my phone records. I made several phone calls, I think I rang like ten times, ten or eleven times to my mother's house—what are you doing? What are you doing—because the guy that she had spoken to is a . . . you don't fuck with him. Just don't do it.'

The 'don't fuck with him' Bandido whom Utah alleges his mother spoke to was Brutus, a senior member of the gang with a formidable reputation for violence, who seemed to have made his way from Sydney to Victoria just like Stevan Utah. Brutus' best character reference comes from Utah, who describes him thus: 'Self-serving. Greedy. Incredibly violent. Incredibly strong . . . I wouldn't take him on.'

One problem with Stevan Utah's claim that he was not in on the second plot to steal from Earl Mooring from the very beginning was that when Victorian police finally caught up with him after this whole tragic weekend was over, he admitted that Brutus had also accompanied him down to Geelong for the supposedly sham burglary on Mooring's house a few weeks earlier. It would be stretching credibility a little to say that a cold-hearted, violent thug like Brutus would travel 2000 kilometres to Melbourne to help out Earl Mooring in winning the favours of

Utah's mummy. That is probably what the Victorian police thought as well.

The moral of the story behind this saga is not just that one should not tell bikies where large sums of money are stashed and hope for the best. Any good defence lawyer will also recognise that Stevan Utah's biggest mistake was to talk to police without first getting his story straight. Whether it was mother or son who set Brutus onto Earl Mooring we may never know, but the one thing nobody, at this stage, disputes is that everyone knew full well that when Brutus asked Earl for his money when he arrived on 10 October he would not be polite. Even Utah admits he knew Brutus was going down to Melbourne at least two days beforehand and violence was likely:

Utah: At no time did I know a murder was going to occur.

Q: Did you know that Mooring was going to be hurt?

Utah: Depends how you define hurt.

Q: You knew it was likely he was going to be hurt?

Utah: A smack in the mouth, yeah, sure.

It was all terribly *Godfather Part III*.

Somewhere in the midst of the myriad of bad judgements, Stevan Utah lost sight of the fact that Earl Mooring was now in terrible danger. For all Earl's faults, which by Utah's account were many, he had a family too and Utah surely knew his prospects of getting through the next few days without at least some injury were looking pretty grim. Despite that, he made no attempt to warn Mooring.

Utah says he arrived at his mother's house in Whittington, eighty kilometres south-west of Melbourne, sometime on 10 October, after a brief kip at a roadhouse near Albury on the New South Wales–Victoria border. Finding no-one else at home, and not able to get inside with his keys, Utah claims he then went to a local graveyard a few hundred metres away and put flowers on his grandmother's grave . . . and then went and had a meal of fish and chips: 'A lot of people can't understand that but that's what I did. Had some fish and chips. And when I went back to the house there was fucking blood everywhere. There was just blood everywhere all the way through the house.'

Utah's mother was now home and so was his young sister. Something very unpleasant had clearly taken place in his mother's living room. The white carpet was drenched red with blood. There was no sign of Earl Mooring. As soon as Mum told him that Earl was now 'tied up' at the nearby house of another local Bandido, 'I was like I knew there was problems'. In the parlance of the bikie gangster world, as Utah put it, the person to whose home Earl Mooring had been taken was someone who 'doesn't need six friends to help him out of a violent situation'.

He, like Brutus, has a formidable reputation as a violent enforcer inside the outlaw motorcycle gangs. We will call him 'Stig'.

Earl Mooring's tiny red Nissan Micra was sitting down the rear driveway in the darkness outside Stig's house, which was located in quiet bushland a short drive from Mooring's house. As Utah entered he could see Earl Mooring lying on a plastic tarpaulin on the ground, his legs and arms bound with tape, in a pool of congealed blood. His head was especially bloody and so were his socks. They were drenched red. A small broken ball hammer lay on the ground beside him, leaving all too much to the imagination. Utah left Earl lying there and went into Stig's house. 'I looked at [Brutus] and asked him as a joke, "Did you cut his fucking toes off or something?" [Brutus] replied, "The cocksucker wouldn't tell me where the money was so I had to do something",' Utah recalls.

Earl's toes had been smashed so hard with the hammer, the hammer had broken. Brutus and Stig had tortured him—without success, as it turned out—to find the hiding place for his money. But what appalled Utah most of all was the sight of his killers sitting up at the table, drinking coffee, discussing the forthcoming national bikie run. Earl's dead or dying corpse on the floor no longer seemed to be of the slightest concern to them: 'What particularly got me was just how. Ever put two sugars in your coffee and just given it a stir, you don't give it a second thought?

Well that's what it was like with Earl Mooring. It was just like putting sugars in his coffee,' Utah recalls.

As well as Brutus and Stig, there was a fourth man in the room that night who Utah did not know. To this day police have not been able to confirm his identity. Utah knew this was not the sort of night where one asks the friendly questions about how we all know each other. While his three criminal associates sat drinking coffee and ignoring Earl, Utah went again to where Mooring lay and called his name several times to see if he would respond. There was no reaction from the inert and very battered corpse.

The indignities suffered by Earl Mooring that night were not over. Late in the night, Brutus asked Utah to help him get the body into the back of Mooring's red Nissan Micra. How they got a body into such a small space does not bear thinking about. Once he was jammed in, Brutus pulled out a gun from the back of his pants. It was very similar and perhaps the same as the one Utah had seen in Sydney just a day earlier in Steed's Sydney bathroom. Brutus then shot Mooring in the lower back to make sure he was dead: 'He just pulled it out and went fucking bang.'

Earl's body did not move. Hopefully, by this stage he was already dead.

11

ON THE ROAD AGAIN

Loose ends get cleaned up.
Stevan Utah

If Stevan Utah had not realised it before, he was now totally compromised. He also knew that if he had showed any sign of weakness that night, his bikie associates would not have hesitated to kill him as casually as they had killed Mooring: 'I am of the belief to this day that he was meant to get a smack in the mouth. I wasn't shocked. I was actually thinking that . . . right about now you'd better help out or I just know that loose ends get cleaned up.'

Brutus ordered Utah to dump the blood-splattered ball hammer somewhere where it would not be found. The hammer would no doubt hold Brutus' fingerprints. It was, and still is, a key piece of evidence. Utah admits he, for once, defied Brutus's instructions and kept the hammer safe rather than throwing it away.

Earl Mooring's body dripping blood and body fluids into the boot of the tiny Micra must have concentrated

Utah's mind enormously on the fact that he was in the company of at least two extremely violent men who thought nothing of killing another human. And that he might be next. It would be very simple for him to say now that he did what he did that night because he was scared of dying: 'OK there was strong mitigating circumstances but you know at the same time I was doing what the boys wanted me to do as well and I've got to live with that.'

Sceptics might suggest that Utah shows remorse now because he has a guilty conscience. There will inevitably be the suspicion that his claims to have been visiting his grandmother's grave and eating fish and chips while poor Earl was tortured just do not wash. As explanations go, even Utah admits it is more than a little strange. The doubting observer might take the view that the real story was that, albeit perhaps unwillingly, he was an observer—and hence an accomplice—to a robbery that got out of control. That he witnessed the torture and murder of a man on that awful night and is too scared of life in gaol to admit it. But to this day, Stevan Utah strenuously denies being there during the killing of Earl Mooring. He is also adamant he did not know that Mooring would be killed or even badly hurt. Whether the police believe him or not, only time will tell.

What he does admit is bad enough. Late in the night, Brutus slammed the Micra boot lid over Mooring's body and ordered Utah to follow him in his vehicle. What a sight it must have been—the hulking and genuinely scary looking Brutus driving a vehicle as banal as a tiny Micra with the rear wheel rims no doubt sagging well over the tyres. For hours and hours into the night, as he followed the tail lights of the Micra on its macabre journey, Utah had plenty of time to think about what was going to happen next. And as the Micra turned off the main national highway nine hundred kilometres from Melbourne into lonely farmland near Goulburn, New South Wales, his pulse was racing more than a little:

> I'm like shitting myself for eight hours thinking when's he going to pull over, when's he going to pull over. We're driving around with a fucking dead body. I'm following a car that's got a fucking dead body in it. I'm like not happy. I hadn't slept for two or three days. I wasn't using methamphetamine or anything else to keep me awake. I'm totally exhausted. I'm not thinking straight. I'm trying to remember everything. I remember I kept looking at the speedo so I could find the same location again later on. I knew then that eight hours was like eight years of thinking. I had just been so careful to remember the finer points.

As Brutus finally halted the Micra by a quiet copse of trees just off a dirt track, Utah warily kept his distance sixty to a hundred metres behind him. But no bullet came. He had clearly passed a test. He was not going to die. 'All I know is in the eight or nine hours I was following him that was all that was going through my head. I made a point of not getting too close. I've fired many pistols in and outside of the army and I basically know what their effective range is. Um, as it turns out at that time he had no intention of knocking me off. But I was tipped off a few weeks later that he was definitely thinking about it.'

Brutus dumped the body under a tree in long grass, not even bothering to bury it. 'He picked him up and dumped him like yesterday's garbage,' Utah says. Utah then followed Brutus to somewhere in the western suburbs of Sydney, where Steed lived. Presumably Brutus also returned the murder weapon to Steed's bathroom sponge bag before he eloquently announced to all present: 'The next person to discuss this will get a punch in the mouth.' Then, his night's work over, Brutus went off to fix his motorbike in preparation for the national run, showing little concern about the evening's events.

Later in the night Utah joined Brutus and another Sydney Bandido hang-around in two cars, including Mooring's. Somewhere on a quiet road in a semi-bushland area of western Sydney they ripped all the identifying plates and tags off Mooring's car. Then fuel was poured into the door cavities and the engine and the little red Nissan Micra, along with any of Earl's remaining DNA and the killer's fingerprints, went up in flames. In the wise book of Bandido sayings there is one known as 'The Three Fs'. It is short for 'Fire Fucks all Forensics'.

At first blush it might have seemed an extraordinary risk for the Bandido killers to take a body and the victim's car across the Victorian border on a drive of nearly one thousand kilometres, not least because they dumped Earl's body within a few kilometres of the New South Wales police training academy at Goulburn. But it seems the outlaw motorcycle gangs also know police procedures better than most people. 'Unfortunately policing in Australia they don't like communicating with each other and this is well known throughout all motorcycle clubs. It's the same if there's some business to be done. If it's immediate the chapters in various states will take care of that business. If it's a little bit nasty you'll find somebody out of state will do it,' Utah explains.

When Brutus turned off the national highway and drove up the narrow dirt road to dump Earl Mooring's body, he knew exactly where he was going. The choice of location was very deliberate. Even if Mooring's body was discovered, there was no DNA database to allow state police forces to share information on missing people. New South Wales police back then would rarely consider asking Victorian police if the corpse, even if it was found, was one of theirs. According to Utah: 'So what you've got, you've got a victim from Victoria. You've got a body located in New South Wales. And you've got a principal offender from Queensland. So you've complicated the matter further by having three states. You find the body . . . if they find the body, they can't identify it.' This alarming hole in police procedures has now, we are assured, been addressed.

Back in Melbourne, Stevan Utah's mother was in a panic about the massive bloodstains across her living room carpet. Utah suggested it was time for urgent renovations: 'I explained to her that she was out of her depth, that the best thing she could do is shut up at that time. Don't talk to anyone. I said whether you like the stuff that's in your house or not, I said it's got to go. I said get rid of it. She actually rang me the following day and she said she'd cut it up and thrown it in the bin. The following day was the garbage removal day and that's about all I know about it.'

When Mooring failed to turn up for work his employer reported him missing. It didn't take long for police to find that Mooring and Utah's mother had been in a relationship. She was inevitably a prime suspect for investigators. Police came calling on Utah's mother within days, to find the house stripped bare of carpet and relaid with cheap linoleum. She had also thrown out the clothes she wore that day.

Across at Earl Mooring's house, it was clear the place had been searched for the money and any other valuables. Brutus and his Bandido outrider associates had done little to conceal their tracks. They used Earl's bank card to make substantial cash withdrawals seven times on the way to Queensland. So brazen was their path that police could follow the transactions from Melbourne, through Sydney, into Queensland and finally the inner Brisbane suburb of Hamilton. Unfortunately, none of the ATMs captured a photograph of the person using Earl's card. The crims were wise to that. Later, police were able to place Brutus elsewhere during some of the withdrawals, but whoever was using the ATM card was acting almost as if he wanted the police to know where he came from.

For all practical purposes, Earl Mooring had disappeared off the face of the earth. He was by now an inside page headline in the Melbourne *Herald-Sun* newspaper, just another missing person:

The mystery of Mr Mooring's disappearance dates back to the night of Tuesday, October 10, when the 54-year-old left a friend's house in Norlane to travel to his girlfriend's house at Whittington, on the other side of Geelong.

According to homicide head Det-Insp. Andrew Allen, the *Spirit of Tasmania* security guard never arrived there, although his car—a red 1996 Nissan Micra—was seen in the area about 1.30 the next morning. That vehicle has also since disappeared.

'We're now two months into the investigation and so far we haven't been able to track down Mr Mooring,' Det-Insp. Allen said.

'We are concerned about his welfare because nothing has been heard from him, although his credit card has been used in a number of transactions. We are now treating it as a possible homicide.

'[The ATM transactions] happened within a short

time after his disappearance, within the first four or five days.

'Large amounts of cash were withdrawn ... and our inquiries have led us to believe it's not him. That type of transaction—taking large amounts of cash out—is out of character for Mr Mooring.'

Mr Mooring's son, Danny, said he and his family were fearing the worst.

'All we know is he's missing and it's been over two months and it's not looking too good. The family's devastated,' he said.

'I had a birthday a couple of weeks ago and I thought I would have got a card or heard something from him but nothing ever came through. It's not like him to go off anywhere without letting anyone know, especially family or friends. We're starting to think it's a homicide.'

One thing that was discreetly let slip in the news reports immediately after Earl's disappearance was the admission by police that it was all probably something to do with the large amount of cash Earl had in his house. One newspaper reported that his family (who didn't live with Mooring) had found a brick-sized lump of cash hidden inside Earl's home shortly after the original burglary. Earl had had the last laugh on Utah, Brutus and their criminal associates on that awful night—but at a terrible cost.

Behind the scenes, Utah's mother was charged a few weeks later with being an accessory to murder. The removal of the blood-splattered carpet from the lounge room was just too hard to explain away. At her son's suggestion, she fled from Victoria to his home in Dalby and then on to Mackay in the far north of the Sunshine State. Her request for an indemnity in return for her full cooperation with Victoria police was knocked back by the Director of Public Prosecutions because there were just too many holes in her story. Extradited back to Melbourne, she ended up pleading guilty to a lesser charge of perverting the course of justice—for which she got a suspended sentence. She now lives under an assumed name with Utah's sister.

Ominously for Utah, at his mother's sentencing hearing the prosecutor Boris Kayser said her son had given 'different accounts of what had occurred at the house'. Victorian police were now very much on his tail. As her beloved son was about to learn, Mummy had also made a statement to police implicating him and Brutus in the botched robbery. Whatever happened to keeping it in the family? Utah was maintaining a low profile back in Dalby, scanning news reports from Geelong and no doubt feeling increasing pangs of guilt each time he read stories on the Mooring family's distress: 'We would really like to get dad's body so we can put him to rest and have a place to visit and mourn,' Mooring's son told Melbourne's *Herald-Sun*.

Years on, Utah admits that he feels overwhelming remorse for what happened to Earl Mooring. He also knows that Earl's family and no doubt many readers of this book will think his present display of a moral conscience is all a little too convenient: 'I am sorry for what happened to Mr Mooring. I am sorry for the circumstances, for my actions, but sometimes you are put in a position where you have to do something for another reason and I know this might sound really strange but the man was already dead.'

By late 2000, when Victoria's homicide squad began investigating Earl Mooring's disappearance, there had been an appalling three-year spate of violent bikie crimes that had jolted police forces around Australia into some degree of momentum on the outlaw motorcycle gangs. Since the November 1997 murder of Bandidos president MKK Kulakowski and two others in Sydney, bikie violence had become an increasing staple of the in-brief columns in Australia's daily newspapers. When bikie gangsters had occasionally killed each other in the past, it rarely generated public concern. 'Who cares if bikies kill bikies?' was the common refrain. But the growing frequency and ferocity of bikie murders, and the murder of a former policeman, were about to arouse a hysterical moral panic in both newsrooms and police ministerial offices across the country.

Following MKK's demise in the basement of Sydney's Blackmarket nightclub, in July 1998 Hells Angel David Newham had been murdered in Sydney in a drive-by shooting. Then, a few months later, Perth Coffin Cheater Mark Chabriere was also blasted to death. In June 1999 in Bendigo, not too far from Earl Mooring's home in Geelong, Vicky Joy Jacobs was shot dead and the nearby Thomastown headquarters of the Nomads was later raided by homicide detectives. In August that year the tortured body of Commanchero Peter Ledger was dumped at his ex-wife's Sydney home. It was a bumper year, because in September the former Rebels chapter president Paul William Wheeler went missing, feared murdered, from Queanbeyan near the Australian Capital Territory. He was quickly followed that same month by Rebel gang member Paul Summers, who died in a machine-gun ambush at a club in Gosford, New South Wales.

Barely a month after that three Rebels were shot dead in an Adelaide ambush and in February 2000, Jacqueline Hinchliffe, the wife of senior Coffin Cheater Mark Hinchliffe, shot dead her lover Michael Wright. The court heard how Hinchliffe had compelled his wife to murder Wright. Then in June 2000 the body of Joseph Flanagan, who reputedly had close links to gangs, was found in forest south of Perth. In August, a couple was murdered in the ACT. A Rebels Motorcycle Club nominee was later charged with their murder. And in the same month as Earl Mooring's disappearance, a woman named Lisa Govan was reported missing and feared murdered, last seen outside the Kalgoorlie headquarters of the Club Deroes motorcycle gang.

Within days of Mooring's murder in Geelong, across the country one of the most momentous events in this recent cycle of bikie violence took place at a small outback town called Ora Banda near Kalgoorlie in Western Australia. A Gypsy Joker gang member, Billy Grierson, was shot by a sniper. Police investigations would later suggest that the gang members blamed a retired top cop, Don Hancock, who owned a pub nearby, and they were absolutely right.

By the time Victorian police began to suspect in late 2000 that Earl Mooring had been murdered, public outrage about violent bikie crimes had moved on to the front page. Unfortunately for Stevan Utah, the suspected bikie murder of Earl Mooring was about to become a major priority. The killings had not stopped at Earl Mooring either. In March 2001, Hunter Valley Bandidos boss Rodney Partington was killed when a bomb blew up in his hands at a Gypsy Jokers' compound in Kurri Kurri, New South Wales. Then national outrage flared again in September that year when Don Hancock, the former Western Australian policeman who had allegedly killed a Gypsy Joker the previous year, was blown up by a car bomb with his friend Lou Lewis outside Hancock's family home. Public outrage poured forth again, then abated just a little when it was realised that Don Hancock had started it by coldly killing one of them.

By the time police revealed in December 2001 that Earl Mooring was the victim of a Bandidos hit squad, the tabloids had already had a field day in the previous weeks with revelations that a former Rebels member and amphetamine dealer, Terry Falconer, had been abducted in New South Wales. His dismembered remains were found in a river. It was one of a series of particularly nasty and lurid murders, and murdered and murdering bikies were great tabloid copy.

Stevan Utah still maintains that without Earl Mooring's corpse to prove he was dead, the Victorian police investigation was going nowhere. But what had happened to Earl Mooring had rattled Utah's admittedly slightly quirky moral code. Earl's four children were now without a father because Brutus and Stig wanted his money and thought nothing of killing him for it. If there was a moment that flicked Utah's switch and sent him down the path of cooperating with police to combat outlaw motorcycle gangs, it was that awful sight of Mooring's battered body on the tarpaulin.

Utah had made a decision. He was prepared to rat on his bikie colleagues: 'The average Bandido one on one is nothing. As a group, they're very fucking dangerous, very dangerous. Just for once, just for once, why shouldn't the tide be turned and let them bastards be looking over their shoulder and always be in fear rather than everyone else in society?' The only issue for him now was when and how to do it.

12

THE HEAT OF THE KITCHEN

What crack is to cocaine, so ice is to amphetamine.
Dr Shane Darke, Illicit Drug
Reporting System

Warning: don't try this recipe at home. Actually, don't try this recipe ever. The exact measurements have been omitted. From 'Cooking with Stevan Utah':

To cook is simple, the threat is real. The cops, other cooks, the gangsters, the greed.

Whilst the methodology to remove pseudo-ephedrine from blockers and other chemicals is easy, it does take time.

Cough medicine—I need 2 x 20 litre buckets, [xx] litres of cough medicine, [xx] litres of hot water, [xx] caps of caustic soda, [xx] litres of toluene. One could extract between [xx] grams of pure pseudo ephedrine (E) by this method in literally 15 minutes. That is enough to make $30 000 wholesale in Australia.

THE HEAT OF THE KITCHEN

The pills and blockers, hydrochlorides require PH altered and intense heat to separate blockers. You need a bucket of water and ice, various tubing, a pressure cooker or flash with burner and a condenser. Chemicals needed are caustic soda, hydrochloric acid and water. This method took up to 2 hours to obtain steam off [fluid from condenser] to acquire 15 grams of E. This would be in [xx] litres of run-off which would be boiled away until the crystals appeared. The crystals are your E. One box of cold medication has 24 tablets containing 30 mg per tab. This gives a max of [xx] grams of E per packet. This method you could remove about [xx] a packet.

The threat: you get caught doing this and you will get five years first offence.

The cops: they will weigh everything to come up with a street value.

Other cooks: they want your secrets and attempt to build alliances, but they are already aligned with crooks outside the circle. Many cooks also use their own product while they work to stay awake and get the job done. Unfortunately your body will eventually begin to shut down and you 'tweak'—this includes paranoia, and hallucinations [*the men in dark black suits coming at you in your peripheral vision*].

The gangsters: will kill you for your product, your knowledge or even harm what is around you to extort and blackmail. Secrecy and protection is always required.

The greed: the end product is there for all to share in equally. Some overcut the same batch product to greater their profit, at the risk of making the team look bad. This is why the right cook will have one cutter. No-one else touches the product.

The cook's cut is approximately 1 to 1, this is because pure product will melt plastic. A cook's cut is also said to be pure as it is obvious it is a 1 to 1 cut to stabilise the product to prevent loss and meltdown. It is cut with glucose, so 112 gms of meth is 224 or 8 ounces of pure.

As we have said before, do not try this recipe at home or anywhere else. When you hear of 'meth' labs exploding you know they got the recipe wrong. Or, as Utah suggested, they dabbled in their own product and the level of care slipped. For Utah, he was pretty lucky. An occasional flirtation with his product was just that. He had the brains to avoid getting hooked on the stuff.

When asked about the difficulty of buying the raw materials to make the drugs, Utah chortled, 'How easy is it to buy cornflakes from Woolworths?' He went on, 'There's 30 milligrams per litre of pseudo in Benadryl [cough medicine] in Australia'. Picture, if you will, bikies motoring up and down the east coast of Australia, in cars and not dressed in the usual bikie ensembles, buying cough medicine that they pour into new petrol cans in their boots. If stopped, Utah reckoned, correctly, that it was highly unlikely a gas can would draw sufficient attention for the cops to open it and take a good sniff. As Utah said, 'Police would hammer you if you had six hundred bottles of cough medicine in your car. That quantity would make two kilograms of pseudo in about six hours.' Legitimate drugs neatly recycled into illicit and highly profitable drugs.

In the aftermath of the Mooring murder, a few things were crystal clear, if you will pardon the pun, to Stevan Utah. He was definitely 'on the inside' with the gangs. He also knew that getting away from the gangs, despite the 'do not touch' assurances of senior members, wasn't going to happen without a lot of pain and suffering on his part. He literally knew where the bodies were buried. On the inside with the bikies he was reasonably secure. If he moved out of their ambit, could they then rely on him to keep quiet?

The only dissenting voice in this cosy circle was Brutus's. Utah heard that Brutus wasn't deeply fond of living witnesses to his crimes in general, and his battering to death of Earl Mooring in particular. Word got back to Utah that Brutus was 'a little worried' and was saying openly to some in the higher echelons of the gang that he was going to see Utah and shut him up. Utah knew that this was not going to be just a vigorous discussion. If Brutus came visiting, then Utah would be joining Earl

Mooring, at least in spirit if not physically side by side, in a lonely patch of bush. A long drive crammed into the boot of a small car was not the future Utah had planned. In what is a testament to his ability to inveigle his way into even the hardest of hearts, Utah's higher-up mates sprung to his defence. One, from whom even Brutus took orders, told him not to go near Utah. Another trusted ally of Utah and Brutus gave him the ultimate accolade, 'I know Steve, that guy's transported money for us'. Utah was safe.

Utah very sensibly decided to stay close. The fact that he still got a bit of a thrill out of life with the gangs, albeit no longer a vicarious one, may have added a little more comfort to his decision. And hell, the money was good, the hours were short, and he could still keep up his nine-to-five lifestyle. For both sides that was good cover and for Utah it was a grasp at life outside the gangs. He wanted to go straight, but it just wasn't going to happen.

Utah's skill as a cook was well known throughout the bike gangs in that post-Mooring world. Thanks to the invention of the internet, Utah had found a recipe and been 'dabbling' since about 1994. He'd heard about the drug, heard how easy it was to make, and how profitable it could be. Utah, in the early days, hadn't wanted to be a major player because, as he said, 'you generally get killed if you do that'. He did it as a favour for some mates, and to make a little for his own occasional use. Years of practice and honing of his recipe and skills meant he did not make mistakes and he could deliver on time. He was utterly reliable, fast, loyal, efficient and didn't dabble too much with his own product. Perfect for the gangs and perfectly timed to take advantage of a booming market.

Around that time, Dr Shane Darke of the Illicit Drug Reporting System told the Australian media that the potent form of amphetamine known as 'ice' was on the rise across Australia. 'What crack is to cocaine, so ice is to amphetamine.' Potent, easy to get and relatively cheap. Lots of bang for your buck. Customs were working hard and having some success. In December 2000, seventy-nine kilograms of ice were seized in Sydney after being imported from Hong Kong. In July 2001, two hundred and forty-two kilograms of ice were found on a yacht at Mooloolaba on the Sunshine Coast, Queensland, only a short drive from Caloundra, and in a townhouse on the Gold Coast. Much safer to source locally was the obvious decision for the traffickers.

By early 2001, the Australian Bureau of Criminal Intelligence was reporting that Queensland, the 'Smart State', was leading the country in amphetamine production. They estimated that production was worth $400 million, and that thirty of the one hundred and thirty-one clandestine labs seized across Australia in 1999–2000 were in Queensland. In the previous twelve months, eighty-five thousand people over the age of fourteen were estimated to have used amphetamines compared to only seventeen thousand users of that very sixties and seventies drug, heroin. Business was booming, and Chef Utah was working wonders in the kitchen. His fate was to be drawn even deeper into the action.

What had become obvious to him, even as far back as the Kulakowski funeral, was that the local Bandidos had good relationships with their overseas brethren. When Peter Harris was married, Utah, who didn't make the wedding, reckoned that his mates bragged that about half of the Vancouver chapter of the Bandidos turned up for the ceremony and subsequent reception. The Canadian Bandidos, along with the Canadian Hells Angels, were seriously bad news. In the 2003 Annual Report of the Criminal Intelligence Service of Canada, the section on 'organised crime in Canada' reported that outlaw motorcycle gangs, and in particular the Bandidos, Hells Angels and the Outlaws, 'remain a serious criminal threat in Canada and continue to be involved in an array of criminal activities such as murder, drug trafficking, prostitution, illegal gambling, extortion, intimidation, fraud and theft'. It also ominously noted that major organised crime groups all had links to Canada's marine ports.

Yet despite a fair guess that Bandidos weren't exactly the most desirable lads to have visiting, the Australian government gave the wedding guests the visas they needed. The high probability is that they simply had no idea who they were letting in. The Australian government's knowledge of who was who in the bikie world was at best rather parochial. Back in the early 1990s the Federal

Court had ruled that membership of an alleged criminal organisation could be taken into account when considering people for temporary visas. However, it is a fair bet that if you didn't 'fess up on the application form, then the Australian government would probably remain blissfully ignorant and give you a visa. The only gang members who had hit an immigration hurdle were Hells Angels. Quite a few had told the truth when trying to come to Australia for the 'World Run'. This was an annual event that their public relations spokesmen tried to pass off as a civilised gathering. Back in the 1960s, sometime Hells Angels groupie Hunter S. Thompson had described the event as 'a massive three-day drunk that nearly always results in some wild, free-swinging action and another rude shock for the squares . . . It is a time for sharing the wine jug, pummelling old friends, random fornication and general full-dress madness.' Colourful, but closer to the truth in all probability. The Australian government declined to offer visas to the intending tourists.

The only notable Bandido to have trouble with immigration was back in 1992, when Pete Gordon Price, sergeant-at-arms of his local chapter in Washington, was arrested in Sydney's reliably colourful Kings Cross. Poor Pete, allegedly on a three-week holiday, was arrested while on a stroll through the Cross with Australian Bandido Grant Evers. Unfortunately for the visitor, the police decided to search him. Pete, according to his lawyer, weighed one hundred and ninety kilograms, was only one hundred and eighty-five centimetres tall, and was wearing an outfit 'that would have attracted anyone's attention', which is no mean feat in Kings Cross. It seems police may not have approved of his Bandido motifed leather motorcycle jacket in the middle of summer. What was more likely was that the police thought Pete may have been concealing something other than his charm. They were right. His jacket contained body armour, and underneath it was a loaded .32 calibre pistol, a curious addition to the usual camera and tourist guide book.

His solicitor, the sometimes colourful Chris Murphy, claimed the ex-Vietnam veteran had been licensed to carry firearms since he was twelve. He claimed, 'Almost every day of his life since he was 12 he has carried a gun but has no criminal record. He admits he was rather stupid in what he did but for a person who is, by his own admission, a member of a motorcycle gang to be 43 years of age and have no convictions is not bad. This spoils his good record.'

Pete, it would seem, had either been very good or very lucky as he also had a licence in the United States to carry a concealed weapon. The magistrate took pity on the poor tourist noting, 'the fact that you have such a licence says that in your own country they regard you as a person of good character', before fining Pete.

The advantage of a guilty plea is that often embarrassing questions simply do not get asked. Was the need for Pete to have a gun simply a cultural misunderstanding or a clash of cultures? How did he get the gun? Even in the early nineties airlines were not too keen to carry armed bikies across the Pacific. If he got the gun locally, then how did he manage to do so, and why did he feel the need? If he had got the gun locally then the 'how did he?' may not be too hard to answer.

Almost a decade after that ill-fated holiday, guns were still a hot topic. Part of the reason was Martin Bryant and his massacre at Tasmania's Port Arthur in October 1996. But police were also getting even more concerned at the rise of guns as part of the criminal culture. Just like Britain, Australia was not a place, even in the criminal world, where guns were part of the currency of daily life. Peter Ryan, the newly minted New South Wales commissioner of police, said, 'criminal gangs were becoming a little bit more brazen and arrogant' and guns 'were being traded as underworld currency'. He went on to comment, rather accurately, 'when one group of people becomes armed . . . the other group arms up as well, so guns start moving around'.

At about this time the Australian Institute of Criminology's report titled 'International Traffic in Firearms—Emerging Issues', reckoned, 'According to police and other sources, the existing black market in Australia is not an organised underworld. It is mostly divided into criminal gangs, whose main focus are crimes other than dealing in firearms, or small networks of individuals who buy or sell by word of mouth. Nonetheless, firearms traffickers play a significant role in supplying firearms to persons with a criminal intent.'

Ryan was much closer to the truth. And the crooks were much much better organised than they were being given credit for. If Stevan Utah had been talkative at that point, and the police listening, the story may have been rather different.

13

DRINKING FROM THE TOP SHELF

I have bought grenades, explosives, passports, drugs.
Stevan Utah

Thanks to his role as either witness or accessory to a couple of murders, and his ongoing silence, Utah had access to the top shelf of Australian crime. Perhaps it might be more accurate to borrow a quip from Norman Gunston and suggest Utah now had the opportunity to 'open the lid [of crime organisations] and peer into the bowl'.

While the collective cops around the country thought that gun trading was a bit of a cottage industry, Utah knew better. He commented, 'Over the years I have acquired .22 Phoenixes [a handgun], 9 mms, .38s, .44s. Damn, I even once bought a brand new original model 29 Dirty Harry special. I have bought grenades, explosives, passports, drugs. I have bought all types of weapons including hunting rifles, AKs, SKSs [both military rifles from the former Soviet Union], fuck, I bought a Mag 58 machine gun once for eight grand.'

DEAD MAN RUNNING

One frequent stop for Utah was a motorcycle dealer in Queensland. It was a gathering place for the Bandidos and a good spot for discreet meetings, not only with fellow Bandidos, but also the other major gangs. Neutral ground, according to Utah. A tricky place for surveillance by police, and a place where the trusted were received with hospitality and outsiders generally got the bum's rush. It was also gun-running headquarters. Back in the 1970s, the Hells Angels caught on to a nice little earner importing Harley-Davidson parts from the United States. The Bandidos and their mates in Queensland sweetened the deal by adding some extras to the parts. Those extras were guns. And Utah was often there when they arrived.

When asked how it worked, Utah said the guns were 'concealed in parts in relation to Harley-Davidsons, one of the sets of businesses that outlaw motorcycle clubs have are Harley-Davidson shops'. No late-night assignations in dark laneways needed. It is important to point out that the majority of Harley-Davidson and motorcycle shops in Queensland and any other part of Australia are legitimate and honourable businesses and not part of bike gang influenced import and distribution networks. But ... some are.

Utah went on, 'I once saw a box that had the name of a bike shop on it. An unopened box. There were definitely guns in that.' Utah found they were all handguns, imported from the United States. The dealership was only interested in guns and bikes. Utah reckons it's a place where the gang

162

members discussed 'guns, drugs, hits on other people. Can you do this for me? Can you do that for me? Thanks, brother.' What chilled Utah was that the gangs traded not only weapons but favours. For police investigating a serious crime the trading meant the link to motive was removed, making the crime appear, at least on the evidence to hand, random. As usual, the bikies were a few steps ahead of their pursuers.

Utah was there when the senior members of the Australian Hells Angels and the Vikings popped by to chat about business. On one occasion he recalled a meeting between the Bandidos and senior Hells Angels:

> I was sitting at the dealership and there were two senior members of the Bandidos and they were openly brother this and brother that. Embraced each other, the whole bit. And I saw one very senior Bandido say to the vice president of the Hells Angels, 'Oh, I fixed that for you, brother', and they started talking about the Rebels. It was like how if there was going to be a very serious conflict you would probably find in an unprecedented way, particularly in Queensland, that the Bandidos and Hells Angels will all of a sudden become allies. Just for that conflict.

Just like the reason Sonny Barger and his fellow Angels ended up in prison.

When Utah was asked about the level of police

understanding of these 'cooperative' meetings, he noted: 'I don't think the Australian police do know. I don't think that they—I am going to rephrase that. I think a minority of state police do, that have done undercover work. It's like another world. Would senior police understand it? I don't think so. I think they would understand the logistics of the problem but they wouldn't understand the actual cause of the root problem.' What police did not fully grasp was the capacity of the bike gangs to operate both in a highly organised and disciplined manner, or to be capable of impulsive and sometimes both profitable and savage acts. And police didn't think across state borders. The dumping of Mooring's body in another state underlined that problem and the bikies' insight.

Another rather problematic policing issue Utah had observed was the police themselves. In Queensland he had witnessed a police officer tipping off Bandido members about raids on their properties: 'I've been there. I've seen it. I've heard it with my own ears', he claims. And the amphetamine business was booming, particularly on Australia's eastern seaboard. These were the drugs of choice and the drugs of fashion. Utah observed that he was making 'millions' of dollars worth of amphetamine in labs secreted on properties in south-east Queensland, often literally under the noses of police. 'Typically', Utah said, 'it's probably like your $80 to $100000, but even still if they're turning over $80 to $100000 each month, you know you're still taking $1.2 million a year'.

On one occasion as part of a drug deal, Utah calmly motored back from New South Wales to Queensland with $3 million in cash. Aside from the large amount of money, the deal was memorable for one other reason. Utah did not quite understand how attached to their cash these lads were, or quite how urgently they were expecting its delivery, so as he meandered back up the coast he decided to stop over and enjoy a little 'friend's benefits' interaction with an old flame. As a result he was a day late getting back to Queensland. It would be a swift learning curve.

The initial reaction of the bikies was 'to put out a hit' on Utah. Find him, catch him, get the money and get rid of him. Trust only went so far. So when Utah turned up at Gronk's home with the bag of money, all intact, Gronk did the right thing by his mate and told him to keep his head down until all could be resolved. Gronk then went into bat with his feisty colleagues, explaining that Utah had merely 'stopped for a root', and hadn't made off with the bag of cash. Mollified, the hit orders were withdrawn and Utah was back in relative safety. It was a chilling reminder of just how fickle the brotherhood could be.

The deal that really gave him a surprise was truly a whopper. Hundreds of thousands of ecstasy tablets with a street value of $16 million. All cash, and tax and GST free. He said, 'Drugs is a currency and a power and when you have power and currency you seem to have all these people that will cater to your every whim and any whim'. That power forged new alliances in the gangs and their associates. In Queensland, aside from growing closer to Sava Cvetkovic, president of the Bandidos Gold Coast chapter, and the lads at Caloundra, he grew closer to the soon to be in trouble Bandido Gronk. So much so that he was called to a meeting with Gronk and a couple of Bandidos and associates at the Cooyar Hotel, a classic wide-verandah Australian country pub in Cooyar, a small town just out of Dalby on the way to the Sunshine Coast. A discreet and convenient spot for a chat.

The chat was about Gronk and his problem. He reckoned he was 'red hot'. Gronk had been told he was the subject of a telephone interception by Queensland police and they were now busily investigating him. Gronk thought the intercept related to 'fixing up' a problem with a witness. Gronk produced a copy of what he reckoned was the transcript of the intercept. Utah took the view that the Queensland police might have been a bit leaky. What he also thought was that Gronk was talking about the murder of the 'informant' by Jonker in Dallas Devine's case. He also believed that the evidence, both what the cops had and what Gronk now had, was quite scary, particularly as Utah had been a witness to the murder. Utah left the meeting a very troubled man.

But business kept chugging away. On his frequent visits to New South Wales he often stayed with a gentleman we will call 'Bobo the Croatian', and members of his gang. Bobo was about fifty, short, thin and with a shaved head and long grey moustache. He was a big distributor of ecstasy and marijuana, with Utah at one time seeing about thirty thousand tablets in his house.

Another on the visiting list was the dealer Milad Sande, who plied his trade in Sydney's more fashionable east, and almost inevitably around the fleshpots of Kings Cross. Utah met him at Bandido Steed's place. Utah was no fan of Sande, and was not deeply moved when Sande was murdered a few years later in a very nasty falling out involving the Bandidos.

Utah developed a good working relationship with Russell Oldham, a fellow Bandido cook of great repute as well. 'Best mates', according to Utah, the two got on so well, they often worked side by side in the kitchens of the east coast. Utah would, 'do a cook-up with him. He was a "tweaker". When he started to "tweak", like anyone on ice, he would hallucinate about the black shadows coming from the side of his head. The bikies would talk about guys in black coats—that's the effect of the ice when you're tweaking. Russell was a big user.' One of those times in the kitchen when the chef's prerogative of tasting isn't such a good idea.

Utah got to know Felix Lyle, head of the Bandidos Sydney chapter and also very close to Russell Oldham. Lyle was doing well, in that very Sydney way, with a growing real estate portfolio. In an odd twist, the softly spoken Lyle decided he wanted to buy a slice of Bandido history, the Blackmarket nightclub in Chippendale. When he approached the real estate agent handling the sale, the agent saw before him a 'pretty sizeable bloke' with long hair plaited down his back, and one who 'didn't appear too concerned about the $3.5 million price tag'. When told that some locals wanted to buy it and an adjoining building to redevelop the site as home units, Lyle said he wanted to preserve the building as a hotel/bar, for 'sentimental reasons'.

Sadly for the sentimental Felix, the New South Wales Crime Commission came visiting in May 2001 and charged him with drug offences. And as they had with Alex Vella a few years earlier, they took a long look at his and the Bandidos' assets. At the time, they included a block of units in glamorous harbourside Double Bay, a suburb in which a Bandido would stick out even more than dog's balls, a unit in Kellett Street, Kings Cross, and a terrace house in inner-city Pyrmont. The value was over $3 million. Poor old Felix didn't get Blackmarket, but he did get a lot of trouble coming his way.

Utah managed to find himself rubbing shoulders with prominent Sydney identity Tony Vincent as well. Tony has been described as a restaurateur, when he owned Lady Janes, a 'lingerie restaurant', to be polite, and one fancied by Bandidos, crooks and the bent former copper Roger Rogerson. A place to enjoy good company and a good meal, perhaps, but just be careful when you go looking for the strawberries and cream. Tony was also a mate of Alan Bond's financial adviser, convicted heroin dealer and habitué of various courts, the unforgettable

Jim Byrnes. He counted the late Mr Big of Australian crime and sometime mate of Fat Vinnie Teresa, Lennie McPherson, as a mate, too. A friendly fellow was Tony. When last interviewed by police he was calling himself a 'pensioner'.

Within a few years, many of the contacts Utah made in Sydney would turn into rather significant players in his life. Many would be dead.

14

RATS IN THE RANKS

Do our children need to grow up and live in fear?
Stevan Utah

If there was one fact very clear in Stevan Utah's mind, it was what happened if you upset the Bandidos. He'd seen Joseph Jonker swiftly and cold-bloodedly shoot a man who just might have been an undercover cop or an informant. From decision to execution was as quick as the fluttering of an eyelid and bugger the consequences. He had also seen the results of the Bandidos at their most brutal, having torturing the hapless Earl Mooring to death, inch by gore-soaked inch. And just for money. What Utah knew was that one wrong step from him, and a similar fate awaited.

Becoming an informant against individual criminals or criminal organisations happens sometimes for just one reason, and sometimes for a collection of reasons. The classic motivation is self-preservation. In America, the mafia found itself in murkier than usual waters when the godfather of all mafia informants, Joe Valachi, rolled over. Joe was a veteran of the bloody wars between 'families' that saw Charles 'Lucky' Luciano as the ascendant gangster of his time. Unfortunately for Joe, he had been caught peddling narcotics for the 'family' and had headed off for a fairly long stretch at the Atlanta Federal Penitentiary.

If the chain-smoking, gravel-voiced Valachi was the typical mafia foot soldier, the Atlanta Penitentiary was the typical prison of your cinema-influenced nightmares. Joe shared a cell with Vito Genovese, then head of the family after Luciano's deportation back to Sicily. Prisons are a great breeding ground for both paranoia and rumour, and Vito soon came to the view, incorrect at the time, that Joe was a rat. He gave him 'the kiss of death'. Joe, equally as paranoid and rumour fuelled, heard of his impending demise, but mistook another prisoner as his would-be assassin and promptly beat him to death with a lump of iron. When a conviction for murder was added to Joe's record, he decided to turn and tell all. In a lovely piece of public relations, Senator John L. McLellan, leading the senate investigation, televised Joe's testimony in September and October 1963. It was riveting broadcasting.

Almost two decades later, Jimmy 'The Weasel' Frattiano took a similar course. Unlike Valachi, Jimmy was at the top of the mafia pile, acting head of the Los Angeles family. He boasted that he had killed eleven people. When Jimmy found out in the late 1970s that a contract was out on him, he promptly gave himself up and started talking. It was a breathtaking insider's view of the mafia, and included tantalising insights into the CIA's Operation Mongoose, which saw them in league with mobster Santo Trafficante Junior in a plot to assassinate Fidel Castro. The old botulus toxin in the cigar trick. Jimmy also chucked in a little J.F.K. legend to give the conspiracy theorists a thrill. Unlike Valachi, Jimmy went into witness protection, got kicked out for behaving badly and became a talk-show regular and co-author of *The Last Mafioso* and *Vengeance is Mine*. He died of natural causes, not lead poisoning, in 1993.

And, of course, in Australia we have had great opportunists, like Arthur 'Neddy' Smith and the sly and devious James McCartney Anderson, the Iago of Kings Cross. Smith, when arrested, promptly started babbling. In return for his information, he got the 'green light' for criminal enterprises from some members of the New South Wales police. Part of the deal was to share, and to keep talking. Very hard if you're ratting on competitors. Anderson actually sought out the National Crime Authority to further his quest to topple his former boss, Abe Saffron, from his perch as the 'Boss of the Cross'.

Other informants come forward out of a sense of responsibility, sometimes for absolution for their complicity and sometimes from a bursting need to unburden. Some, of course, just want the attention. If you have worked in law enforcement or in the investigative end of the media, then these people can be tricky to deal with. Their stories are plausible, they present as earnest and honest. But if you've been around the traps a while that sixth sense kicks in—if you're lucky, that is. The light bulb comes on above your head and you start probing a little harder. Quite often the penny drops soon into the conversation and you realise you're dealing with someone whose grip on the plot is either skewed or missing.

All informants can expect a bit of due diligence. Do you have documents to support your claims? You push the chronology of events to see if it tallies. You listen with a hard objectivity. Does the story make sense? Can it have happened the way you're being told? If the answer is yes, then you move on. On the flip side, informants have expectations, some reasonable and some unreasonable, of their handlers. Compassion and respect, either real or feigned, are high on the list. It's a bit of a master/servant relationship, but the master has to be a fair one. Anyone with some experience will know that one thing is true about all informants: it is unlikely in the extreme that you will get the whole story first time around. No matter how motivated they are, a little seduction is needed, and the closer they get, the more you get.

When Stevan Utah decided to start talking it was for a mix of reasons and he would sail through the due diligence with flying colours. He also would not have handed over everything on the first date. His marriage was not faring too well. Regular trips into New South Wales and Victoria on his drug-related activities did not help. Neither did police turning up at his retreat in Dalby and searching the property for evidence that might pin him, or his mother, to what was then, in the police's eyes, the disappearance and probable murder of Earl Mooring. Even though Utah had popped into the Dalby station and alerted his tea-sipping acquaintances of the probable request to search his house, having big-footed coppers, even amiable ones, tearing your house apart is not good for domestic bliss.

Another little problem chucked into his path was a serious car accident, a near-fatal crash in February 2001. Swerving to avoid an erring P-plate driver, Utah's car plunged off a bridge about ten kilometres west of Dalby. He damaged his knee badly and eventually picked up a settlement of $128 000. The lawyer's bill quickly whittled this down to $72 000. When he was ready to return to work, it was to a round of menial jobs like supermarket shelf stocking in the area. It was an unsettling time for him that eventually saw him working again with timber and his hands as a carpenter.

Utah also knew that the gang had him by the balls and would not hesitate to squeeze and squeeze hard if it was to their advantage. Utah had seen enough of Mooring's blood to know that he didn't want to go through that again.

When thinking about a specific motivation for his actions, he found words tricky: 'It's actually a . . . it's very difficult to answer. It's in my head. It's like when you've seen too many people that aren't able to defend themselves, they live in fear, constant fear, all the time, something just like says, you know, why do you let these people [the Bandidos] get away with this?'

Into that dreadful mix was still the young man who, almost two decades earlier, had decided not to go on a joyride interstate with two mates. Utah had wanted a future, and that ill-fated journey would have kiboshed it. Still in him also was the boy who had once put a knife through another boy's hand in defence of a sad and vulnerable child. Two decades on and Utah still clung to the hope of a future, and it was a future that specifically didn't feature Bandidos. That love affair with the strength and purpose the gangs offered to the damaged goods that had been Stevan Utah was nearing its end run. In Utah's eyes, the gangs were growing too strong, too violent and too powerful. A counterpoint to the hope of a future. He said:

Australia is truly a unique country, the land of fair play, give a bloke a go, the land of opportunity. We have the most wonderful oceans, world renowned diverse flora and fauna, and great weather. We also have outlaw motorcycle groups, the one percent fraternity of murder, drugs, extortion, prostitution, arson, theft, assault, deprivation of liberty, kidnapping, torture and many many more. The Bandidos, a North American based organisation, the Hells

Angels, a North American based organisation, the Outlaws ... should I continue? Australia is my country, it is mine. Do our children need to grow up and live in fear? I have personally seen four new Bandido chapters open in the last eight years. That doesn't sound like much. One every two years. Okay, minimum eight members per chapter, that's thirty-two new groups in the OMG [outlaw motorcycle gang] world of organised crime. Oh, and the 'hang-arounds' and criminal associates, let's double that number to sixty-four living, breathing, cunning, logical thinking criminals. They know the police and they know what they can get away with, they know the methodologies. That's a new criminal every six weeks.

When it was suggested that cynics might think that Utah decided to start talking because police were on his tail for the Mooring case, he scoffed, 'The Victorian police didn't have shit. I knew it. They knew it.' For Utah, the circumstances had conspired to give him the courage to stand up and have one last grab at a better life. Of course the problem he had, aside from the enormous danger to himself, was danger to his family members. He had made up his mind, but it had to be done carefully.

Utah was well aware of the problems he would face in talking to the Queensland police. Though they were the only game in town at this stage, he was not a huge fan: 'They're scared, they're pathetic, they're lazy, they're ineffective, they're inefficient and they're just self-serving and they like to waste the taxpayer's money. But I'm very biased about my opinion of them.'

Bias notwithstanding, Utah was receptive when two Queensland detectives and a squad of local uniforms came to Chez Utah in late November 2001 for a further chat about the still missing and presumed dead Earl Mooring. They also did one search of the property to see if they had overlooked any potential evidence lying around. Yet again, the house and the outbuildings were thoroughly searched by the detectives and local cops, and yet again they didn't find a thing. Nor did their intrusion rattle Utah. He was very much aware of what they wanted.

In the post search chat, the detectives were pushing for information, hoping that Utah might roll over or offer a tantalising slice of information on which they could move the investigation a little further. Utah did not dismiss them out of hand. He was very close to the point of no return. What the Queensland police did not know was how close they had come to stumbling over an informant who had the potential to unlock a treasure trove. Of their visit, Utah commented, 'I just had too many links to my life and I needed to push everything away . . . I actually said to them, I said, come back and see me in six months. And they said, what? I know you fucking done it. They said, you do a deal with us today or there's no deal. And I said, well, there's no fucking deal then. And anyway, then he and the other detective said to me, look, he said, think about it. He said here's my card, give me a call.'

Rather than handling Utah like a potential source to be nurtured, the detectives handled him like a punter in a used car yard. Many police make the same error, using the strength of their office to bully instead of using some basic humanity to coax. Bullying may work with the none too bright or the desperate, but neither of these descriptions fitted Stevan Utah.

Utah admitted that the trick almost worked, but he knew what he could bring to the table, and he knew there was a deal to be had. Somewhere. After a night with very little sleep, Utah followed up, ringing the number on the card. He told the detectives he had a bit of thinking to do and would ring the next day. He didn't want to blow his chance, but he also didn't want to make a deal with the police holding all the cards. Part of the motivation for talking was to put some control back in his own hands.

He was good to his word, and rang the next day. One of the detectives had headed off to investigate a murder in the country. Utah said to his partner, 'Mate, you just got to understand something. I said there's too much going on around me and I said they're going to come at everything around me.' Utah had a very good grip on the downside of his actions and was determined to minimise the risk both for him and for his family. He went on, 'Come back and see me in six months'. They didn't come back. Utah later commented: 'This conversation definitely occurred because the Victorian police repeated the exact same conversation to me in December 2004. So they obviously got the message. No, but the key point here is nobody came back and saw me six months later. I still had to approach them. Um, you know, fourteen, sixteen months later, whatever it was.'

What neither the Victorian police, when they had popped up shortly after Mooring's disappearance to chat to both Utah and his mother, nor the diligently searching Queensland police knew was that Utah had kept a little insurance policy in case any problems came his way in relation to the murder. Rather than getting rid of the bloodstained hammer that had been used on old Earl, he had kept it as insurance. It was wrapped in plastic, tightly sealed and hidden in one of the outbuildings on his Dalby property. And it was missed during both searches by the cops. This rates as a major investigative 'oops'.

The two detectives came back to Dalby in late 2002 and had a brief chat with Utah at the Dalby police station. They took his mobile phone and that was it. No offers, no cajoling, nothing but hard ball. A little respect and perhaps even a little empathy might have given Utah the nudge he needed. In hindsight, the Queensland police had fingers like Errol Flynn. Everything they touched they fucked.

15

INTO THE ARMS OF THE CRIME COMMISSION

After what I've done to them they'll want to cause me some serious pain.
Stevan Utah

Queenslanders have always prided themselves on being different from the rest of Australia. It is a hedonistic place of often astonishing beauty but, just like Florida in the United States, whose character it most resembles, it has an apparently disproportionate representation of carpet-baggers, dodgy developers and politicians, and homicidally amoral gangsters.

Perhaps that perception is more to do with the fact that older states like New South Wales and Victoria cherish their criminal milieu as 'local colour' and take a certain civic pride in the affectionate cronyism which passes for representative democracy in their states. Queenslanders—bless them—always react with mock horror when anyone suggests they might have an organised crime problem, so the rest of the country delights in pointing out they are just the same as everywhere else. Heaven help anyone south of the border who points this curious anomaly out. The Sunshine State's ex-Premier Sir Joh Bjelke-Petersen once neatly represented much of the Queensland public's general hostility to investigative media questioning by opining that: 'The greatest thing that could happen in the State and the Nation is when we get rid of the media. Then we would live in peace and tranquillity and no-one would know anything.'

A week after Earl Mooring was bludgeoned to death on a Geelong floor by Queensland Bandido Brutus, three hundred Bandido bikies travelled from interstate on a three-day holiday to the Gold Coast. Gold Coast tabloids had been warning that the event would result in riots and tarnish the tourist strip's family friendly image. Score one in the public relations battle went to the outlaw motorcycle gangs as 'Tina—a 53-year-old Bandido wife' was given photo and page lead status to decry those who had warned locals to 'lock up your daughters' from the 'unpredictable and often violent' gang members. 'I am very tired of this rubbish that I hear', Tina told Gold Coast papers. 'It's not true. They are family men. They've got children, they look after their children. They look after their wives and girlfriends. They are lovely people.'

While the good citizens of the Gold Coast were no doubt reassured by Tina's protestations that bikies are lovely people, illicit drugs such as ice and cocaine continued to exact their grim toll of addiction, despair and misery along the seamier strips of their coast. Whether Queenslanders wanted to know about it or not, it was business as usual among many senior Bandidos involved in serious organised crime.

Within weeks of the Bandido's family weekend on the coast, the gaoling of Bandidos sergeant-at-arms Dallas Devine barely rated a mention in the local papers. One of the principals of the Sunshine and Gold Coast trade in illicit drugs, Dallas had been busted selling speed, cocaine, hash, LSD, handguns and even stolen guitars to an undercover police officer. And somewhere up the road, near the Beerwah cemetery, one of those suspected of having shopped him to the police was, according to Stevan Utah, lying undetected and unmissed with Hombre Jonker's bullets in him.

A little further up the Queensland coast, towards the playground of the Great Barrier Reef, in August of 2001, the Cairns Supreme Court was meting out justice in the trial of another group of Bandidos. They were allegedly caught in a 'massive' drug operation around Mission Beach and Tully, a few hours south of Cairns, trafficking amphetamines, LSD, cannabis and hash. This was an important case to Queensland police, who had made much of how it demonstrated the force's get-tough attitude against organised crime. But it is also significant because of what it shows about the willingness of the police to offer indemnities to witnesses who are sometimes themselves as dodgy as the people in the dock.

It is also very possibly a case that mortally influenced the Queensland police's attitude to the use of Stevan Utah as a protected witness when he was to offer them information a few years later.

In the Cairns drug trafficking case, the former president of the Bandidos' Cairns chapter, Maxwell Patrick Geary, was given a stiff twelve-year gaol sentence, along with three of his patched members who got lesser sentences. One of those three was a man whom Utah knew well as a notoriously successful amphetamines cook. We will call him 'Tank'. An intimidating sight, Tank is a solid six-footer with a long goatee beard and a shaved head, weighing a delicate one hundred and twenty kilograms (and suffering from gout as a consequence). Tank is also a very persuasive fellow. As well as being gaoled for drug trafficking, he was also sentenced to three years for kidnapping a man and taking him to the clubhouse where he tortured him and threatened to kill him to extort money.

Tank and Utah had got to know each other in the mid 1990s when both were plying their craft as drug cooks. And because Brutus, one of the senior Bandidos around Brisbane, had a brother—Cleaver—who had joined the Cairns chapter after leaving the army, there was a very close relationship between the clubhouses. When Tank got out of gaol in 2004 he moved to the Sunshine Coast hinterland. His reunion with his old cooking pal, Stevan Utah, was to end badly.

But for the moment, in 2001, Tank and his Cairns clubhouse chapter president Patrick Geary were going to gaol. The witness largely responsible for sending them there was himself a former senior Bandido—Peter Klarfeld, aka 'P.K.' In return for his evidence P.K. was, controversially, given a full indemnity from prosecution. He now lives on a secure farm in splendid isolation in the Atherton Tablelands rainforest behind the town where he once reigned as chapter president, no doubt watching his back very closely.

The moral ambivalence behind the decision to give him a get-out-of-gaol-free card in return for his evidence remains, to those who know P.K. well, a highly questionable judgement—to say the least—by someone in the Queensland police hierarchy. For Mr Klarfeld, on his own evidence, is not a nice person at all. As well as fingering Geary and others for their role in the drug racket, he admitted to getting his hands dirty. In 1998 he led police to the lonely burial site of a murdered Cairns bouncer, Jason Tyler. In 1995, Tyler had been lured from a Cairns nightclub to the Bandido's clubhouse and shot in the legs. A sock was stuffed down his throat and he was then kicked to death before his body was dumped in a creek bed. Utah says the word around the clubhouses was that Tyler had given evidence to police about the Bandidos, and that: 'What happened to him is what will happen to me if they ever catch me. Except in my case they'll drag it out a bit, make me suffer. After what I've done to them they'll want to cause me some serious pain.'

Klarfeld fingered two men for the murder, Michael Anthony Rousetty and David Barry Houghton, saying Rousetty had told him Mr Tyler 'deserved it, so I whacked him'. He also claimed to the court that he was not present on the night but helped bury the body later. P.K.'s full indemnity from prosecution was justified to jurors on the grounds that 'little fish must be used to catch big fish'. But there are claims to this day that there is something very wrong about the way P.K.'s evidence against his former Bandido mates was not questioned more rigorously by the police and prosecutors who chose to rely on it, and that the police should have known full well that P.K. was a much bigger fish than he let on to the court.

The Bandidos charged with Jason Tyler's murder admitted their role as accessories after the fact in disposing of the body but they flatly deny to this day that they were the ones who committed the murder. The court was told it was in fact Klarfeld and another bikie, Grant Clear, who pulled the trigger—a claim put to P.K. under cross-examination, and which he denied. 'I would suggest you have a powerful reason for concealing the murder, that's because you and Clear killed him?' Klarfeld was asked in court. The former Bandido president replied: 'That's a figment of your imagination.' His alleged accomplice, Grant Clear, had killed himself in gaol while on remand. Efforts by the defence to label Klarfeld a 'practised liar' failed. His evidence swayed the jury.

But then new claims surfaced. A new trial had to be ordered because a witness came forward to say one of the accused, David Barry Houghton, was not at the clubhouse on the night of the murder. This dramatic twist cast severe doubts over Klarfeld's evidence. That new witness, Tracey Hancock, told the court that Klarfeld was in fact at the clubhouse on the night of Tyler's murder, despite his sworn evidence, and that he had warned an associate not to speak to anyone about the killing or he would 'get the same'.

A judge subsequently directed the murder trial jury to find Houghton not guilty on the murder charge. A mistrial was also declared in the case of Michael Anthony Rousetty. Both men still went to gaol for their alleged role as accessories and Rousetty was subsequently found guilty of murder on a retrial, implying that the jury again accepted his evidence despite hearing Tracy Hancock's account.

Not surprisingly, Patrick Geary's mother Carol and his brother Shane have long protested that Klarfeld's evidence against him on the drug bust was as suspect as Klarfeld's evidence in the murder trial. Whatever the truth of the claims of P.K.'s alleged far greater complicity, the concerns about giving people like him indemnity stuck. The case was being discussed in legal and police circles all through 2001 and 2002 as appeals questioning the reliability of Klarfeld's testimony wound their way through the courts. And within the Queensland Police Service there were concerns being raised about why Klarfeld's evidence incriminating his own Bandido colleagues had not been more rigorously questioned before he was given his indemnity. As it happened, unfortunately for Stevan Utah, this debate was taking place as he was wrestling with the huge decision of when and how to roll to police.

Back at his Dalby farm, Utah was trying to be as inconspicuous as possible, tending to his two Rottweiler dogs, Caesar and Cleo, and working as a carpenter. 'I was normal me. Living with my dogs. I was so normal I wasn't noticed.' But despite the assurances that Brutus was no longer coming after him to keep him quiet, Utah was spending a lot of time looking over his shoulder. Who could blame him, knowing Brutus's propensity for mindless and sadistic violence? It also didn't help his paranoia when his farmhouse at Dalby burned to the ground in January 2002. The only luck Utah had was that the outbuildings were unharmed. Police forensics investigators decided it was an electrical fault, but he wasn't so sure. He suspected it was a warning: 'I don't share their view. I again lost everything I owned.' Utah moved into a rented house in Dalby. He reckoned that with the fire and the recent demise of his marriage, he walked out of his farm with only about $20 000 to show. 'I got fucked', he groaned.

Down in Victoria, Detective Sergeant Tony Thatcher was not going to let the appalling events of Earl Mooring's brutal murder on the night of 10 October 2000 go unpunished. Utah's mother had admitted enough about her son's involvement for him to get warrants for Utah's bank records. And what the records showed was more than enough to raise a reasonable suspicion. For what Stevan Utah had to explain was just how it was that $782 000 had found its way into his bank account around the time of Mooring's death.

Utah claims he parked the money in his account as a favour for an employer who wanted to keep some money away from a messy divorce. The way Utah tells it, the employer had never previously made any complaint to police and it certainly took him two years to come up with a statement to Queensland police. But within a month of the Mooring murder, Tony Thatcher was questioning Utah's former boss about the money. When Queensland's fraud squad finally began investigating at Thatcher's request from Victoria, the boss suddenly alleged Utah had stolen his money. In February 2004, Stevan Utah was finally charged with one hundred and sixteen fraud offences. All the charges related to the curious $782 000 deposit in his bank account. He was bailed and put on reporting conditions, and had his passport taken off him. Tony Thatcher now had the excuse he needed to put pressure on Stevan Utah to tell what he knew about the murder of Earl Mooring.

Utah now decided to play his hand, instructing his lawyer to approach Queensland police with information: 'I told him to go to the highest levels of the police because I was already worried about corruption issues.' All through his time with the Bandidos, Utah was aware of questionable and probably corrupt relationships between some police, especially in the Queensland state police, and senior Bandidos. Even the street-hardened Utah was shocked to discover how close one senior Queensland police detective was to senior bikies, seeing the man on several occasions fraternising at the clubhouse:

> I said very early on that I didn't want the cunt near me. He was pretty heavily involved with [a senior Bandido's] boys. If there's a cop that deserves a prison sentence it's him. He sells information to the bikies. To me, to be a cop in a clubhouse having a free beer and watching a stripper is a form of corruption and that's what he did. I hate him. I just want to punch his face in . . . that's how he made me feel. He stands for everything I hate. I've been in the room when he's there and I've walked away from him. You know when you stand next to somebody and you can feel their aura. His aura makes me want to vomit. He's like a bad fart.

The policeman Utah saw cannot be named here because he may face unrelated charges arising out of another matter. 'This officer was a hang-around [at] the Gold Coast clubhouse and I saw him in Brisbane and the Sunshine Coast. He speaks to the Spinks a fair bit. Nobody likes him. He's like a 1930s Al Capone corrupt cop', Utah says.

The relationship between police and criminal informants is a delicate one at the best of times. A recent Queensland inquiry by its anti-corruption body, the Crime and Misconduct Commission, reportedly identified several police officers and prisoners who have unexplained cash in their bank accounts. In late 2007 Brisbane's *Courier-Mail* newspaper told how members of the Queensland State Crime Operations Command—major crime investigators—and the armed robbery squad were embroiled in the scam. What it allegedly involved was police and criminal informants splitting the cash after criminals were paid for information about crimes.

One of the wearying facts about police corruption is that what goes around eventually comes around again. The informant payments scam is not new. While the Queensland police put out a press release promising a review of its accountability controls, the very same problem had been highlighted over a decade earlier by the watershed investigation into police corruption, the Fitzgerald inquiry. It had also expressed serious concerns about how informants were being paid as well as the transparency of the practice.

Police can always argue that they can only monitor the organised criminal activity of bikie gangs by having officers who are prepared to court contact with often undesirable types. But there is no doubt in Utah's mind that nothing this officer did, or several others he saw during his time inside the outlaw motorcycle gangs, could be justified as good policing:

Well corruption comes in many forms. You know it doesn't just have to be information. It could be . . . it could be favours. It could be . . . police officers in clubhouses . . . well, consorting with criminals. Okay, it's not an offence but you know to me, it's morally corrupt for a police officer to be seen in a supposed outlaw motorcycle club clubhouse enjoying the strippers, the beers, and consorting. I wouldn't let the Queensland Police Service walk my dog. I wouldn't tell them a thing.

To borrow from the notorious femme fatale at the centre of England's 1960s Profumo scandal, Mandy Rice-Davies, a man in Stevan Utah's position would say that, wouldn't he? But his concerns about corrupt police links with bikie gangs are much more substantial than witnessing them enjoying the odd friendly beer or stripper. Few events inside the club rattled him more than what happened to Bingey Douglas, Utah's old bikie mate from prison who had watched out for him on the inside, and dabbled in high-end wildlife trafficking with him and Kaos Kulakowski on the outside.

As Utah became a hang-around in the club chapters along the east coast he watched on as Bingey lived up to his name and spiralled out of control through drug abuse and mounting debts. Back in 1998 Bingey had caused no end of grief for Utah when he turned up at his Dalby property with a caravan in tow. A hopeless addict, Bingey owed too many violent people a lot of money and Utah, unwisely, allowed his mate to live in the caravan on his property. It turned out the caravan had been stolen from the landlord of a building which was, at the time, the Bandido's clubhouse. Not a clever place to pull a heist at the best of times. And when the theft was reported to police, Bingey's clumsy trail had led police right to Utah's property. They assumed that the large quantity of building and electrical equipment Utah had there was also stolen material to be used for an elaborate bunker to cook up drugs, so a lot of what they found on his property, including Bingey's stolen caravan, was carted away on semitrailer. 'They thought I was a major drug dealer setting up an operation. I was an honest guy setting up a house in a rural setting', Utah recalls, without a trace of irony. He is adamant that, Bingey's hot caravan excepted, all the other property was legally obtained and the Queensland police had to give it all back in the end. But Bingey was a recurring headache for his good friend: 'I would die for my beliefs and friends! . . . He tried to sell me a boat for a grand. I told him to fuck off. Then the club was kicking him out so he stored his bike under my house so they wouldn't take it.'

After one too many transgressions, Bingey had been thrown out of the gang because it was suspected that he had also become a police informant to get himself out of trouble. Sadly for Bingey, if he was indeed helping police, someone had talked and the Bandidos knew about it. If he wasn't actually helping police, that really didn't matter anymore. He was a marked man anyway. Utah recalls the talk around the club from as early as 1999: 'They referred to him as double agent Bingey . . . he was already a flog on sight.'

Utah waited for the beating he thought would come if anyone discovered the complicated facts about his continued friendship with Bingey Douglas, but once again the Utah luck held: 'They turned around and they said the only thing you're fucking guilty of is being his friend.' But what alarmed Utah most of all was that in around 2003 the club was twice tipped off, allegedly by serving Queensland police officers, that Bingey was a police informant. One tip alerted a senior Brisbane based Bandido to the fact that there was about to be a police raid looking for drugs at his home—and that Bingey was the informer. Another warned that the drug squad was also about to raid Brutus's property looking for drugs— and two days later Brutus was raided as predicted. Utah also claims to have seen more direct tip-offs from serving police to the bikies: 'I've been there; I've seen it; I've heard it with my own ears.'

Not long after the tip came into the club in 2003 that Bingey was an informant, Utah learned, to his dismay, that his old friend had apparently killed himself: 'I got told by a senior member that he hung himself. He was an ex-Bandido. He was kicked out of the club for drug abuse, debts, things like this. When I got told he'd committed suicide, though, the person started giggling. Now the person who told me just doesn't giggle. You know ... I knew there was something wrong.'

Utah's worst suspicions were confirmed months later when he began working as an inside mole for the officers of Australia's Crime Commission. He had already seen enough inside the clubhouse to be suspicious about corrupt elements inside Queensland's police force. It made his decision to approach police with information all the more dangerous. But the fraud charges laid against him in early 2004 meant that, whatever the risk, it was time to show his hand.

16

TROPICAL TURF WARS

Tell them what you need to to get what you want
from them and then fuck them off.
Anonymous police officer

Utah had enough money set aside for a good lawyer and in June 2004 that lawyer hired one of Queensland's most respected criminal barristers, Terry Martin SC, to approach the Australian Crime Commission's representative inside the Queensland police force, Detective Inspector Marty Michelson. Utah felt he had important information to offer and indeed he says that when his lawyers came back from meeting the police to negotiate a deal, the ACC was 'salivating'.

What Utah wanted was ACC help to allow him to relocate to a secret overseas location, and for all charges against him to be withdrawn, including an indemnity from prosecution for the fraud charges and any offences committed after the murder of Earl Mooring. He also wanted his Rottweilers, Cleo and Caesar, delivered to him as part of the deal. What he dangled in front of the

ACC to get them interested was the location of a hidden drug laboratory tucked away in the mountains around the Yarraman National Park, north-west of Brisbane. He revealed that there was an underground bunker beneath a private house which had already been searched by police once before in June 2003: 'One of the principal offenders before that, you know he actually sat there and he laughed at me after his last raid and he said they were standing right next to the door. They didn't even see it.'

The owner had recently had a marriage break-up and taken up with a new woman. His jealous spouse had tipped off police that there were drugs on the premises. But as Utah told police: 'The police were at the time fooled by the jovial nature and the general image and standard of living of [the residents]. They accepted the explanation offered and although standing next to the [bunker] did not detect it.'

Utah's detailed information told police how under the front landing of the house, in an area where garden tools were stored, there was a secret entrance to the bunker behind a noticeboard on the wall. He also explained how when police had done an earlier search they had failed to find a huge amount of Sudafed tablets (used to extract the pseudo-ephedrine for amphetamine manufacture) and a large amount of cash totalling tens of thousands of dollars. He gave the location of a separate bunker a few kilometres away from the house, which was accessible through a secret opening in the floor of a small shed. Utah also told police how, as well as cultivating hydroponic marijuana and cooking up amphetamines in the underground bunkers, the residents were storing a huge shipment of heroin that had recently been smuggled in from Vietnam.

Rarely do police get such detailed tips on such a substantial potential bust. Utah knew his information was good and he expected that because the approach was made to the Australian Crime Commission's secondee in the Queensland police force, the information would be passed on straight away to the ACC for action. Utah was to learn later how the maps showing the locations of hidden bunkers were handed over to the Queensland police drug squad—who promptly did nothing about it for over four months.

If he had known what the police were *not* doing with his information, it might have given him some foreboding about any hopes of a workable deal with the Australian Crime Commission. Stevan Utah was under the impression his lawyers had been able to secure a deal with the ACC: 'Several things were asked for. Nothing that I wasn't entitled to. I wasn't greedy. It was whatever I would have lost by doing what I was doing. There was no profit involved. Ah . . . things were agreed to.' But here is a friendly tip to any criminal contemplating approaching Australia's prime crime-fighting body for a deal: get it in writing—or in blood, preferably. In the words of one very senior state police officer willing to speak anonymously, the ACC is notorious among other police forces for its treatment of criminal witnesses: 'The attitude seems to be: tell them what you need to to get what you want from them and then fuck them off.'

To folk not familiar with the vagaries of investigating organised crime this attitude might sound fair enough. Why should a criminal like Stevan Utah get any special treatment? For starters, any observer with an eye for history would recall that the ACC's predecessor, the National Crime Authority, had long recognised the need to woo informants from inside criminal organisations—especially someone like Utah with his astonishing recall and memory for detail. What many have long questioned, however, is the NCA's judgement, because it historically showed no queasiness about offering indemnities and buckets of money to sometimes highly dubious witnesses. As dirty as it may feel, sometimes it takes a crook to bust a crook. As we have already seen, though, sometimes too little effort is put into testing those witnesses' stories before they are offered a full indemnity as a key Crown snitch.

In 1987 the NCA, desperate to score a hit against organised crime, arrested Sydney's so-called 'Mr Sin', nightclub owner Abe Saffron, on tax charges and for allegedly conspiring to bribe a police officer. The integrity of the key witness, James McCartney Anderson, a former Saffron intimate, had by then already been lambasted by former New South Wales Premier Neville Wran, who quipped: 'You wouldn't convict a dog on the evidence of Jimmy Anderson.' Even one of the NCA's own lawyers had warned: 'It should be borne in mind at all stages of the investigation that Anderson is a liar.' Eventually, the bribery charges, by far the more serious, failed at least in part because of Anderson's doubtful credibility in the box. There is more than a whiff to the Jimmy Anderson story that he told police what they wanted to hear, and made most of it up along the way.

Whatever the merits of Jimmy Anderson's evidence, the NCA spared no expense in giving him rolled gold protection for his assistance. Not only did they pay relocation expenses for him and his wife to the Philippines, but they were flown first class and stayed in the very best of hotels. It all got a little embarrassing, though, when a joint parliamentary inquiry decided to investigate the relationship between Anderson and the NCA. It was a tender matter of a little $30 000 bill for some of Jimmy's food, travel and accommodation costs while in witness protection that had finally blown the NCA's largesse in to the open. Even the NCA had refused to pay this bill.

In the subsequent inquiry, quite apart from the huge bills mounted up by Anderson, the committee found good cause to question the NCA's decision to use a witness like Anderson in the first place. Not only was he, they found, a 'very marginal proposition' as a witness, there was doubt his evidence was ever needed to convict Saffron at all. For the expenditure of hundreds of thousands—if not millions—of dollars on Anderson's relocation and protection, the crime-fighting body was only ever able to pin Saffron for tax evasion. Their witness thoroughly discredited, the NCA assured parliament that it had changed its procedures to ensure that problem witnesses like Anderson would not happen again.

What did happen then was a total overreaction to the parliamentary criticism. The NCA and its eventual successor, the Australian Crime Commission, did a one hundred and eighty degree turn in its attitude to its informants. Far too many witnesses who were rolling to the federal crime fighters were complaining about the government welching on its own deals. In 1999, a witness we will call 'Bill' was persuaded to roll over to the NCA, revealing the dark secrets of the villain dubbed 'Mr Big Enough'—drug dealer Ian Hall Saxon. Bill was a suburban Sydney accountant who had quite literally fallen in with the mob by accident, thinking he was just laundering money from Saxon's music business—a nice, gentle, white-collar crime. When he was finally confronted by police with the fact that he was washing drug money, he was shocked and terrified—and immediately cooperative. In his head were the secrets of what was to become Australia's first-ever major investigation into the criminal tricks of offshore money laundering.

The man who persuaded Bill to roll was Police Superintendent Bob Small, who was on secondment to the NCA from the New South Wales police. Bob got Bill to agree to wear a wire in one key conversation with drug dealer Saxon and this blew the whole syndicate open—a chilling recording in which several murderous threats were made by Saxon should the accountant fail to get him money frozen by police. In the subsequent bust and trial, Bill was a superb witness for the prosecution. Even better, his evidence led police to a garage in the Sydney suburb of Coogee where they found a treasure trove of ill-gotten loot: four kilograms of cannabis resin, three gold bars, $50 000 of Krugerrand gold coins and a suitcase stuffed with $5.5 million in cash.

For reasons best known to the NCA, Bill was about to be dudded. Right at the beginning of the operation, Bill was given what he had thought was a cast-iron assurance that he and his wife would not only be given full witness protection but that neither of them would suffer any financial disadvantage as a result of the loss of their business and having to be relocated under a new name. What happened instead, according to Superintendent Small who went public on their behalf, was that the NCA reneged on its promises. 'It's been positively evil. They've used up his evidence and then they've dropped him. To put it in the colloquial, they've squeezed the orange dry and put it in the dirty garbage,' Small admitted at the time, at considerable risk to his own future career.

It was a brave act for the now retired copper to speak out against his former masters but he was moved to do so because Bill was dying of cancer, stricken with anxiety that his rolling to police would leave his wife in penury when he died. It took a decent cop to get Bill and his wife the settlement they deserved, but the NCA only settled at the door of the court. The warning Superintendent Small gave on Channel 9's *Sunday* program in 1999 has as much application for Stevan Utah and witnesses like him today, who might be thinking of coming clean with what they know:

> Unfortunately, I really do have to say this. Anybody that contemplates giving evidence against major drug importers where their lives are in danger would be silly in coming forward until such time as legislation is in place to protect their rights . . . It's absolutely awful. Like all it's going to do is stop key witnesses coming forward in the future. The only explanation that I can think of is that his usefulness is now finished. The bean-counters have moved in and they are just trying to get out of it as cheaply as possible . . . leaving ethics and morals out of it.

It was a prescient warning indeed, but not one that Stevan Utah was aware of as his lawyers negotiated with police for the best deal in return for his cooperation. There was and still is no such legislation to regulate how protected witness informants should be treated by Australia's premier crime-fighting body. By October 2004, whatever deal Utah thought he might have had was not legally binding on the police. He was already starting to get worried because the police had not raided the properties he had tipped them off as containing illegal drug laboratories and heroin. What he did not know was that Queensland police had not even passed his information on to the Australian Crime Commission. His tip was lying in an in-tray somewhere in the Queensland police drug squad.

Utah was also unaware of what the Queensland police also doubtless knew: that Tony Thatcher was finally about to make his pounce to get Utah talking about Mooring's murder. The Victorian detective had been patiently assembling the limited evidence they had against Utah in the case, but the fraud charges had helped provide enough of a whiff to get a murder arrest warrant across the line. In early November Thatcher turned up at one of Utah's Dalby Court appearances for the fraud charges, a bevy of Queensland police in tow, with a murder warrant and an application for his immediate extradition back to Victoria. 'It was issued on the grounds that I was supposedly likely to abscond. The fraud charges were used as a leverage to persuade the magistrate to allow my extradition to Melbourne and he didn't even want to hear the police case. He just signed the papers and I was on the plane with Thatcher', Utah recalls. 'Thatcher later said to me that that was the first time he'd never had to give evidence to support an extradition.'

At this stage Utah still believed he had a deal with the ACC. As he cooled his heels in the Dalby police station, his lawyer arrived to discuss the arrest with Detective Tony Thatcher. The notes he made of that conversation clearly record police offering a deal: 'Know that he is not the main player. Prepared to drop fraud charges, re-location overseas and witness protection if he cooperates.' The one complication had been the fraud matters on which Utah had been charged earlier in the year. Thatcher spoke to the Queensland police's representative at the Australian Crime Commission, Inspector Marty Michelson, and by the end of that day the fraud charges had been withdrawn by the Queensland police service. His extradition to Victoria for his alleged involvement in the murder of Earl Mooring could now go ahead.

Clearly Utah believed that in return for his cooperation with Victorian police on Mooring's murder, the Queensland fraud charges would be dropped for good. And so, in all likelihood, did Victorian police, who do seem to have done all they could do to honour their promised deal. But it seems the Queenslanders had other ideas. In the minds of the Queensland police bosses, it looked as though Utah's fraud charges were only being dropped because he faced a likely sentence of life in gaol if he was convicted for his involvement in the Mooring murder. This was a crucial misunderstanding, which was to come back and bite Utah a few years later. As he sat next to Thatcher on the plane to Melbourne, being arrested for Mooring's murder was in Utah's mind the best thing that had happened to him in a while. It represented an opportunity to come clean about what he knew—which was extensive—and get a new life, away from the outlaw motorcycle gangs.

TROPICAL TURF WARS

What Utah and the well-meaning Tony Thatcher were to fall foul of was the arcane and absurd jurisdictional boundaries between police forces in Australia. If ever there was a gift to organised crime, it is the lack of cooperation between police forces when police from one state want to run a witness like Utah inside the turf of a fellow police agency in another state. Forget any notions of collegial cooperation, for quite apart from the legal hurdles that have to be jumped through, there is more than a lot of male testosterone and bristling self-importance that all too often impedes such police investigations. Victorian police efforts to exploit the information locked up in Utah's head were to be no exception.

Utah was by now behind bars in the Victorian Police Custody Centre in central Melbourne. Aware that Utah's bikie mates, including Brutus, would soon know he had been arrested for Mooring's murder, Thatcher's major priority was to take the by now cooperative Utah to find Earl Mooring's body in New South Wales as soon as possible. Utah was happy to help. He thought he had a deal, agreed upon by both Queensland and Victoria and the Australian Crime Commission. Ah, if only life were so easy.

Initial attempts to get Utah released from gaol to help find the body were forebodings of the jurisdictional mess that was to haunt the case. Being charged with murder meant Utah could not be taken across the border into New South Wales where Utah had already told Victorian police the body was hidden. If he had known about it, Brutus would have been laughing. He probably still is. So for weeks Utah languished in gaol, growing increasingly frustrated at the lack of action. During this miserable time he did bump into his uncle's old mate, notable crim Kevin Taylor, who was still inside.

What was clear to the warders was that the Queensland prisoner was something special to the Victorian police cold-case unit because a succession of police were coming and going on a daily basis:'The word "dog" was mentioned. Some of the staff there used to call me a super-rat. They put me in isolation for a few weeks. I don't actually call it isolation because at one stage there in a six by eight cell there were seven of us. And when they'd hand me my cigarette each day, they'd call me a super-rat.'

One day, a minor Victorian gangster with a wee bit of a heroin problem decided to give Stevan Utah a little smacking. Utah found himself coming second, waking up in the St Vincent's Hospital prison ward. 'Ah, I got beaten from behind. My eye was split open and the old brain was rolling around the melon and had to go to hospital and get sewn up.' Things were not going well for Utah. Repaired after his biffing, he was sent back to the remand centre and placed into another small cell for his own protection—often with up to five other people, who were also beginning to take a curious interest in this Queensland hood with a conspicuous number of police friends.

It did not seem possible but things were about to get worse. Utah learned that efforts by the Victorian police to get the Office of Public Prosecutions in Victoria to agree to an indemnity had been rebuffed by the prosecutors. He was staring at a murder trial, with the real possibility of life in gaol at the end of it. In late November he had been moved into the protection wing of the Melbourne Assessment Prison but in early December Utah found himself in Port Phillip prison, with the future looking extremely bleak.

The Victorian police had given Utah an assurance that they knew he was not the main player in the Mooring murder. They wanted Brutus and the other killer, badly. And in early December Utah got a visit from Thatcher making an offer that scarcely seemed possible. 'He told me that if I put my statement about Mooring's murder on audio I'd be out of gaol by the next morning', Utah recalls. He did, and Thatcher was true to his word.

Against the protestations of the Victorian prosecutors the police had used their power to withdraw the murder charges before they got to a committal hearing. Detective Tony Thatcher had stuck his neck out for Utah. Now it was time to deliver Earl Mooring's corpse: 'Thatcher again stated to me, are you sure I can get a body. I said I will not stop looking until we find him.' After a swift court hearing to get the charges withdrawn, under the glare of angry prosecutors, Utah was then walked straight from the courtroom to an unmarked police car, and driven for six hours to central New South Wales, to the farm track where Earl Mooring's body had been dumped. Utah recalls:

> We looked for approximately three hours and I couldn't get my bearings. I was basically physically and mentally exhausted. Thatcher was pissed off. We went up there and we looked for a day and a half, two days, and nothing looked the same to me. I remember Thatcher was so disappointed. He thought he was coming back with Mr Mooring's body and I remember we stopped . . . on the way back to have a coffee and I said to his partner, I said nobody's getting a fucking thing out of me until Mr Mooring's body is found. So I said even if we have to go back and do it ten times then we'll go back and do it ten times.

The problem for Victorian police was that no matter how serious a crime Earl Mooring's murder was, they could not throw endless resources at a case that was now four years old when Stevan Utah could no longer locate where they had dumped his body.

For any policeman, there always has to be the suspicion that a criminal like Stevan Utah had made the whole thing up about Earl Mooring to try to get the indemnity from prosecution that he wanted so badly. Back in Melbourne there were a lot of senior Victorian police officers now watching Utah very closely. One of those he claims to have met him was Simon Overland, now the Assistant

Commissioner of Victoria Police, in charge of Operation Purana, Victoria's investigations into the spate of killings in Melbourne's criminal underworld. What Overland saw must have convinced him to give Utah another chance, for Stevan Utah's cooperation with the Victorian police was allowed to continue. Four years on, in tribute to the Victorian assistant commissioner, Utah has a pet piranha whom he has dubbed 'Simon'—as in 'Purana'.

Victorian police did not have the money to keep on looking for Mooring's corpse so they got in touch with Australia's premier crime-fighting body, the Australian Crime Commission. Utah's handler, a man we'll call 'Laurel', escorted the amazed Utah from Victorian police headquarters to the luxury Radisson Hotel on William Street in central Melbourne. 'He walked in, gave me 500 bucks for some clothes. I had nothing—$500 to go and get laid and a drink, told me to do what I wanted in the hotel and charge everything to the room. Then he left.'

For a week Utah savoured the pleasures of the Radisson, letting Victoria's gaol system become a distant memory. Then in early December the ACC took him on another trip back to Goulburn, where they searched every country road for hundreds of kilometres around where Utah remembered the corpse being dumped. Again, no luck. 'I said the same thing to the ACC, that you're not getting shit until we've got his body. I said the family deserves some peace.'

Then shortly before Christmas 2004, Utah went back one last time with another ACC officer. They searched all day and then, as the end of the day drew near, Utah's minder was pressing him to leave to make it back in time for the return flight to Melbourne. 'I recall saying to him, I felt stupid. He said to me you are suffering displaced memory. I said well I feel like a dickhead. He said we all know you know. We will just keep looking. You know what a displaced memory is and I said yeah. I drew everything I could remember. He was on the phone to an acting detective inspector. We were about to go back to the airport. And I said to him, hang on, let me go back.'

What Utah had not realised until the third visit was that the trees under which Earl Mooring's body was dumped by Brutus had grown hugely in the last four years. They had gone past the spot several times in previous searches. Utah looked again at the map he had drawn from memory and suddenly realised he was standing somewhere near Earl's body: 'I remember I was sitting back and I had this plan and the ACC officer is saying to me, no this is not the place and I am saying yeah, look it is. You know like that hill's there. That hill's there. The grass is there. Look, I said, I have even got the turns in the road right. Everything's right. I said no, fuck it. Give me ten minutes. And it was just strange then. I just walked over and I realised that was where the body was dumped. And there was this one big tree. And when his body was dumped there I remembered there was like this sapling and then I saw this tree and it was like yay round and I thought he's at the bottom of that tree. And then I walked over there and the undergrowth was pretty thick and I looked in there and there were some legs sticking out of the ground.'

The Australian Crime Commission investigator rushed over to see what Utah was pointing at. He slowly realised that, four years on, the secret of Earl Mooring's last resting place had finally been discovered. 'He said to me—are you sure that's a body? That's what he said to me. Are you sure that's a body, and I like looked at him and I said to him, man, it's not a Darrell Lea chocolate fucking factory. I said look: femur, patella, patella, tibia, fibula. I said, what do you want? And I said, they're clothes.'

Forensics police were brought in from Sydney to go through the crime scene. Utah was quickly hidden away. Having proven his story, the ACC investigators now realised he was going to be very useful indeed and they did not want their key witness being eyeballed by New South Wales police.

Back in Melbourne, shortly before Christmas, more confirmation came of Utah's credibility. His tip-offs about an illegal drug lab, which had been passed to Queensland police, had finally been investigated. Police found an illegal methamphetamine factory and hydroponic marijuana. But the heroin was gone. 'I said—what about the Harry [heroin]? He said we didn't get it. I was rather annoyed. I said to him, you think when somebody hands a map of a place of interest, particularly when warrants have been issued on the premises before without detection of these labs, it should take seventeen weeks? I went on to ask how many crimes were committed and how many people died from these drugs. He said, well, mate, personally I am happy with the result. I was angry. I asked why it had taken seventeen weeks.'

Utah's handler Laurel told him, 'Well, it was a good score and you have been right on the money about everything'. The Australian Crime Commission now knew Utah's information could be taken seriously, indeed. Discussions began about Utah going back into the very group he had walked away from several years earlier. The ACC wanted him to return to Queensland and penetrate the Bandidos' clubhouses—to capture evidence of organised criminal activity as it happened.

For Utah, the decision to cooperate was momentous. He knew any slip-up, any detection of his role as a police informant, would see him swiftly dealt with by his ruthless former associates. But he assumed he had a deal, and he had made the decision to cooperate. Not only was it good for him, he had realised it was the right thing to do.

17

WIRED FOR SOUND

*She found I was intelligent and always passive
unless provoked . . .*
Stevan Utah

Being an informant ranges from the moderately
dangerous, like those who offer a snippet now and then
to law enforcement in return for a favour, a few bucks
or a kind word, through to the perilous. To willingly
become an informant against outlaw motorcycle gangs is
perhaps at the top of the perilous class. To then willingly
throw yourself back into their orbit and record their
shenanigans is to hover on the precipice of suicide. An
error, a misinterpretation, even a hint of a problem can
result in unpleasantness akin to that of the Mooring
murder. These are guys who deal in suspicion and
mistrust, hiding behind their notions of 'brotherhood'.
A little spice is added by the use of their own product
which brings with it an unhealthy dose of paranoia.

What Utah was doing took guts, and talent. For
someone who had long harboured suicidal inclinations, if

it all went to hell then going out with a bang rather than a lonely whimper might not be too bad either. In television, film and actually in the recent past of the real world, being wired for sound is a dangerous undertaking. The obvious problem is being caught wearing either a microphone and recorder, or wearing a microphone that broadcasts back to a nearby listening post. The chance of being searched for these devices was quite high, and being found with them could be disastrous.

A lesser known but equally clear and present danger was the device itself. In less technologically advanced times, a battery to power the device needed to be hidden on the mole's body. The most popular place, based on the blokey assumption that one gentleman wouldn't probe too closely around another gentleman's genitalia, was to secret the battery in that particular location. The wearer walked with a little more care than usual, but the real problem was that the earlier model batteries could be both unreliable and temperamental. Thus when the quite reasonably nervous wearer started to perspire, there was the chance that the battery would react badly. Many an informant darted back to their handlers with some trickily placed acid burns—an unseen hazard of a most hazardous undertaking.

Luckily for Stevan Utah, the ACC had at its disposal some state-of-the-art digital equipment so there was no need for him to risk life, limb and other vital parts. Neither did the recording device he was given require nearby listening posts, so there was no need for any back-up to be on hand. Utah was effectively on his own. He could operate up and down the coast, communicating as necessary with his Melbourne based handlers—although not much fun if he ran into strife in Queensland. The device looked like a run of the mill alarm blipper for a car—one quick poke and the car alarm was deactivated and the central locking popped the doors open. Utterly innocuous unless you pushed the button and held it down for a few seconds, in which case the digital recorder inside would activate its microphone and run for about twelve hours, capturing every golden word.

Around Christmas 2004, Utah began his new career as an informer in earnest. The start was bumpy and, unfortunately for Utah, and perhaps fortunately for his handlers at the ACC, Utah missed the warning signals. The sad truth is that Utah's tip about the drug lab and heroin deal languished with the Queensland police until December 2004. When they finally raided the premises, the lab had moved on and a tiny amount of drugs was found. Utah was convinced that as a result of their failure to act quickly, the Queensland police had inadvertently unleashed a massive supply of drugs onto the street. 'I am certain, absolutely certain', he said.

Over the Christmas break in 2004 Utah slipped overseas to discreetly advance his escape plans for life after the ACC. While overseas, his home at Dalby, where he had moved to after the fire on his farm, was ransacked.

Utah suspected a former business associate, a tradesman who had fallen on hard times. This former associate was involved in the amphetamine cooking business. He also thought the culprits may have been some inquisitive Bandidos wondering if Utah had left any incriminating mementos lying about.

Whoever did the search was more competent than the Queensland police. When Utah got back to Australia and did an inventory, he couldn't find the murder weapon he had so carefully hidden. Though it had survived the fire at the farm and the move into town, it became a victim of the burglary. What he also found, however, was that about $86 000 worth of equipment had gone, including ride-on mowers and 'every carpentry tool you can possibly think of'. Utah took the news of the missing hammer stoically. He reckoned there was a fair chance most of the property taken from his house had been sold. As for the hammer, well, 'he's probably using it to hammer in nails'.

To add insult to injury, his pride and joy, a $52 000 Holden SS ute was also missing in action. At the time he was carted off to Victoria he only had about $3000 owing on it. 'There's $49 000 of my own cash tied up in that asset and I have no fucking idea where it is. No-one will tell me. It just disappeared. I don't know what happened to that vehicle, but I can only assume it was repossessed because I missed a few payments while I was in gaol.' In what was now a very complicated life Utah just didn't get around to finding out what had happened to his beloved ute.

In February 2005 the ACC belatedly carted him off to see a psychologist for a spot of psychometric testing to make sure he was up to the rigours of what lay ahead. He said, with some amusement, 'She found I was intelligent and always passive unless provoked, and had an extreme amount of forcefulness and will. Extremely high.' Utah was chuffed when told he was 'very cool, a fast thinker'. Handy attributes for a high-risk lifestyle, and attributes that would be overlooked by his handlers. After the testing Utah went back up to his old stamping ground in Queensland. His brief was to again grow close to his acquaintances in the gangs. The emphasis was on drugs and guns. As for other crimes, like murder, Utah chuckled, 'They didn't give a fuck about Mooring being murdered!'

Utah rapidly found that he was welcome back in the Bandidos' orbit. Few questions were asked about his absence, as it had been typical of him to work hard and then disappear into New South Wales for 'funerals and shit' for extended periods. So warm was the welcome that he took the opportunity to introduce an undercover police officer, who we'll call 'Plod', to the lads in the gang. Plod would go on to become a so-called 'Bandido hang-around' in Queensland and be an occasional contact for Utah.

Utah's fastest point of entry was his old acquaintance, Gronk. He was very glad to have his mate back in the business. Gronk was your archetypal bikie—hard, sly, vicious, loyal, and not spectacularly bright. He thought the world of Utah, which was soon to prove a very big mistake. Utah introduced Plod to Gronk, who then introduced Plod to the gang, vouching for him, which also meant that any problems caused by Plod would rebound on Gronk. Both Utah and Plod kept their noses clean while operating in the gangs. No drugs, and no crimes. As Utah noted without much in the way of guile, 'He was part of Stevan and Stevan never did that. He was part of me, the man they could not root, shoot, or electrocute!'

Plod did, however, find himself a little socially compromised at one stage. He and Utah were at the fiftieth birthday of a bikie called 'Mads' at a Bandido clubhouse. The featured event of the evening was the almost inevitable stripper—a 'seriously hot stripper' in the view of the ACC's newly recruited infomer. The stripper in question took a fancy to him, but Utah wasn't interested. 'Don't fucking touch me', he uttered eloquently when declining her advances. He said, 'Plod was standing next to me so I said, take him, so Plod was rolling around the floor with this stripper—I laughed very hard inside'. After the usual backslapping and male bonding, Utah said to his mate, 'I don't do strippers and whores' to which Plod replied, 'I thought that would have been a fringe benefit'.

Another fringe benefit of their working relationship was that Plod had a high regard for Utah. His handler once told Utah, '[Plod] has told me straight up he would back you and anything that comes out of your mouth anytime'.

One outing for the informant and his undercover mate occurred shortly after Utah's return to Queensland. The venue was the opening of the Ipswich chapter. The two lads were chatting with a bikie, Jamie, who had just moved up from Geelong to join the expanding Gold Coast chapter. Utah recalled that Jamie gave 'a riveting dialogue' about disgraced former Victorian copper Detective Sergeant Wayne Strawhorn. Strawhorn was, at the time, on bail for a pile of drug-related offences for which he'd end up in prison. According to the bikie, Strawhorn was a 'close friend' and was busily moving pseudo-ephedrine—'no pseudo, no meth', quipped Utah.

The conversation didn't come as a surprise to Utah, but it gave Plod a bit of a start. Utah had met Strawhorn in about 1999 when he was spending some time in Melbourne and rubbing shoulders with the various Bandidos. Strawhorn was then deputy head of the Victorian drug squad. He'd been dubbed the 'golden boy' of that state's police—the man most likely to succeed. A handsome angular face that worked well with the camera, well-barbered salt and pepper hair, an athletic shape and great talents as an investigator had made him a local legend. Utah was present when his companion, a senior Melbourne Bandido, met with Strawhorn. Utah didn't get out of the car and didn't hear the conversation, however he commented that the Bandido was known as 'a great cook with a lot of contacts to get effy [pseudo-ephedrine], so I guess it was a meeting to get "effy".'

Unfortunately for Strawhorn, his rise to the top was cut short in 2003 when he was arrested after a lengthy internal investigation. He was charged with a pile of offences related to drug trafficking. Strawhorn, like Roger Rogerson in New South Wales and a stack of lesser detectives, had succumbed to the lure of the vast amounts of money that could be made crossing the line. Strawhorn and a hand-picked few of his fellow drug squad detectives had made a stack of cash by obtaining the raw materials through unauthorised police 'buys' and then onselling to the Bandidos and to the late Melbourne gangland notable Lewis Moran. The buys were made from pharmaceutical companies, and the idea was that police undercovers and informers would sell it into the marketplace and police could then trace the labs and distributors. At least that was the theory. A nice plan that was wide open to corruption.

At the hearing of charges against him, the prosecutor alleged that Strawhorn could buy pseudo-ephedrine for $170 per kilogram and then sell it on the black market for $10 000. A six thousand per cent profit was good business. One of Strawhorn's transactions alone involved 5.5 kilograms of pseudo-ephedrine, 3.5 kilograms of which allegedly went to the Bandidos and the remainder to the late gangster Lewis Moran's son, Mark, now also the late.

The coppers investigating Strawhorn and his colleagues did a good job and, like Utah, were able to get recordings.

Stevan Utah

Utah with his pet piranha 'Simon'—a tribute to
prominent cop Simon Overland

Michael Kulakowski modelling his range of bikie accessories

Bikies United—the funeral procession of Michael Kulakowski

Beerwah Cemetery—rest in peace

Behind Beerwah Cemetery—a fine place to hide a body

A busy social calendar

Things that go 'bang'—the rocket launcher supplied
by Shane Della Vedova

The late Earl Mooring

'...boot space. It's okay for light shopping expeditions but the lack of length prohibits bigger items.' A review of the Nissan Micra on www.drive.com.au
—handy for transporting the deceased Earl Mooring, however

SPECIAL REPORT AUSTRALIAN

Drugs, guns and vicious attacks. Just where do bikie gangs fit?

BANDIDO BLING: Unidentified Bandido, 2000.

Gangs targeted across country

FROM PAGE 1

IT was targeting "OMCGs in the jurisdictions".

While the investigation was continuing, the ACC said from previous and on-going operations it had concluded that "the size, profile, geographical spread and level of sophistication of OMCG criminal activity presents a significant threat to Australia and its interests".

The ACC intelligence team has identified 3500 "full patched" members of OMCGs currently spread across the nation, but said the number would "expand signifi-

"new generation" of OMCG members were emerging who appeared "less interested in the historical ideals of OMCG membership and more interested in using the OMCG club to facilitate criminal enterprise".

It ACC found that members were involved in a "large number of criminal activities" which they claim are "primarily designed to generate income and protect gang interests".

But the ACC also claims that OMCG involvement in legitimate business enterprises had the poten-

THE woman's injuries were horrific.

A broken nose and cheekbone. Concussion. Gravel grazes and cuts all over her body. Staples were needed to stitch a gash together, which ran from one side of her head to the other.

Blood freely ran down her face and dripped on the road, where she lay moaning.

But it wasn't a car which caused these injuries – it was something almost unthinkable.

The woman, believed to be in her 40s, had allegedly been bad-

'The end begins'—*Sunshine Coast Bulletin* article

The dead man starts running—the lonely spot where
Utah nearly met a sticky end

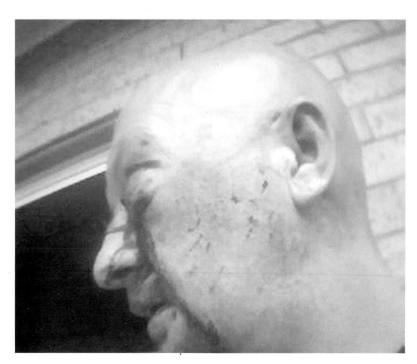

Upsetting the Bandidos can sometimes be a bruising affair—
an almost unrecognisable Utah

Pity the poor informant who recorded Strawhorn saying: 'It doesn't pay to be a whistleblower. As I tell people, if they ever come to me and say, "look, I have discovered corruption", tell 'em to fuck off, tell 'em to talk to someone else.' Not the sort of news you like to hear from someone like Strawhorn. The detective took a similarly feisty view of those responsible for his incarceration, stating in a recorded conversation that he would 'not rest until [the investigator] is dead' and later commenting that the 'only way to get satisfaction' was to kill the investigator himself. These are not the sort of words that engender comfort for an informer.

Neither Utah nor Plod, nor their evidence, was used in Strawhorn's trial. The charges arising from his alleged association with the Bandidos failed. However, he was convicted and gaoled on some of the other charges.

18

BANG BANG YOU'RE DEAD

*I will look like a big-noting wank stain and that is
not a good thing.*
Stevan Utah

The morning of 18 June 2007 was a typically chilly
morning in the depths of a drab Melbourne winter. At
least until about 8.15 am, anyway. In King Street in Melbourne's CBD, a young woman believed to be an exotic
dancer from the nearby Spearmint Rhino, was seen to
emerge into the morning light from a nightclub called
Barcode. Emerge is probably a bit understated. Closed
circuit television revealed, according to press reports,
'a man picking up the dancer by the hair, hurling her
onto King Street and throwing her suitcase, handbag and
make-up kit at her head. As she tries to get to her feet, she
is kicked in the head and appears to fall unconscious.'

A few moments later another woman emerged from
the club and saw her friend on the pavement. One
eyewitness noted the attack was 'brutal and unexpected'.
What happened next was far worse. The other woman,

222

Kara Douglas, was grabbed by the hair and dragged along the street by the man while she tried to hail a taxi. Two men ran to the woman's assistance, whereupon the assailant calmly turned to them, pulled out a handgun and shot both men. He then shot Ms Douglas. One man was badly wounded; his fellow good samaritan, 43-year-old solicitor and father Brendan Keilar, died almost instantly.

The alleged gunman was Christopher Wayne Hudson, a member of the Hells Angels, a former member of the Finks, and a habitué of south-east Queensland. It seems Hudson was no stranger to strife. He'd been arrested for identity fraud while trying to purloin $100 000, and was a suspect in New South Wales for assault and forty fraud related offences. In Queensland he'd been at the Royal Pines Resort at Southport on the Gold Coast at a kickboxing tournament in March 2006. Things didn't quite go according to the organisers' well-intentioned plans as the Hells Angels and Finks had turned up and got a little testy with each other. Hudson ended up being shot in the jaw, two others were also shot and two were stabbed. The Victorian police had also been keen to chat to Hudson after a shooting incident earlier in June 2007 when they'd pulled over a car and a gun had been fired. Luckily no-one had been hurt that time.

The moral of this story is that Hudson's weapon of choice was a heavy calibre handgun, one of the many illegally obtained firearms that drift about in Australia. The criminal underworld has long had access to weapons like this. Some are as old as God and arrived as souvenirs of war in times when border controls weren't terribly rigorous. Some are the proceeds of robberies. Some are obtained through military sources, and some come from the police themselves. In many instances they are recently imported, often, according to Utah, in boxes of motorcycle parts, or in Harley-Davidson tyres. Once in the underworld network, the guns can live for years, passed from one crook to the next for a tidy profit.

One light-hearted view, unless you're the hapless crook, on gun recycling was told to young detectives in New South Wales back in the bad old days of the 1970s and 1980s. The story involved a detective famous for his quiet and gentlemanly behaviour and his rather deadly (metaphorically, of course) reputation. The detective was in the witness box, solemnly telling the magistrate that he'd found the pistol on the felon he'd arrested. He theatrically produced the pistol as Exhibit A. The magistrate took all this in good stead and, with a sly grin, quietly told the detective, 'This is the last time I want to see this exhibit', and promptly sent the felon in question off to prison.

Underworld trafficking in firearms was a criminal target the ACC had in mind for Utah's skills. It is quite possible that the heavy calibre pistol might not have found its way into Hudson's hands if our law enforcement professionals had got their act together when dealing with the information provided by Stevan Utah.

The very first deal to come the way of Utah and his recording device happened moments after he'd returned to Queensland. The source was Gronk, who was offering brand new heavy calibre handguns for sale at the bargain price of $2000 each. He told Utah that he had sixty for sale. This was a great opportunity for Utah to prove himself and to get involved in a major weapons trafficking operation. In late March 2005, he told his mate that he would take two and bragged he could onsell them for about $3000 each.

Gronk took the bait. Utah still has the emails he received from his ACC handler on 21 March 2005, in which Laurel said: 'I'll be up there to see you on Thursday and hopefully we can reach agreement on the issues. We will not be buying those items this week unfortunately even though everybody is very keen to do so. I will discuss the reasons for that and a strategy for the other party today.' They did chat, and the next day, 22 March, Utah emailed Laurel: 'You still want those 45s from [Gronk]? I will have to call him Tuesday or I will look like a big-noting wank stain and that is not a good thing!'

What Utah also found out at this time was that the ACC was having email problems, and some of his were being eaten by the ACC's internet security filter. Not exactly a situation that filled him with confidence. Unluckily for Utah, some of his emails were about trying to get funds from the ACC rather than operational matters. He'd started off on a tight financial leash of $400 per week, and life wasn't too easy. It was a far cry from the Rolls Royce treatment of Jimmy Anderson by the ACC's predecessor, the NCA, and discontent with the financial arrangements would grow quickly and destructively. Laurel, responding to Utah's problems with technology and gun buying, offered, 'I guess you need to be careful how specific the information is in them. We are secure at this end (I guess) but I don't have the technical knowledge to comment on what happens whilst the message is en-route.'

About now anyone in Utah's position should have been feeling a little disconcerted, but luckily for the ACC, Utah was the epitome of gung-ho. In his return email banter, he tried again to get the deal happening: 'I have been sent a text message by [Gronk] asking if "I still wanted the 2 tool boxes".' A cute subterfuge but unlikely to confuse law enforcement for too long. Utah went on, 'I will call him later tonight as discussed and let him know I am busy and generally out of mobile range. I will tell him that I definitely want these items and get a "rain check". You may find he may even source them for me and hold them until I return. This is not an unusual thing ... if I say I want something then that's exactly what it means to them and I will take possession of them, so that's all good.'

Utah and Laurel spoke by phone about some troubles with the buy. Utah was getting a little concerned about Laurel's evasion and his own reputation with Gronk. He enjoyed his hard-earned respect and intended to keep it, both for his own vanity and for his safety. The problem that confronted the ACC was the matter of operational certificates. If the ACC's investigators and their sources like Utah were planning on doing something like a gun or drug buy, this would inevitably entail them committing an offence under federal laws, or the laws of the state they were operating in, or both. What the operational certificate did, with certain limitations of course, was to sanction the operation and provide immunity from prosecution for the offence. Easy, you'd think. All the ACC had to do was seek an operational certificate from their colleagues in Queensland and Utah could then go happily shopping at the 'House of Gronk, Firearms to the Gentry'. However, as the ACC and Utah would soon find out, the Queenslanders were none too keen to play ball. So much for Australia-wide cooperation in the fight against organised crime and unpleasantness.

According to Utah, his handler had been told that at one stage the Queensland police weren't even returning phone calls from the ACC, which made discussing the operational certificates rather tricky. The ACC, he reckoned, were 'dirty. They were very dirty' with their Queensland associates, so much so that Utah, members of the ACC and the Victorian police met with Queensland's anti-corruption body, the Crime and Misconduct Commission. They gathered in a hotel for 'a bit of a chat', and then, later, without Utah, they met again to try to drive the investigation. The result was zero. The Queenslanders wouldn't move. Utah thought it was primarily a turf war, 'the most petty, pedantic, pathetic thing I've ever seen in my life'.

When Utah got the hurry-up text message from Gronk he reckoned there was a fair chance that things weren't going to happen with his handlers, so he thought on his feet, trying to keep the deal alive. Just in case. He emailed Laurel:

I rang [Gronk] and advised him that I was busy with other horticultural interests in Dubbo New South Wales and would be for a few weeks. I further told him that it's a long drive for me to take possession and could we put it off for a few weeks. He wasn't pushy in any way but he did say 'that new stuff is as rare as rocking horse shit'. He said he will hold them with a deposit if you're serious, you know him. I said my mate is down the road getting a pizza and will be back in about an hour but he has the cash and is keen. I will let you know tomorrow morning before we go back out bush. History tells me that [Gronk] is a man of his word in relation to these matters. I strongly suggest a deposit of say $2000. It's like leaving a burley trail so the fish stay and eat. By handing over $2000 we will also be gaining back the old trust and integrity I had with them. Let's call it an investment. I do have some fears if we don't hand over some form of deposit we may not be in a position in the future to access these services. Bottom line, it's not my money. If it was mine,

I would pay it without question or thought. Don't ever lose sight of the fact this guy will also vouch for me to anyone and has in the past. This is not strictly localised to the group in interest. There are obviously suppliers of all kinds of things that this group knows. What makes [Gronk] important to our needs is he is also one of four surviving members of an old group of Saddists, the others are Packles, [Brutus] and [Stoat]. These are four very influential men.

Laurel, wisely sensing a problem with the star recruit, emailed Utah later that night:

The money has nothing to do with anything, it is against the law for us or you to engage in any negotiations regarding illegal activities without a controlled operations certificate which is a document that I had alluded to yesterday during our phone conversation. If we give you money for let us say expenses and you choose to use that money, no matter how well meaning to further the investigation by leaving a deposit for the guns, someone is very likely to charge you with conspiracy to traffic firearms. These matters are not negotiable, no certificate, no jobs. As I explained these certificates are a bit of work but once we get the first one up the process will be streamlined from then on. Our main problems in this one are Easter and you not being here after Monday.

Crime fighting and bureaucracy don't make for a healthy mix.

Utah took the problem, at least at that point, with good grace. He wrote back to Laurel:

> I must say though it is both annoying and disappointing that there isn't a uniform set of legislation that allows activities in all states and territories. God, bring back the republic debate. And just so you know, if you gave me money for expenses then that's the way I would expend it. If you give me money to fly to Pluto then I would fly to Pluto. I would never jeopardise my position by being foolish. I don't play games with other people's money. We will be okay. It will just take time.

Utah, at that point, seemed to have bonded nicely with the authority of the ACC and Laurel.

With Gronk taking him at face value, Utah slipped briefly out of the country again to do a little more groundwork for his life after being an informant. If he made it that long, of course. Very little happened to our informant until mid June 2005. Gronk and he met on 16 June for a chat, but guns weren't on the agenda. The opportunity to trace a significant supply of brand new guns had now passed thanks to bureaucratic bungling. It may be that the Queenslanders were a little apprehensive, thanks to the Geary case, of taking a bikie informant too seriously. The only problem with that was Utah had proved his worth to his ACC handlers. He'd shown them Mooring's last resting place, he'd provided high quality information on the drug cache even if the follow-up had, again, been bungled by the Queenslanders. They plainly had not got the message or were just playing small-town politics.

What is incredibly sad is that the guns Utah could source from Gronk were of the same description, and very possibly the same source, as the gun used by the bikie and sometime Queensland resident Christopher Wayne Hudson in his indiscriminate Melbourne shooting spree two years later. It is impossible, given the provenance of Gronk's guns, to categorically state that Hudson's gun came from the same stash, but there is the chilling possibility that it did. Which of course leaves a question hanging in the air: could swift and definitive action on Utah's evidence have prevented the Melbourne debacle? Yes would be a pretty fair answer. What Utah later found out was that the guns had disappeared at a rate of knots within three weeks after initially being offered to him. Sixty more illegal handguns in the hands of precisely the people who should not have had them. At least for Gronk, business was good, and Utah's welching on the deal did not bother him one little bit.

At their June meeting, Gronk was distracted. Utah, somewhat apprehensive about his failed attempt to buy Gronk's wares, used the distraction to talk about anything other than guns. He vaguely tossed in 'what happened to that guy in Caboolture', referring to Hombre's homicidal evening some years before and trying to tease out some information for his handlers. It seemed that Gronk was a little worried about a rat in the ranks. To his surprise, Gronk started talking, but not, as Utah would soon realise, about the murdered undercover cop or alleged informant. Gronk was talking about a much more current issue.

Utah was baffled at first, asking pointedly 'who' and 'what' Gronk was on about. He observed Gronk's body language and that he 'sat straight up and rigid, his eyes rolled and he turned his neck upward to the sky. Utah took this to mean 'are you trying to convince me you don't know about this? Obviously he had my attention.' Utah decided to play it cool and let the recorder run, thinking that 'I would prefer time to take its natural course. I have do doubt I will be given this information in the near future.' He was.

The Caboolture incident was about Utah's late mate Bingey Douglas. Utah was already suspicious about Bingey's alleged suicide. The other slight problem that Bingey had, aside from his drug addiction and light fingers, and this probably accounts for Gronk's interpretation of Utah's question about Caboolture, was that Bingey was thought to be a rat. Double Agent Bingey was a suspected snitch from back as far as 1999. Bingey was lucky to have survived the intervening years. The timing of Gronk and Utah's conversation corresponded with the coroner's inquest into Bingey's alleged suicide.

As a consequence of that conversation Utah did a bit of sniffing around himself, and came to a very different view to that of the investigating police and the coroner. Utah reckoned that the Bandidos had gone to visit Bingey, thinking it was about time they did a bit of risk minimisation. A solid beating, at the very least, was on the menu for the visit. Bingey certainly hanged himself in his own garage, but it wasn't a decision he came to solely on his own. He had a choice. A brutal beating, if he was lucky, or just do the right thing and save yourself a whole world of pain. Bingey took the least painful way out and his former colleagues watched and waited until he was dead. This information, of course, Utah passed on to Laurel and his colleagues up the line. There does not seem to have been a flurry of activity to follow up this allegation.

Utah was a popular chap that week. Gronk had given his contact details to a colleague we'll call 'Arthur'. Arthur had a business proposition. At their meeting, Arthur showed Utah what looked like one kilogram of pure methamphetamine. Just a sample, and there was plenty more available. He told Utah that Gronk reckoned Utah was just the bloke to move it in Queensland. When he asked Arthur how much he could get his hands on, he replied, 'How much do you want, lots?' Utah played noncommittal, drawing more from Arthur. Arthur told him that the kilogram was worth 'eighty, but if you get more than that the extra is yours, we want eighty'. Utah, not exactly inexperienced in these matters, thought eighty thousand dollars a kilogram was 'an average price'.

In his report to Laurel he noted the drugs were in a large plastic ziplock bag, and they were 'light to dark brown claggy looking stuff. I know my description sounds inconclusive, I will admit this, I have seen pure amphetamine on many occasions and this looked by texture and feel of pure amphetamine. When I held the bag it looked like a kilo. The bag was of reasonable size.'

Utah put the deal with Arthur on hold, using Gronk's impending drug vending tour into New South Wales as an excuse. When Gronk returned, he would get back to him. Unfortunately Gronk ran into a spot of bother in New South Wales.

As for following up on the potential to take one hundred kilograms of a very destructive drug off the street, Utah and his handlers hit the same wall as they had in the gun deal a few months earlier. That wall was the Queensland Police Service and its reluctance to issue an operational certificate to the feds, allowing them to commit crimes on Queensland soil. No certificate, no deal. The ACC were banging their heads against a brick wall. As Utah later observed about the impact if the deal had gone ahead, it would have been:

I believe significant. Others believe significant. If I was to use figures. Let's say ... Let's say there's a hundred Bandidos. Let's say the ACC was successful and they had the operational certificate and they had the support of the QPS. Let's say of the hundred, let's say they put fifty away. That is half. That is 50 per cent. Let's say they control five per cent of the methamphetamine trade in Queensland, which they do. You take 50 per cent reduction in the Bandidos, five per cent methamphetamine trade, it would go down two and a half per cent mathematically—a two and a half per cent drop in meth alone.

More pithily: 'It would have fucked them.'

The medical staff in emergency rooms around the country might have spent quieter Saturday nights if the Queensland police had played ball. At the same time as the Queenslanders were saying no, the National Drug and Alcohol Research Centre reported that seventy-three thousand people nationally were addicted to methamphetamine, about one and a half times the number of people addicted to heroin. Between 2003 and 2004, three thousand one hundred and ninety users had been hospitalised for mental and behavioural disorders. At Sydney's St Vincent's Hospital, close to the life of many parties, Gordian Fulde, the director of emergency care, stated that in his hospital 'violence associated with crystal meth had risen fivefold between 2000 and 2004'. By December 2005, the *Sydney Morning Herald* was reporting an estimated twelve thousand young Sydneysiders were believed to be dependent on 'ice'.

While the ACC had not had any luck with its confrères in Queensland in running an operation against Gronk and his cache of guns, they had been a bit luckier with the New South Wales police. When Gronk arrived in New South Wales, he had eyes all over him. What the police didn't know was that the sixty handguns were well and truly in the possession of their new owners. Gronk was travelling around New South Wales with something more old-fashioned: marijuana. While motoring along a quiet road about one hundred and fifty kilometres north of Sydney, the New South Wales police pounced.

Gronk had been blissfully unaware that he'd been followed from Sydney. Utah recalled that Gronk later told him he had taken a wrong turn, leading him onto a quiet stretch of road. Poor Gronk got the shock of his life when he became the star turn in a paramilitary style operation by New South Wales police. Rather than sirens and chase cars, the police landed a helicopter across the path of Gronk's truck. Gronk hit the anchors and realised two things very quickly: firstly, he had nowhere to go. Secondly, he had ten kilograms of marijuana in the back of truck. Life was about to get even more complicated. Gronk later told Utah, 'They had machine guns at my fucking head and they landed a chopper in my way'. Utah responded, 'You are full of shit, you cunt'. The dubious Utah later asked Laurel about the story and Laurel commented, 'No, everything he said is true'.

Police dragged the hapless bikie out of his truck and pinned him to the road. The potential of interdicting the trade in illegal guns was driving their operation. What they did not know, of course, was that they were long gone. Old information in a vigorous market is not worth much at all. What they also didn't know was that Gronk was planning another gun deal. According to Utah, Gronk said: 'I was glad I fucken got lost because I didn't stop off at a guy's place where I was supposed to pick up the weapons'. Ten kilograms of high quality marijuana was a nice catch, but nowhere near as much fun as the guns. They weren't deeply interested in trying to turn Gronk in order to trace his source of dull old dope. Gronk would end up on bail, and then, thanks to ten kilograms' worth of solid evidence, to prison. The amphetamine deal with Arthur went south along with Gronk.

What was very disturbing in the wash-up of the incident was yet another missed opportunity. Utah later found one of the sources of the guns, saying: 'What's crazy is that I had LD [listening device] recordings from Bobo the Croatian's home which totally fucked Gronk. I was conducting his affairs for him while he was in gaol. I and the ACC knew everything about him. [Gronk] was buying firearms off the Croatians.' That evidence seems to have gone the way of much of Utah's evidence, simply gathering dust somewhere.

19

MOVING RIGHT ALONG

*I could have had more fun sitting at home today
cutting off my toes with a teaspoon.*
Stevan Utah

Even though he'd had mates like the late Bingey Douglas, and had been arrested and chucked, albeit briefly, in prison for the Mooring murder, the Bandidos were still big fans of Stevan Utah. His cooking skills were the toast of the gang and they wanted to bring him a little closer to their hirsute bosom. They were keen for him to cast off those last vestiges of life in the straight world, and join them both as a member and full-time cook.

For Utah it was a chance to join the life he had toyed with for years and finally turned against. It was both ironic and a little threatening—and he admitted to being a little interested. Then a call had come from Packles—Mick Reed—inviting him down the coast to Caloundra for a few drinks with him and another biker called Pedro. Sava Cvetkovic, then head of the Gold Coast chapter, was also showing interest, and that interest had been stimulated by Gronk. Utah was now being courted by two chapters which, if not handled with good political skills, could be a little dangerous. Sava and Brutus were not close after a dispute almost ten years earlier.

Utah was more interested in getting away from the Sunshine Coast and heading to the bright lights of the Gold Coast. The Sunshine Coast literally had too many bodies buried for his taste and the Gold Coast was where he thought the main game might be happening. Mick Reed's blessing would be needed and Utah had no trouble getting in. It was, next stop Australia's playground.

The ACC was keen on Utah being accepted. So keen that they gave him $1200 to cover car hire costs, accommodation and spending money so he could motor about checking out possibilities on the Gold Coast and pressing the flesh with the locals. Naturally there were conditions. Laurel stated, 'this is on the proviso that you are not required/expected/pressured to say yes on the spot. From our conversation it appears this will not be the case as there has to a period of assessment and acceptance by the membership. This suits us while we negotiate with our partners.' Those partners were people like the Queensland Police Service and their compatriots in other states.

Utah wasn't exactly dazzled by most of the compatriots in other states. He had seen what the Victorians like Strawhorn and the Queensland coppers were capable of, and 'confident' was not the word that came straight to mind. One other issue that the partners had to consider was the investment of about $12 000 in that essential piece of bikie clobber—the big bruising motorbike. With Gronk having no need for a bike for the foreseeable future, his bike was available. A confluence of needs. Oh, and hand over $1000 deposit to Gronk as a show of good faith or, as Utah more colourfully put it, 'It's a lot of money to justify and account for when an informant is handing it over to a fat scumbag'.

This tweaked another lingering problem. On a management level things had been a bit tense. Utah's emails to the ACC, including one he'd recently sent Laurel containing plans and diagrams of Bandido clubhouses, homes and labs, were still occasionally bouncing. At least the recording device seemed reliable. Money was also an ongoing issue, one of those niggling things causing Utah a lot of grief. On 30 August 2005, Utah had met with Laurel in Brisbane. Laurel dropped Utah at the airport before flying back down south, and the cash-strapped Utah took three hours to get himself home to the Sunshine Coast. It wasn't helped by heavy, soaking, chilly rain. Utah wasn't even remotely happy. All his concerns, like lack of action on his information, lack of money, poor email connections and so on, got the better of him. He was feeling very second class and Laurel copped it:

> I felt totally crapped on yesterday after you dropped
> me at the airport. I have told you a hundred times I
> socialise with these monkeys to achieve a common

goal with obvious mutual benefits. I don't socialise with them so I am forced into a position of giving someone $1000 for a culturalistic bikie debt that has absolutely no moral basis or legal justification. I handed that money over to better both our positions after others had let us down. All I was doing was staying in the game and maintaining credibility and a safe environment to operate in (as safe as it can be).

On a roll, he continued: 'I know I feel offended but I am not sure exactly why it is I spend 20 to 40 hours a week with these mongrel children and getting nothing for it?' He concluded: 'Shit mate I could have had more fun sitting at home today cutting off my toes with a teaspoon. But I wanted to have a face to face with you to clear the air about a few issues.' He signed off a little more lightly, 'Cheers Mr Hypothermia'.

Laurel was also expecting detailed accounting records for the piecemeal payments he was giving Utah, even down to signing for a loan of $40. It might have done wonders for public accountability, but it was not a confidence builder for Utah, who viewed matters on a somewhat larger scale. Perhaps the ACC was lucky that Utah was blissfully unaware of the lifestyle of the rich and famous led by Jimmy Anderson. A cold and wet trip home via public transport and hitching is a world away from first-class airfares and five-star hotels all paid for by the unwitting Australian public.

Laurel's email response to his pissed-off informant was not exactly helpful. He commented: 'We will assist you with money to do what needs to be done and in some cases in matters of emergency we will advance you money to keep you out of strife but your day to day living is your business.' What was emerging was a battle for control between informant and handler, neither giving an inch. A pissing contest is not the way to run that sort of relationship. Laurel ended the email saying, 'Don't do anything silly to get money in the meantime. I'll see about sending you $100 of your $400 before then. Take some deep breaths.' A pat on the head might work with someone not so bright, but that certainly wasn't Utah.

By early October 2005, Utah was still in discussions with the Gold Coast chapter to become patched. The lack of funding for the bike was still an impediment to him becoming a 'patched' member but this problem had been reduced by his need to travel interstate regularly and in particular his support of the incarcerated Gronk. Fraternal support in tough times is a big plus in the bikie world. From 16 October he was in Sydney holding, metaphorically, the hand of Gronk, who was about to be sentenced for the marijuana bust. For Utah it was a chance to delve a little deeper by contacting his old colleagues, Steed, and a chap we'll call 'Peel'.

Gronk and Utah were due at Bandido HQ in Sydney on the night of the 17th, and then in Court on the 18th. Utah was calm about the trip, emailing Laurel: 'I have no idea where I'll be staying, I will send you a text to let you know when I can. Going to the clubhouse Monday night, and court Tuesday. Possibly departing Sydney Tuesday night or Wednesday morning at the latest. I feel OK about going down there and I don't feel intimidated or feel anything naughty would occur. If I had a reservation it would be that I will be limited as to where I can stay. Limited options can alter a man's mojo.'

Utah also knew, particularly after the disaster of the operational certificate saga, that getting involved with things like a 'criminal act' in Sydney could land him in extremely hot water both with Laurel and with the New South Wales police. He told Laurel: 'Unfortunately this is a possibility. The part that is an impossibility is me committing an offence. Sydney guys are moving violations. Bandidos typically use "out of towners" for nasty stuff. Ciao Stevan.'

Laurel's response was terse: 'Who is [Peel]?' he demanded. Utah didn't linger in replying: '[Peel] is most definitely an accessory after the fact in relation to Mr Mooring. He further aided in the disposal of both his property and was present during the vehicle being dumped and burnt out. He is a trusted person to all members of the Steed family and a very long term hang-around of the Bandidos.' As for other problems, Utah commented: 'In relation to the police I just won't say anything to them they will have to let me go sooner or later if I haven't done anything wrong. I think things are getting warmer down there than what they are on the Gold Coast, but that is only my opinion.' It would soon be proved to be an uncannily accurate opinion.

Utah put in five hours' work stacking supermarket shelves before being collected by Gronk in his Ford F100 just before midnight on the 15th for the journey south. It was raining heavily. Utah had the listening device ready for action, recalling, 'I thought ten hours in a car could produce some wonderful listening'. They didn't get off to a great start. When Utah slipped into the passenger seat he noticed that Gronk was showing signs of 'heavy drug and alcohol intoxication'. Not exactly ideal for a long and wet drive. He told Utah he'd had 'a couple of big lines' and 'could go all night now', and he was smoking a large joint while talking.

Utah didn't share his optimism. Chances of spicy conversation went down the drain as Utah observed, 'his voice was impaired and he was mumbling very badly'. Gronk chained-smoked joints all through the night. Utah's offers to take the helm were rebuffed.

Aside from stops for fuel and a snack, their only port of call was in Port Macquarie and Kempsey on the New South Wales north coast, both times so that Gronk could chat briefly to fellow Bandidos by phone. Then it was on to visit the new clubhouse in Port Macquarie. It was getting like a royal tour. Utah duly noted the address, descriptions of the cars and the hefty security at the clubhouse, which included three sensor activated external security cameras.

Utah was getting edgy and asked Gronk where they would be staying in Sydney. Gronk was evasive. He was dog tired and his behaviour was getting odder. When they stopped for fuel at Nabiac on the New South Wales mid north coast Utah got creative. While Gronk was out of the truck Utah dickered with the wiring under the dash, causing a fuse to blow and disabling the vehicle. Utah got a well-deserved shower and some sleep at the local motel while Gronk, still chain-smoking joints, waited for the repairs to be done. Utah managed to undo his handiwork before the auto electrician arrived. A $1 fuse later and they were back on the road.

They drove straight through to south-western Sydney and on to the city's rural fringe. Gronk brought the F100 to a stop outside a nondescript house on acreage. Again Utah noted the cars parked there, along with two old boats, and two large and potentially grumpy German shepherds. They were expected. Sort of.

As they entered through the back door, Utah saw a woman coming towards them, armed with a heavy calibre handgun that she was waving about. Though they hadn't met, he soon found she was Bobo's wife—Bobo being an old mate of Utah's. Her husband was in Croatia. Utah recalled:

> She does have major issues with the English language although sitting in front of her you can understand with the aid of hand movements and gestures. She

was armed with at least one handgun possibly around .45 calibre. It was large, black. I recall thinking how out of place such a large handgun looked in a small hand. Later that day we were talking about someone they believed was an informant. She was waving it around saying, 'I see, you believe, I shoot da fuckin' cunt, you believe, I see'.

Not the ideal conversation to be having with someone who was secretly working as an informant.

As the day unfolded the reason for the visit became apparent. Gronk and the Bobos were keen to use Utah to open up their marijuana business in Queensland. Mrs Bobo took him outside to a shed where seventy plants were growing nicely. Utah noted: 'I have seen lots of hydro crops and this was a very clean operation and the plants were the best I have ever seen. They either have very good knowledge or an exceptional strain of plant.' The troupe then went to another house nearby. It had one hundred and twenty plants growing merrily, and all about a month away from a bountiful harvest. Utah was told this crop was earmarked for the Bandidos in Queensland, and it would yield about ninety to one hundred pounds.

What Utah also discovered was that when Gronk was caught, the ten kilograms in the back of his truck had been destined for Queensland, not the reverse. Gronk also commented that over the last three years he had made about thirty trips to Bobo's to collect. Utah was now pondering where Gronk was keeping his stash of cash. The F100 was old, he had debts and certainly did not look affluent, but Utah reckoned Gronk was 'very money conscious down to the last cent'. Therefore his lucrative horticultural business interests meant he should have money stashed.

Utah also noted that Mrs Bobo had five mobile phones. She bragged that two of the phones were not in their names so 'the police wouldn't be able to work out who owned them'. He managed to note down the numbers.

As the evening wore on, it was down to business with Utah being offered thirty-three per cent of the crop if 'I watched it and processed it for the next six weeks, or $35 000 cash upfront for six weeks of babysitting'. Utah told them he'd get back to them. As the talk got a little looser they told him that some of the crops were swapped in Bribie Island, not far from the Sunshine Coast, for meth. Utah knew the contact and thought slipping past for a quiet beer when he was back in the area could be handy. The contact up there was also doing a bit of debt collection for Gronk. Six pounds had not been paid for, and Utah would collect the money from the contact and deposit it into Gronk's bank account. Any problems in recovering the money would be looked after by the East Brisbane Bandidos. Apparently they had a certain knack for the debt collection business.

The next morning, Mrs Bobo was bragging about their business, commenting that they owned twelve houses and had stacks of cash in Australian and Croatian banks—all nicely recorded by Utah. He reckoned that over the last three years, they had made millions. Over the last twenty-four hours he had seen drugs with a street value of about $500 000 and about $70 000 in cash.

About 10 am that morning, the lads motored into the city so Gronk could meet with his solicitor. While Utah was waiting, a member of the Sydney chapter turned up so they went across the road from the Downing Centre courts to the pub for a cleansing ale. The day then went pretty much as planned. Gronk got nine months and had to serve a minimum of six. Utah got custody of the F100 and a pleasant solitary trip back to Queensland. Of the trip he commented to Laurel by email: 'I hated every second of that trip! I admit seeing the cash did make me wonder if I was on the right side. You'll just have to trust me when I say I am not a criminal and I want my life'. He did not get to catch up with Steed or Peel.

A few weeks later, he was back on the road to New South Wales, in a hire car courtesy of the ACC. The destination was Bobo's to see what further information he could collect. Mrs Bobo had stayed up, and when Utah arrived on 3 November shortly after 10 pm, there was a vast pile of that Croatian staple, meat and potatoes, on the table. Enough for six people, Utah reckoned. She also gave him a very affectionate hug which he hoped was a 'cultural thing'.

He was disappointed to find the drug operation had closed down after one of the co-workers had got cold feet. He commented 'she is a strong woman, she simply shut it down. The harvesting and processing of the mature plants just stopped'. Well, not for long as she then showed him about another two hundred juvenile plants under cultivation in the shed out the back. A dope nursery. A colleague would use them, she told him; 'they have ten houses going, would you believe'.

After a good night's sleep, Utah slipped outside to ring Laurel and let him know what he had found. Just before he left that day, Bobo had called from Croatia, and they'd chatted, planning on catching up when Bobo returned. Mrs Bobo gave him a few sandwiches and a bottle of Coke to tide him on his way. He also got a hug and noticed Mrs Bobo was 'wet around the eyeballs'. 'What kind of an asshole am I?' he later observed with a laugh. Utah then motored off, collecting some 'socks and jocks' for Gronk, who was then in prison near Tamworth on the New England Highway, about one-third of the way back toward Brisbane.

The visit to Gronk proved useful. He was very happy to see Utah and even happier to find the debt collection had gone smoothly. The money was in the bank. When Gronk asked about Bobo's drug business, Utah told him it had been delayed but would continue a little later. Gronk, pleased that the wheels hadn't fallen off, gave him a list of his customers. They included numerous Bandidos at various chapters and of course the contact on Bribie Island, who took two pounds of dope per week in return for two ounces of pure meth.

Gronk also told him that all the dope came from the Bobos. Around five to ten pounds week in, week out, and the same amount went to their contacts in Melbourne. Utah did some quick maths. One house with eighty plants equalled forty pounds. Ten houses equalled four hundred pounds of dope every fourteen-week cycle. Three cycles equalled one thousand two hundred pounds. Good business. Gronk was buying at $2500 per pound and selling at $3200 so Utah reckoned Gronk's annual income was about $300 000.

After more 'supportive' conversation, Utah headed back to Queensland to spread the word that Gronk was doing just fine. Utah wasn't, and in his report to Laurel he commented: 'I am feeling rather used and highly unappreciated at times. I spend a lot of time with people and it's my personal time; don't think I'm having fun because I'm not. I don't have any time for the Bandido nation or the members as individuals. They can all go to gaol and commit suicide for all I care. When will the balls bounce back in my court for a while?' Utah also gave the ACC something that many intelligence professionals dreamed about: a list of the names and mobile telephone numbers of eighty-seven Bandidos and their associates. This was gold.

Despite his great work, the issues over money, as might be expected, accelerated. Hand to mouth wasn't suiting Utah, and the ACC did not intend to take a blank cheque approach. They were keeping Utah lean, and in

Utah's view too lean. Rent was regularly in arrears. Most expenses were quibbled over. The hours with the gangs were growing. Work as a shelf-stacker or anything else to turn a quid was getting hard to fit in, and the ACC were not overly happy when he suggested he could work as a driver for strippers and prostitutes. The ACC wanted details to the last cent of his expenses, even motorway tolls. Money was ruining the relationship.

To add to the problems, Utah regularly visited Gronk, now residing in the palm-fringed surrounds of Long Bay Gaol, known with bleak humour as the Malabar Motel, on the coast just south of Sydney's CBD. Utah thought the trip worthwhile as 'a lot of girlie shit' was happening locally, so a visit to the trusted Bandido, and maybe a quick grip and grin moment on the way at the Gold Coast clubhouse, would be good public relations. The lads were still keen to see him patched, and get a bike. They were pushing and Utah was running out of excuses. The ACC had promised him $15 000 to buy one.

On the lack of a bike he recalled: 'It was one of the reasons why I never took the patch. You needed a bike. I didn't have one. Because of the ACC's promise, I approached the chapter sergeant-at-arms and he offered to sell me a $19 000 bike for $13 000. Ten thousand down and $1000 a month thereafter. Then they refused to give me the money from the ACC. I really lost face over that one. It was the start of my problems in the club. I had to make a lame excuse not to buy the bike.' He commented to Laurel, 'I fear this issue will not go away and I refuse to borrow money off these people. The highest levels in this group are watching now. I am saying not too much and being noncommittal.' The lack of decisions on the bike purchase and patching were obviously gnawing away despite the bold façade.

In mid November Utah was further unsettled by the introduction of another handler to the team, in addition to Laurel. We'll call the new man Hardy. He met Utah in Brisbane and told him that he was there to 'put a fresh set of eyes onto this'. Utah's view was 'too much talk, not enough action here. The fresh set of eyes can go and take a jump.' That said, he quite liked the new set of eyes. Utah reckoned Hardy was a decent person but looked and acted like a copper. During the meeting Utah got a call from his contact on Bribie Island, and Hardy complimented him on the switch in persona. Utah enjoyed the praise of his acting skills.

The introduction of the new man meant that there was yet another person at the ACC who knew who he was and what he was doing. The more people who knew, the more the chance of a slip-up. And Utah was not completely sold on the security of the ACC's operations either. He knew a former police officer who had worked at the ACC and had resigned amidst corruption allegations. Utah believed the officer had used informants to set up drug busts and then ripped off the proceeds, both cash and product. What had given Utah a turn was that he had recently bumped into the former copper, meeting him with Brutus, another Bandido and a 'Lebanese gentleman'. The former copper and the Lebanese gentleman were doing a drug deal at the time. When Utah passed the information on to Laurel, Laurel went pale. Utah reckons that while he had no doubts about the integrity of Laurel, he did harbour some doubts about whether the information was passed on.

Disquiet notwithstanding, Utah was soon off to Sydney to hook up with the recently returned Bobo. He got there late on the evening of 18 November. Bobo was knocking back the scotch and Utah joined him with a demure VB or two. According to Utah, Bobo had a good grasp of English, but favoured 'fuck', 'cunt' and 'shut up' as his words of choice. Conversation wasn't exactly lyrical. They spent the night drinking and talking drugs. Bobo, the drunker he got, bragged about his tourist developments in Croatia on the shores of the Adriatic. Would Utah like to pop across and lend a hand over the Christmas break? 'Ask me again when you're sober' was the reply. Bobo also bragged about his local area being called 'Bobopool'—known more widely as Liverpool, a city on the south-western fringe of Sydney.

The next morning, brutally hungover, Bobo and Utah motored around Bobopool and it was soon obvious from the smiles and free drinks that Bobo was a notable local. The wandering also included a brief but non-contact visit to a local brothel. During a stop at a pub, Bobo segued back to drugs, asking if Utah knew anyone who was interested in ecstasy. A large chunk of generations X and Y would have yelled 'yes'. Utah asked about price and says Bobo offered, 'If you buy many thousands you could get them for $2 or $3 each'. Utah told him that the local product was a bit dodgy, 'lower MDA', and compared to the imports it was 'shit'. That didn't worry Bobo as he reckoned it was fine German product, imported to Australia via Victoria. The deal was tasty and certainly an excellent opportunity for the ACC to snag a major distributor and their supply line.

Utah told him no-one would buy thirty thousand to forty thousand tabs without 'sussing' them out first. Bobo was okay but wanted cash upfront at the time of the deal. No credit even for friends, it would seem. Utah played hardball, saying, 'Get fucked—when the drugs are in front of me so will the money be, if they don't like that they can eat a dick!' His gut feeling was that the drugs were already in Australia, imported through Bobo's Croatian mates. He had heard rumours of Bobo's mates being involved in mid-level deals with rival gangs like the Rebels. Utah thought that if he played along and obtained a sample, they could source the origin of the drugs. Bobo, in Utah's view, was getting very careless. Too careless to be a successful drug dealer for much longer.

Later that day, the tour took them to a local plant nursery, where they were shown the usual commercial plants. Secreted at the rear near a dam were eighty marijuana plants. Utah thought, 'Wow, talk about balls, doing this right in front of the public'. And then it was back to Bobo's for a few more essential drinks and to meet yet another drug supplier. Bobopool was looking a bit like the epicentre of Sydney's drug culture.

The supplier was a Croatian, and in the boot of his vehicle was about fifteen pounds of marijuana which he offered to Utah for $40 000. Utah declined, giving the reasonable excuse that he'd soon be visiting Gronk and parking a car full of dope in a prison car park was asking for trouble. The bloke then bragged that he had a further one hundred and twenty pounds to get rid of. He and Bobo chuckled about the hundred people they knew in the business, and how they could fill any order. Bobo also offered Utah a sawn-off shotgun, just in case. A gift. Again Utah declined, using the Gronk excuse. Later that night he duly recorded his observations of the day, including vehicle registration numbers. What he also noted was that Bobo and his family seemed to have direct connections to Bandidos in a few Queensland chapters.

Fun over and back in Queensland, Utah noted in one of his many email reports to the ACC: 'Dude I am depressed, work is pissy at me and I have lost out again. I think I need to reassess my situation again.'

20

SWANSONG

I would like to take this opportunity to thank the taxpayers of Australia for taking twelve months off my life through gross intoxication.
Stevan Utah

In mid December 2005 Utah took himself to Mad's fiftieth birthday party. His mate Plod went along with him, encountering the randy stripper mentioned a little while back. The guest list included the cream of the clubs—national president Jason Addison, Brutus, Sava and so on—some one hundred members from five chapters and about fifty others. Addison asked Utah to be the barbecue cook for the night as a favour.

Later that evening Utah sat down for a drink with Addison. Addison said, 'You haven't changed a bit', to which Utah replied, 'You have', and when Addison laughed, Utah pressed on: 'Have you chosen names for the quads you're carrying!' The good-natured banter continued. Addison introduced him to the Ipswich president, Pig. Pig had married into Bandido royalty, marrying the late

Snotgrass's wife. Addison asked Utah, 'Ever thought of living in Ipswich?' Recruitment was back on the agenda and Utah recalled thinking, 'I am in over my head at this point in time—no money, no bike and out of excuses'.

Utah told Addison he had given his word to Gronk that he would visit every two weeks. Utah looked rather civilised in comparison to the average bikie so he would not set off alarm bells in the prison. Gronk had a business that needed a hand outside the prison and that would be Utah. He was winging it. He even suggested he'd move to Sydney to make life a little easier. Addison wasn't having a bar of that idea. He wanted Utah in the club. As for Gronk, he offered to get someone else to take over from Utah. Utah's only escape was the respect that the Bandidos expected from each other—when it suited, of course. He told Addison that he'd given his word and intended keeping it. Luckily it struck a chord and Addison understood; however Addison added, 'You are welcome in any chapter down there, you know'. Snookered.

The evening wore on, with Utah again being prospected. One president said, 'I spoke with Jason last week. I wish you had a patch—I want you as my sergeant'. Utah was a hot property. Luckily for him their odd code of honour supported his commitment to Gronk. He had a few months' breathing space until Gronk made it out in April 2006.

Toward the end of the evening, after the usual commitments for Christmas drinks and so on had been made, Steed pulled Utah aside to discuss, out of the blue, the hiding of Mooring's body. Steed was very cautious and he and Utah went for a walk down the road to chat. Utah offered: 'Bro', do you want to pat me down? I won't be offended.'

Steed looked at him with a little embarrassment, and took him up on the offer. He conducted the pat down, Utah noticed, like you see on television, lifting his shirt, looking for wires or a microphone. Old technology. With Steed relieved, Utah told him the body was well hidden and that he had driven down the road a few years before and the body would never be found. Half true in hindsight. Steed then chatted about his family, the Sydney chapters and current events down there, and gave his new phone details to Utah for a future hook-up.

In his report Utah commented: 'Despair is the only word that comes to mind! On behalf of my liver and brain cells I would like to take this opportunity to thank the taxpayers of Australia for taking twelve months off my life through gross intoxication. (That's a joke!)'

At the end of his first year on the inside Utah was decidedly unhappy. With tongue in cheek he likened himself to Johnny Depp as the FBI undercover in the 1997 film about the mafia, *Donnie Brasco*. That took a bit of licence as the similarity in looks is elusive. He felt he wasn't getting the support he needed, that he was isolated both mentally and physically, and suicide was in the back of his mind: 'There's not a day that goes by I don't think about knocking myself and have to find a reason not to'. At night he dreamt of Bandidos or, as he put it, 'When I try and get some sleep all I can think about are those cunts'.

He was also a little concerned about the lack of obvious results from his work. In addition to his numerous recordings he had given the ACC two very tasty bits of information. One concerned a Queensland-based European diplomat who Utah reckoned was providing various crooks, including some Bandidos, with his country's passports for sale. All genuine except for the name and the personal details. As well, he had given the ACC an original Queensland driver's licence, in a fake name of course, sourced through his gang mates. Things like these gave crooks the opportunity to move around under the radar of law enforcement domestically or internationally, and if they were of a mind, they could get up to all sorts of undetectable shenanigans. As far as Utah knows, the trade in dodgy documents continues unfettered.

His handlers at the ACC were not doing him any favours either. Utah reckoned he'd been putting in about twenty to thirty hours per week meeting, partying and socialising with the Bandidos. He did not have much of a life for himself. His capacity to earn an income was dramatically impeded, to the point where his wages did not cover his rent and cost of living. The $400 per week from the ACC was not filling the void. Plus he had legal expenses and regular court days arising from the fraud case.

After a long chat with his handler, Utah reckoned Laurel commented, 'I thought $400 was enough and we were going to produce a sealed document to the courts so you don't get a sentence on that fraud matter'. A little hope for the future, but not too much. Laurel's only other reaction was to arrange a quick meeting in a park with the psychologist who had tested him earlier that year. A little due diligence in case things went awry. Backsides covered. Utah was still on the hook, though wriggling hard.

'Those cunts' who were constantly in Utah's mind did, briefly, come in handy. In mid December Utah was back from Sydney and out of cash. The ACC had given him money for the rent but they were a day late in making the payment and so his landlord seized the opportunity and gave him his marching orders. Utah reckons his landlord later told him he had received a phone call from a Queensland copper who wasn't a member of the Stevan Utah fan club. The copper didn't give Stevan a glowing endorsement.

Utah was homeless, at least until his unlikely fairy godmother appeared. A one hundred and twenty kilogram, six-foot tall fairy godmother called 'Tank', now out of prison. He offered the virtually destitute Utah somewhere to live. More precisely, he offered Utah a room at a property in remote Delaneys Creek, about half an hour's drive from Caboolture. Also in residence were a few other bikies. The lads were running a familiar cottage industry, cooking up amphetamines almost daily.

The property was perfectly located in the lee of a hill and completely hidden from the road. The drive to the house was a couple of hundred metres over a hill, and the house had a good line of sight to the closest property, and to cars breasting the nearest hill as they came in from the main road.

When Utah reported this offer to the ACC they were ecstatic. Utah was less so. The frying pan was trying enough. Leaping into the fire was going to be very unpleasant. However, his choices were limited. When he moved in the ACC did something really dumb. They discontinued his rental support. In the short term, it committed him to living at Delaneys Creek and getting more involved. What it also did was accelerate the failure of his arrangements with the ACC. There was also a lack of an operational certificate for activities on the property that the ACC had overlooked. Utah stood a fair chance of ending up on his own with his future whistling in the wind.

Suddenly the prospect of moving down to Sydney was looking good. But not for long.

21

RAT-FUCKING THE FEDS

Would your boys have any issues if we did Legs?
Alex the hit man

There are no half-measures in becoming a member of an outlaw motorcycle gang. If you're in, you're in—and if you are asked by them to do something nastily crook, you do it without question to prove your cred with the club. By late 2005, Stevan Utah was beginning to get very worried that his police handlers just did not understand this. They had asked him to 'go back across' to the biker life he had tried to put behind him. He had been working now as a secret informant for the Australian Crime Commission for over a year, but his credibility with his outlaw motorcycle gang 'brothers' was starting to wear a bit thin. Lots of excuses but no patch. And in his mind it was all the ACC's fault.

As an informant, he felt he had delivered, in spades. But every time he had passed on information, at considerable risk to his own safety, it seemed the ACC did not 'give a shit' about it. From the start he had told his handlers about the drug stash hidden in the hills behind the Sunshine Coast, and yet their man had squandered the opportunity by flicking the information to a disinterested or maybe overworked Queensland drug squad. A chance to take a massive haul of heavy calibre handguns off the black market had also been lost because the ACC could not get the vital operational certificate from the Queensland police. Not to mention the blown chance to bust a huge amount of methamphetamine. What the hell was going on?

Utah had also seen close up turf wars between state police agencies and the federal Australian Crime Commission that would make a biker brawler blush. He strongly suspected, for instance, that the information in the request by the ACC for an operational certificate to allow Utah to buy the heavy calibre handguns had been ignored by the Queenslanders just to blow off the feds. He suspected the Queenslanders had then used the information in the ACC's request to alert New South Wales police to stop Gronk in the helicopter bust across the border, a failed operation in that it only put Gronk inside for minor drug charges. Perhaps if Queensland had cooperated, that weapons smuggling racket might well have been shut down.

Utah had the awful feeling that state police agencies liked 'rat-fucking the feds' as much as possible and if that meant compromising the hard-won intelligence he passed on to the ACC from time to time, then so be it. It does not inspire a crook trying to go straight with a great deal of confidence in the battle Her Majesty's constabulary is waging against organised crime. Then there were the nagging worries about bent cops he had encountered along the way. What if one of his bikie 'brothers' knew or had even picked up a whiff that the ACC had someone on the inside. They would not be sentimental about putting a bullet in his head on the merest suspicion of him being a police informant.

Laurel had assured him his cooperation was being kept very tight inside the already secretive crime-fighting body. But the ACC had done nothing with his evidence incriminating the now former—and bent—deputy head of the Victorian drug squad, Wayne Strawhorn, already in gaol for dealing in drug ingredients with a Melbourne crime family. Even though, courtesy of Utah, the ACC had secretly recorded a senior Bandido admitting Strawhorn was a source of illegally procured pseudo-ephedrine, the Victorian court never got to hear that evidence. Strawhorn was acquitted on the charge of supplying the Bandidos. Somewhere inside the ACC an incriminating transcript that would have nailed Strawhorn was burning a hole in the desk of senior management. Why was that, Utah was starting to ask himself. If the concern was to protect Utah's usefulness to police as an inside source then what exactly was he useful for if they were not going to act on any of the information he gave anyway? It was almost, Utah was starting to think, as if Australia's crime fighters were too scared or just too hobbled by legal restrictions to do much with what he was offering.

Utah did not need to be sniffing the bubbling barrels of methamphetamine now sitting in his house to start getting increasingly paranoid. A lot of the officers working in the ACC were then and still are seconded from state police forces, including Victoria's, and there was always the risk someone might talk—perhaps boasting about 'the ACC's man on the inside of a motorcycle gang' to some as yet unacknowledged corrupt cop. Utah had also told Laurel about the now former ACC policeman whom he had witnessed criminally dealing in drugs with his Sydney Lebanese drug dealer mate. Surely Laurel had passed that on? But if the ACC knew about that then why had he not been asked to give a statement? Utah trusted Laurel but was it possible that the higher-ups did not want to risk the blow-back from using Utah—that his penetration of the Bandidos was revealing some uncomfortable truths about police corruption that no-one wanted to hear too much about. These kinds of worries were now beginning to weigh heavily on him.

Added to the mix were his more immediate concerns. Until now, Utah had always been able to keep a distance from his bikie mates. It kept him sane to go home to his dogs, Cleo and Caesar—but he had been forced by the move to Tank's remote house at Delaneys Creek to give the care of his dogs to a female friend. Then came the heartbreaking news that while he was on one of his many trips to Sydney gathering information for the ACC, one of his beloved dogs had died. Worse still, the supposed carers had decided to put the surviving dog, Cleo, down because they could not cope with looking after such a big animal.

This all sent Stevan Utah into a blue funk. Already prone to depression, Utah was also becoming increasingly anxious about Chez Tank at Delaneys Creek. Wherever he looked there were hulking bikies lugging tubs of ingredients for the massive methamphetamine factory they had now constructed in Tank's garage. Worse still, if Stevan Utah was busted by Queensland police with all this drug paraphernalia—and illegal weapons—lying around, he knew he was going to gaol for a very long time. This was because, nearly a year after he had started helping them, the ACC had still not come up with an operational certificate which would have allowed him to commit crimes to help police bust the gang. As life sentences' worth of crystal meth slowly stacked up at Delaneys Creek, it was wearing on Utah's mind that he was the only one there who knew for sure that the police knew all about it.

What bewildered Utah most of all was that Australia's peak crime-fighting body did not seem to understand the significance of his being offered a full patch as a Bandido. He was also getting a little worried that his mates at Delaneys Creek might be wondering why he hadn't taken up the Bandido offer. Despite these niggling concerns, Utah continued to fire regular detailed reports to his ACC minders. To make the point about his growing frustrations with the apparent lack of interest in his inside information, Utah boasted in one email in early January 2006 how: 'continuous telephone contact was kept with numerous people including Mouse, Harry, Packles, Ivan and Bobo. To speed up identifying those names it equates to 1 x National Secretary, 2 x Chapter Presidents, 1 x Sydney Croatian and a clown. Whilst I was never physically with these people for a week, I maintained top order contact over this week. There was nothing special about this contact, it was all very friendly.'

One possible explanation for why the ACC was hamstrung using their inside source at this time is that the Queensland Police Service was persisting with its fraud charges against Utah, re-instated in May 2005, and the ACC could not get an okay from the Queenslanders to use Utah on their patch. While neither the Queensland police nor the ACC are talking, it seems very likely that these charges were a major stumbling block. The ACC needed Queensland police's support for an operational certificate which would have allowed Utah to commit crimes in that state as part of the police investigation. But someone senior inside Queensland police had 'shit on his liver', according to Utah, and was insisting he face trial for the outstanding fraud charges. For reasons neither New South Wales, Victorian nor federal police could ever understand, the Queenslanders took the view that Utah was not someone they were prepared to work with. Even the Queensland Crime and Misconduct Commission, the state's anti-corruption body, was asked to help break the police veto on using Utah, but the appeals fell on deaf ears. As this extraordinary legal limbo dragged on, Utah's pre-trial committal hearing on the fraud charges began in mid January 2006. 'That was about as exciting as having your eyes removed with a fork', said Utah.

While the coppers dithered and wrung their hands over whether a criminal like Utah could be used in an operation, the real criminals were hard at it—including Bobo the Croatian, who in early 2006, Utah discovered to his horror, had dispatched a couple of fellow Croatian hit men to Queensland to knock off an old pal of Utah's called 'Legs', who was not a Bandido but a local drug dealer known to the gang. As far as Bobo was concerned, Legs had not paid up on a drug debt so he had to be killed as a warning to other clients. Business is business. Bobo's clients had to learn their obligations. By now Bobo so trusted Utah that he had suggested to the two Croatians that they ring him for help in tracking down their troublesome target.

Utah, no doubt ever mindful that he probably had both Queensland police and the ACC listening in on his phones, made a full and immediate report to his handler by email: 'I telephone[d] Bobo and during the conversation he told me, "They are there to fix that Legs fella up". I do have knowledge of why this would occur. Bobo also made it very clear to me that Legs would die because of what he had done to [Gronk] and a previous 30k drug rip-off. This was not the only time Legs had ripped [off] Bobo ... Obviously this could not be allowed.'

In the cold, hard world of high-level drug crime, knocking off a bad debt like Legs was routine and necessary. Utah was in a bind. If he did not help Bobo, he could just as easily be bumped off or smacked around himself for being unhelpful to Gronk's Sydney mate. If he did help Bobo's hired killers, then he would be an accessory to murder. Arranging to meet the men at the Deception Bay pub north of Brisbane, he contacted Laurel, his ACC handler, telling him he would record the conversation if safe to do so:

I went and sat in a Keno bar and had a rum and awaited further instructions from [Laurel]. I recall sending him a text message with words to the effect of 'I intend using the device tonight unless advised otherwise'. I got a reply, 'Yes, use it'. It was obvious to me [that Laurel] had a few issues his end he couldn't quite sort out [Queensland Police Service]. I decided to head home and get changed and pick the device up. A few minutes after I left home Laurel rang and told me under no circumstances was I to enter the hotel in question prior to 7 o'clock.

Behind the scenes Laurel was frantically trying to do the right thing by Utah, attempting to arrange some kind of assistance from Queensland police to protect their man just in case the meeting went bad. Not for the first or the last time, this was proving difficult for the ACC officer. As Utah entered the Deception Bay pub just after seven o'clock that night, he did not know whether anyone was watching his back as he walked in to meet the two hit men. Utah describes the scene as:

> He is a hit man. He was there to kill Legs. I had said to him that I am not taking part in this shit. He said it's got to be dealt with. I rang [Bobo] and said what's the go here. [Bobo] wanted him dead ... I have two Croatian hit men here that want Legs knocked off. I said this is a bit of a nasty business and that I would have to go and meet the hit men. [Laurel] told me to go along. It was the day of my hearing and all the ACC would pay for was a taxi for me to get [to] the hearing on time. They couldn't find any Queensland police prepared to help out in case things went bad. So I went down to this pub ... by myself ... and I was carrying an ACC bug.

Alex the Croatian hit man wanted Utah to come to them in a quiet motel room but Utah's instincts for self-preservation saw him insisting they meet at the pub: 'I do not enter areas such as motel rooms, cars, alleyways, etc. I believe police call it a secondary crime scene or something like that. I call it an act of lunacy.'

There was the added problem that Utah did not know what Alex looked like:

> I walked around the pub and couldn't find anyone I could identify as being Croatian looking. I actually recall thinking to myself I didn't like being in there. It was dark in areas; it was a rat's nest of corners, poorly lit beer garden and car park. I chose to sit in the TAB section as the entire perimeter wall was made of glass and anyone outside could clearly see me and who I was with. It was also probably the noisiest section, unfortunately.

Alex entered the pub with an associate from central casting—a hundred and five kilogram Croat as wide as he is tall. To borrow from a colloquial metaphor, he is a man who could be described as 'a brick with eyes'. 'I noticed he had a funny looking nose not unlike that of the sixties, seventies Victorian wharfy "putty nose Nicholas",' Utah chuckled. He had spotted them as soon as they walked in the door but to be sure he kept on watching the television, ignoring both men, until Alex rang him on his mobile, identified himself and came over to the table.

Clearly the man known as Alex was the brains in the team and his associate, John, was the muscle. In the report he wrote to the ACC later that evening, Utah provided copious detail: 'Alex was a very smooth talker. He tended to place a hand over his mouth while he spoke, and he also had a short conversation with John in a language other than English. John was a smug type, just nodded, smiled, made gestures and said very little. His [aura] reeked of danger. I really didn't like this guy.'

For Utah, the approach by Bobo's hit men was a classic illustration of just why the stalemate between the ACC and Queensland police about whether to use him was getting very dangerous. When Utah had taken the call from Alex earlier that day, he was thrown off guard: 'I recalled speaking with Alex earlier that morning and when he asked me, "Would your boys have any issues if we did Legs?" I replied, "No they wouldn't. It's none of their business".'

To preserve his credibility with Bobo and his homicidal associates, Utah had assented to something extremely dangerous—and not just for the unwitting Legs, but for himself as well. 'I had seriously screwed up that morning', he admits. He belatedly realised the implications of what he had said to Alex on the phone. What he had effectively done was sanction the murder of Legs on behalf of the Queensland Bandidos—precisely the kind of criminal activity an operational certificate was required (and highly unlikely in any event) to sanction. The problem was, that certificate was exactly what he did not currently have— especially with small-minded Queensland coppers wanting to 'rat-fuck the feds'. Now he was sitting in a bar opposite two aspiring killers with cheesy grins on their faces, scheming a way out. Thinking fast, Utah played for time:

Alex asked me where [Legs] lived; I said I didn't have the details on me. Alex went on to say how they had been to every club and pub in town looking for him, everyone knew him but no-one knew where he lived. It was at this point I told them he was not to be touched. He owed [another Bandido] some money and he wanted it. 'You should both do yourselves a favour and go back to Sydney.'

Alex became agitated with this and John had this stupid shit-eating grin on his face and just glared at me. John said nothing. Alex looked at John and said to me, 'It's nothing like that, we just want to go and see him'. I again said I didn't know how to contact him at that time.

What Utah knew was that Legs lived just three streets away from where they were sitting. And Bobo's message earlier in the day had made it clear that Alex and John were there for more than just a quiet chat. John had the malevolently happy glint in his eye of someone who looked like he would enjoy nothing more than mashing Utah's head into a nearby pokie machine if he did not hand over Legs. But Utah followed his old dictum, never to show fear to your adversary. He played cool and stared right back at the brick-with-eyes.

'The conversation took a turn towards availability of drugs in Sydney and what they could assist me and members of the Bandidos with', Utah's subsequent memo to the ACC explained. What the Croatian hit men told him was golden information for police. It showed the Croatian dealers were looking to cooperate with the Bandidos and other bikie gangs in the distribution of massive amounts of ecstasy, pseudo-ephedrine, marijuana and 'goey', or methamphetamine. Happy to be discussing something other than Legs' current home address and imminent demise, Utah bought himself some time with the Croatians by promising to come down to Sydney in a couple of weeks to discuss doing business. To Utah's great frustration, here was another opportunity the police subsequently failed to take up: 'What really annoys me is that if we'd continued the Bobo relationship we could have busted him because the ACC device recorded them saying they could deal with me in Sydney. Nothing ever happened on it. Bobo's still selling his drugs.'

To the ACC's credit, later that night handler Laurel insisted Utah find Legs and warn him to stay out of sight from prowling Croatian hit men. Ever mindful of the need to cover himself just in case they did find Legs, Utah kept his covert digital voice recorder running: 'I walked up the street and asked Legs to leave home for the night. I then went home. The device would have captured my comments to Legs as I left it on for the conversation. I stated to Legs that if he compromised me I would hit him in the head with a bat. Just for the record I don't hit people in the head with bats.'

It had been one hell of a day. Utah left the now full digital recorder in a Brisbane luggage locker to be collected and transcribed by ACC staff. For good measure, Utah also dropped in on Brutus at one of the Queensland Bandido clubhouses. Brutus wanted to use Utah's knowledge of the Sydney drug scene to help him in negotiations with a visiting dealer. Utah told his handlers:

> We spoke about drugs and what's the go in Sydney, etc. He specifically asked me about ecstasy. I said I knew of some imports and locals, but hadn't seen any as yet. He asked me about imports and then went and saw a guy sitting at the bar. I have seen him before, I know he is a drug dealer on a large scale and certainly someone who has the protection of the club. I don't know his identity and I did not ask. I will find out over a few weeks and report on this later.

Inside the clubhouse Utah constantly had to feign disinterest in anyone else's dirty business, unless told: 'When crims do stuff you don't look like you're interested. You don't care what's going on, even if you do. If someone gets shot next to you, you are just having a cigarette. Don't get involved in somebody else's shit.' That is how the chapter clubhouses work—a very blokey safe ground behind tight security and fortified doors to share information and discuss criminal enterprises—with the odd woman as a decorative accessory for amusement and sexual relief. These are not places for nice girls. A bikie literate enough might describe many of the women who hang around clubhouses as *demimondaines*—women whose sexual promiscuity places them outside polite society. Suffice to say, in the world of outlaw motorcycle gang members such social concerns do not rank too highly. However pejorative the term, a woman hang-around in the clubhouse is usually termed a 'slut'. Utah said that:

> [Brutus] had a slut coming over and asked if I was staying around. I said no I had to work. I then recognised one of the blonde hang-rounds as someone I knew from years earlier. She was with another girl. I decided to buy some drinks and sit with them. Their names were Brooke and Deanne. Brooke was the blonde . . . I must have met her years ago when she was about sixteen. Deanne was a hideous looking creature. Apparently she is about to go to court for assault and is violent for a female. She came across as very flippant. As [Brutus] walked me out at approximately 0100 hours a girl approached. It was the slut. She tried to touch me and I laughed at her and said, 'Fuck him not me'. We laughed. I went to work, I got home at 0700.

Somewhere in the bowels of the Australian Crime Commission's offices in the federal police building in Canberra, there are dozens of detailed reports like these from Utah. Some of the information is of little value but, for a crime-fighting organisation desperate to build up an understanding of how the principal criminal minds in the Bandidos work, much of it was extremely important.

What was not clear to Utah was whether police were actually doing anything with the detailed tips he was giving them. The one thing Utah wanted most, as he daily risked his skin for the feds, was a place to stay away from Delaneys Creek crime-HQ-central but, incredibly, a Queensland police officer was actively sabotaging his (and, indirectly, the ACC's) efforts by frustrating Utah's efforts to hold down rental accommodation. It was becoming almost impossible for him to find a landlord because of that Queensland officers's campaign against him. 'Bail conditions state I must advise the DPP of my change of address, will this happen again?' he asked his police minders about this copper's unwelcome intervention. 'Life is difficult enough without having this anal maggot around. People actually expect me to have patience. It's hard . . . It's very fucking hard! But they can all go eat a dick. I will do the right thing, I will survive and I will not let them beat me mentally. He should smell the roses . . . you give anyone enough rope they will hang themselves.'

Utah was also regularly travelling the five-hour drive to Glen Innes in New South Wales, where his drug dealer mate Gronk was now languishing in gaol. On a typical day, this meant rising after three hours' sleep from a late shift stacking shelves at a local supermarket (no illicit profits for this police informant) and getting to the prison by noon.

The pressure of his double life was getting to Utah. But

he was also enjoying it in a perverse way. It was exciting and it made him feel that for the first time in his life since the army, he was doing something worthwhile. The growing violence among bikie gangs was also making his information more valuable than ever. Everyone was talking in the clubhouses about the awesome shoot-out in early 2006 between the Finks and the Hells Angels at the Royal Pines Resort on the Gold Coast, the melee in which Christopher Hudson had been shot. By luck no-one had been fatally injured. Now, the violence was spreading across the country.

Police were apprehensive as it became clear a major turf war was going on between bikie gangs for control of lucrative entertainment strips in cities across Australia. In February 2006, a doorman learned this to his cost at the Sapphire Suite nightclub in Sydney's Kings Cross. A Hells Angel marched up to the entrance with five of his patched brothers and demanded entry. 'We're Hells Angels, step aside', one told the unwitting bouncer. 'Who?' the naive young fellow asked, to his eternal regret. He copped a bullet for his trouble, as did a woman standing nearby waiting to enter. Luckily the injuries were not fatal.

Another group who had moved into the Sydney nightclubs, claiming them as their own, were the Bandidos, who had opened a Pyrmont clubhouse—the Downtown chapter—in the old wharf district close to the city CBD. They were trying to establish an inner-city presence to counter the dominance of Kings Cross nightclub owner Sam Ibrahim, the president of the Nomads Outlaw Motorcycle Gang Parramatta chapter. The Downtown chapter's founding president was Felix Lyle.

As the heat rose in this simmering Sydney turf war in late 2005, the ACC realised they had a good 'in' with Stevan Utah. He had met Lyle in the Sydney clubhouse many times. He was also a good mate of Russell Oldham, the much-respected and highly intelligent Bandido who had been a fellow methamphetamine cook with Utah over the years.

As one wit in the New South Wales police expressed it in an instance of more than mild understatement: 'There seems to be a bit of a bottleneck' in the Sydney outlaw motorcycle gangs jostling for power. Sydney was about to blow sky-high—and Stevan Utah would find himself right in the middle of things, as usual.

22

SYDNEY GANGLANDS

Expect no mercy.
Bandido book of useful sayings

Barely twenty minutes from the centre of Sydney's business district, a narrow peninsula of coastline juts like an accusing finger into the city's iconic Botany Bay. The barren grassy sandhills from south-eastern Sydney's Port Botany around to Malabar cresting the Tasman Sea have long been a favourite spot for the city's mobsters and gangsters. It is here where they come to do discreet dodgy business and also the occasional killing.

In late November 2005 Milad Sande, a 29-year-old father of two young children, dropped in at his parents' printing firm in Parramatta in Sydney's west. He had asked a friend of his if he could borrow his ute for a job that night, and he had arranged to pick it up at the factory—a request that puzzled his family at the time because he had a car of his own. He left home at about 3 pm that afternoon. It was the last time the family saw Milad Sande alive.

Late that night, residents of a tiny street adjoining Cromwell Park in Malabar, forty kilometres away, were just about to go to bed for the night when they heard a commotion outside their homes. At any other time, the heavily tree-lined Cromwell Park is a beautifully desolate location, bordering a favourite fishing and surfing spot just off the eastern coastline. It is more than a little ironic that the bay adjoining the park is called Long Bay and, as they waited for their quarry, Sande's lurking assailants might just have been able to see the twinkling lights of the maximum security wing at Long Bay prison on the hill a kilometre to the south.

The city's main rifle range is also just a few hundred metres away across the bay. But around 11 pm when the locals heard three gunshots in quick succession, they wisely stayed inside their homes, guessing correctly that these shots were something more sinister. Police were called and Sande's slumped body was found lying beside the white ute with three bullet holes in his head. He had been cold-bloodedly executed at close range, clearly by more than one man, and left lying in the empty street. In the weeks after his death, family members made an emotional appeal for the public's help in finding his killers, saying that Milad had a 'heart of gold' and that he was a committed family man who had worked tirelessly to help run his family's two successful companies. 'Our family is struggling to understand why somebody would want to brutally murder Milad and take him away from us', his grieving brother told the press.

A few months later, in early January 2006, readers of Sydney's *Sun-Herald* flicked open their Sunday tabloid to find a brief article mentioning that Milad Sande's uncle, also named Milad, had once been described by a royal commission as one of the city's biggest heroin dealers, with links to large-scale Chinese importers of the illicit drug. There was nothing to suggest that Milad junior was crook, though, and no lead on who had killed him, or why. To this day, the murder remains officially unsolved. But Stevan Utah knows the real story, and he knows the murderers all too well.

Utah had met Sande several times and did not like him. He knew him as 'Milano', a major drug dealer well known to the outlaw motorcycle gangs who traded in the hugely valuable pseudo-ephedrine market. One afternoon after the murder, at Brutus's remote Queensland farmhouse home, Utah heard the first suggestions that the Sande hit had a Bandido tie-in. In a scene reminiscent of one of Utah's favourite gangster films, Brutus and half a dozen or so Bandidos, including Utah, discussed why Sande had been killed. Typically it was because they didn't want to pay Sande for the drugs:

> The conversation was in [Brutus's] lounge room in his house . . . It was a pretty cold conversation. Think of [the movie] *Donnie Brasco*—it was like that. They were all sitting around a bong on the table. It was after the event . . . The murder happened when Mirhad [sic]

Sande was meeting [a Bandido] with the intention of selling him kilos of pseudo-ephedrine. The only way they could take it was to kill him because the Sande family is well connected.

Utah's detailed report to the Australian Crime Commission on what he had heard went on to name four Bandidos as being responsible for the murder. In what was one of the stupidest murder plots in recent history, the killers had left a long trail of suspicion to their door because for some weeks they had been negotiating with Sande to buy about two kilograms of pseudo-ephedrine, worth as much as $200 000 on the black market.

This suggestion of a Bandido hand in the hit was explosive information inside the tight world of the outlaw motorcycle fraternity, for Sande was extremely well connected. His cousin Danny Sande was the president of the Bandidos Blacktown chapter. And Milad's good friends included Nomads motorcycle gang chief Sam Ibrahim and his brother Michael. A lot of brothers inside both the Bandidos and the Nomads were very angry indeed that someone amongst them had killed Sande. It did not take them long to find out who.

There is another quote in the Bandido book of useful sayings relevant to what inevitably happened next. It is 'Expect no mercy'. Early in February 2006, some of those friends of Milad Sande began their retaliation for the hit. Their information pointed to the murder having been carried out by one Bandido with several others, on the orders of his father, a senior Bandido whom for legal reasons we will call the 'Wiseguy' in tribute to the *Donnie Brasco* movie Utah thinks this saga most resembles. If the outlaw motorcycle gangs are mobsters, as Utah believes, then the Bandido father of the killer was a wiseguy. Not just a 'connected' guy, a 'made' guy, to borrow from the mobster vernacular. It was a huge moment when Milad Sande's avengers took on the Wiseguy because, as mobster Lefty says in the movie, 'A wiseguy never pays for his drinks'. They are not men to be crossed lightly.

What Utah was able to piece together was that Milad Sande's avengers took the approach commonly favoured by the Soviet KGB with people who crossed them—a highly effective strategy of kidnapping their loved ones and threatening to send back bits of them until they got what they wanted. On a hot February summer's night in 2006 the much-loved son of senior Bandido Wiseguy was kidnapped together with two of his associates and taken to a Bandidos Sydney clubhouse. 'I am not exactly sure who was kidnapped with [Wiseguy's son] but I know they were tortured', Utah says.

'When Sande was murdered all hell broke loose', Utah recalls of the reaction from senior members of both the Nomads and the Bandidos. 'They suspected [Wiseguy and his son] because they knew they'd been negotiating a buy. [A senior Nomad] had a conversation with [then Bandidos president] Rodney "Hooksey" Monk where it was made clear that unless the gear came back there'd be war.'

The Nomad associates of Sande who had kidnapped the three were furious at his murder, but—business being business—they also wanted either the drugs back or cash compensation for what they had stolen. Wiseguy was soon ringing around gangland Sydney looking for a large amount of cash, the screams of his tortured son no doubt still ringing in his ears. No-one, it seems, thought reporting the kidnap to the police was a prudent idea. The son and two other very bruised and battered men were only released after the payment of a rumoured $300 000 in cash and a promise to pay much more.

Monk also made what was to be a fateful decision. He stripped Wiseguy of his Bandido colours to keep peace with the Nomads and avoid a war. Utah says, 'Hooksey and others fucked [Wiseguy] off—that's a big call to fuck [Wiseguy] off. It was because [Wiseguy] authorised the fucking hit.' But the sacking of one of the most senior members of the Bandidos angered some inside the gang, who felt Sande was fair game and that it was time for the club to assert its dominance over the Nomads. As Utah eloquently puts it: 'Sande—he was a slimeball. Just a gangster arse motherfucker with too much money. Lived off bullshit threats. There's no waste to the world that man got a fucking bullet.'

There was also another humiliating moment for the now dumped Wiseguy. As part of the code, he had to forfeit his $80000 motor-cycle to the club. But to evade that dictate he had already accepted a $26000 deposit from a prospective purchaser. The Bandidos president Rodney Monk demanded he hand over that money. It was the final indignity for a very powerful member of the gang, now stripped of his colours, and his treatment grated with many in the club. Perhaps Rodney Monk should have borne in mind the other memorable quote about wiseguys from *Donnie Brasco*: 'A wiseguy's always right. Even when he's wrong, he's right.' For the sacking of Wiseguy from the club was eventually going to cost him his life.

Enter Russell Oldham, one of the brightest of the Bandido associates, who shared with Stevan Utah a skill for the complex and dangerous job of cooking up ice. 'I had met Big Russell. Probably the most intelligent man I've ever met. When he was sorted, you couldn't fault the guy. He had a charisma about him. If he had a little bit of drugs in him, he was a totally different guy', Utah says.

Russell Merrick Oldham was not a born-on-the-wrong-side-of-the-tracks biker boy. From a wealthy upper middle-class family, he headed to Sydney University where he boarded at St John's College, the alma mater of cabinet ministers, lawyers and numerous notables. After starting a science degree he won a place in the medical school. He excelled at everything he did. He was a talented cricketer and by the time he was in his first year at university, he already had an eighteen-month-old baby. He was one of those men drawn to the outlaw motorcycle gangs not out of weakness but out of a hankering to live on the edge.

Abandoning his university studies, he soon became a Bandido hang-around. Some media reports have it that he became a Bandido sergeant-at-arms, ironically a position in which the incumbent's job is to enforce the club's strict rules. But Utah is adamant Oldham was never patched into the gang at all. Oldham, though, did develop a formidable reputation for violence, going to gaol for five years for the manslaughter of two men in the western Sydney suburb of Bankstown in 1998.

Joining him in prison for the manslaughter was Arben 'Benny' Puta, a notable Romanian cocaine dealer and at one time a regular at the ironically named Sweethearts coffee shop in Kings Cross. It was not the first time Benny had been in strife over a death. About a decade earlier he had been minding his own business in the toilet at Sweethearts when he reckoned he was shot in the leg by a coke dealer. Benny, allegedly in self-defence, resolved the matter with a house brick firmly applied to the coke dealer's head. Only Benny survived the altercation.

Incongruously, while in prison Oldham also showed his tender side, raising money for charity to help a young disabled child. On his release, it was his good friend and Bandido president Rodney Monk who ordered a limousine to collect him from gaol. Among Oldham's Bandido brothers he was seen as a natural leader of the one-percenters. Oldham had been destined for great things inside the Bandidos, but now he was flaming out badly.

It slowly emerged around the clubhouses that Oldham had been in league with Wiseguy and his son, agreeing to cook up the stash of pseudo-ephedrine stolen off Sande for a quick profit. Much of the evidence incriminating Oldham was passed across by the Nomad members who had extracted admissions from Wiseguy's son under torture. With Wiseguy now stripped of his colours, the club president Rodney Monk was looking very differently at those close to him, including Oldham. 'He was a cook—and a very good one . . . well he was until he had a bullet in his head', Utah wryly recalls. 'The deal with [Wiseguy]—with whom he was very tight—was that he was to cook up the gear they'd stolen off Sande.'

Oldham was becoming a major nuisance to the Bandidos, not least because of his growing addiction to his product. The ice was making him 'tweak'. Oldham was constantly paranoid and violent. But, worst of all, he was increasingly indiscreet. The revelation of his involvement in this clumsy plot against Milad Sande was the last straw. Sydney Bandidos president Rodney Monk decided he had to kick Oldham out of the club. 'Hooksey Monk was the person who fucked Russell Oldham from the club—because of the drugs hit', Utah recalls. 'Hooksey Monk was given the order . . . to fuck him off.'

Bar Reggio in East Sydney is one of the more popular Italian eateries in the restaurant strip straddling

Crown and Stanley streets—renowned for good, honest, nourishing Italian peasant food. It shares a boundary with the once notorious Francis Lane, where forty years ago hookers would give a gentleman or a visiting sailor a knee trembler against the wall. Now the once dirt-poor terrace houses along its length are much sought-after inner-city dwellings, but the Bar Reggio crowd still rubs shoulders with gangsters, prostitutes, drag-queens and, in late April 2006, with bikies. Rodney Hooksey Monk had invited Russell Oldham to Bar Reggio for a farewell supper, where he planned to pass on to his old friend and Bandido associate the decision that Oldham was also to be stripped of his colours and tossed out of the club. Monk's gigantic Samoan bodyguard, Raymond Curry, joined the dinner with his wife, Trish, sitting down with Monk, Oldham and Monk's glamorous girlfriend, Stephanie Roman.

Oldham had greeted his president with a kiss and a hug. But within minutes of Oldham and Monk sitting down to talk, a furious argument broke out between the two men. It was probably over Monk's decision that Oldham would no longer be allowed to ride with the club. The argument became so heated that Monk asked Oldham to step outside so they could continue talking without upsetting other diners. He left his bodyguard at the table—a fateful decision.

Inside the noisy restaurant nobody heard a thing, but in the adjoining Francis Lane, the restaurant's neighbours heard two men arguing and then at least three gunshots.

Within minutes police arrived on the scene to find Monk lying dead on the ground. He had been shot in the head by Oldham with a heavy calibre pistol. Oldham ran for his life. He was not running from the police. They were the least of his worries now. He was running from the outlaw motorcycle gang members who would doubtless want to seek vengeance for the murder of their president.

Utah was in Queensland that night but so well plugged in to the Sydney chapters that within twenty minutes of the murder he got a phone call at work from one of the Sydney vice presidents who was frantically looking for Andrew Nesbitt, the sergeant-at-arms of the East Brisbane Bandidos chapter. 'I was basically told that Big Russell shot him', Utah remembers. 'I went outside and had a cigarette and I rang a person at the Australian Crime Commission and gave it to them and ah . . . told them exactly what had occurred.'

For the police, now frantically trying to piece together what was going on, Utah's tip was one of the first bits of information to explain who the killer was. They immediately went public with pleas for Oldham to turn himself in. At the time, much of the media speculation suggested Oldham had killed Monk because the Bandido president had told him to stop having an affair with his parole officer. But Utah is contemptuous of such speculation:

They would talk about how Hooksey Monk supposedly didn't like this relationship he was having with his parole officer. I mean that's more dramatised bullshit as well because quite frankly Hooksey Monk was not the sort of guy who would give a shit about that . . . I think it just got out of hand. I think that Russell was there to have a conversation . . . in relation to [Wiseguy] and his son and their subsequent kidnappings and tortures for restitution of the chemicals that were stolen. Russell—big, big meth head, well-known cook, good cook. Just tweaking, shot him.

When Hooksey Monk was laid to rest in a massive funeral ceremony at Sydney's Castle Hill cemetery later that month, the Bandidos turned on a royal send-off for their slain president. His flower-draped coffin was driven on the side-car of a Harley-Davidson motorcycle accompanied by 150 other Bandidos on their bikes to a Catholic church in Carlingford. Media reports linking Monk with drug trafficking had soured bikie relations with the press, and gang members glowered at dozens of television cameras, circling helicopters, and prowling journalists recording every step of the event. It was a very public showing for the normally media-shy Bandidos.

Also among the mourners was Nomads boss Sam Ibrahim, the bad blood caused by Wiseguy and Oldham's transgressions with Milad Sande now dealt with. What police also did not know was that keeping themselves deliberately inconspicuous among the funeral guests were members of Bandido chapters from around the world: Vancouver, Washington DC, West Coast USA, France, Denmark and Thailand. If police had been watching more carefully they could have secured photographic evidence of the growing transnational criminal associations between the outlaw motorcycle gangs.

Much nonsense was written in the newspapers covering the event about the comradeship and brotherly support that the gathering for Hooksey's funeral represented. A member of the God's Squad bikie group, not an outlaw motorcycle gang, was naive enough to claim to listening mourners at the funeral service that people like Monk in the outlaw motorcycle gangs represented something that was lost in Australian society—'community and loyalty to your mates.' Utah had hugely respected Monk but there was no mention of the criminal culture permeating the club he helped lead. No mention of Brutus torturing Earl Mooring to death with a hammer or Wiseguy and his son whacking Milad Sande, father of two young children, in a Sydney park. Brutus was in fact among the mourners, one of those Bandidos regarded as senior enough to escort the fallen leader on his Harley-Davidson.

Convicted rapist and armed robber Arthur Loveday, also a senior Bandido and mate of disgraced New South Wales detective Roger Rogerson, told waiting television cameras that the Bandidos had 'put violence behind them'. He also described Monk as a 'sensitive new-age guy', ignoring the claims reportedly made by a police informant to the New South Wales Crime Commission about Monk's role as a major 'cocaine broker' in extensive drug trafficking. Such sentimental drivel was lapped up by the more naive end of the tabloid press as they were swept along by the emotion of the day.

The New South Wales police gang squad were watching on, no doubt in despair at the naivety of much of the coverage. Truth is, they knew little about what was really behind Monk's death, and they had only just learned of the possible connection to the murder of an obscure drug dealer in the sandhills of Malabar five months earlier. The breakthrough came only when Utah arrived in Sydney a couple of days before Monk's funeral to be debriefed by police about what he knew.

Inside a small hotel room in western Sydney, Utah watched on as different state and federal police agencies bickered in front of him over who could use him and how. Until Utah's information on the Sande murder came in to the New South Wales homicide squad, the investigators had been looking in a totally different direction on the murder. Utah sat down with an officer from the New South Wales gang squad, who grew gradually more excited as he realised the insight Utah could offer. It was a great opportunity for the federal Australian Crime Commission to help a state police agency crack an unsolved murder— but it was not to be. 'They said they really needed to see some evidence. But [Laurel] said he's contracted to us, he's not fucking talking to you. The gang squad and organised crime squad in New South Wales were bickering over who was going to run me. It was playing with my life at the end of the day. It wasn't about unanimity of purpose. I lost everything out of helping those pricks.'

Just a few weeks after Monk's death and the saturation media coverage of his funeral, a man waded knee-deep into the surf at Balmoral Beach, a popular family beach on Sydney's wealthy North Shore. It was just after sunset on a chilly May evening and the beach was mostly deserted. Russell Oldham had been on the run for three weeks. He had had enough. The 39-year-old who might one day have led the Bandidos put a gun to his head. He pulled the trigger and fell into the surf. 'Dead man walking. What choice did he have?' Utah comments. 'A few days later, he obviously had some sleep, realised what had occurred. Okay, he's going to face life in gaol. Let's say he gets a 30-year sentence. That's a long time to deal with people beating the living shit out of you and if that hadn't happened, Bandidos would have fucking got him. For sure. He was a knock on sight.'

Utah headed back to Queensland, all too mindful that if anyone in the gang found out he was helping the Australian Crime Commission, he too would be a dead man walking. Having seen the various state and federal police agencies up close and together for the first time, he was bitterly disillusioned about the level of police preparedness for what they had to confront inside the outlaw motorcycle gangs. All too often, his tips seemed to disappear into a bureaucratic morass and petty police turf wars. He had told New South Wales police, for example, that he normally stayed with his Croatian gangster mates when he came to Sydney, and that he knew Bobo and his gun-toting wife had 30 000 ecstasy tablets in their house. 'I was prepared to do an op against him but the gang squad and organised crime squad couldn't agree on who would do the op.'

By April of 2006 the Australian Crime Commission had been nobly attempting to secure the Queensland Police Service's okay to use Utah in controlled operations on their patch for well over a year. In early 2005 they had obtained hard evidence on Utah's hidden listening device of Gronk's involvement in illegal weapons and bulk amphetamine sales. The Queenslanders had knocked the federal crime-fighting agency back. Then, at a second meeting, a very senior Queensland policeman had actually told the ACC an operation using Utah would take place 'over my dead body'. Laurel had then enlisted the help of Victorian police but, in Utah's words, 'QPS again rejected the operation'. A fourth attempt through the offices of the anti-corruption body, the Crime and Misconduct Commission, was also rebuffed by the Queensland police.

Now, in April 2006, New South Wales, Victorian and ACC officers were convinced Utah was the real deal. He had provided some of the first information on the reasons behind Monk's killing, linking it to the previously obscure murder of Sande. A request backed by New South Wales police went again, a fifth time, to the Queensland police, effectively pleading for permission to allow Utah to be used in a controlled operation on Queensland soil. The New South Wales gang squad was amazed because Utah knew the whereabouts in Queensland of a criminal they were chasing to give evidence in a crucial committal hearing. The answer was again no.

'The New South Wales officer—Jason—went straight to the superintendent in charge of the Queensland police drug squad to get his support for a controlled operation using me. He was salivating . . . QPS rejected it', a dejected Utah recalls. He claims the senior officer in the Queensland police drug squad had personally gone higher in the force to get permission to use Utah in Queensland. 'He was told to get fucked and mind his own business . . . [The senior QPS officer] just wouldn't play the game. He wouldn't sign. You know, it was like some bullshit jealous thing. You know, if you can't you can't. You can't come and walk on my turf . . . I think it was the most petty, pedantic, pathetic thing I've ever seen in my life.'

For those sceptics who believe there must be some plausible reason, not yet disclosed, which explains the hesitance inside the Queensland police, Utah makes the point that much of his evidence was caught not only on a hidden listening device but also in the presence of an undercover Australian federal police officer. 'The Australian Crime Commission came back to me and actually he said that guy backed you to the hilt. Anything that comes out of your mouth is the truth.' There is no doubt that within the ACC there was huge alarm at the Queenland police's resistance to using Utah. Laurel, Utah's handler, was furious: 'He said words to the effect of "We can't let this go. We'll get them all with this. We'll fuck them." I don't think you could imagine his frustration. It would have fucked them', Utah claims.

If that was not bad enough, on the Queensland Gold Coast police officers were in open rebellion against an edict from senior police management which allegedly directed them to lay off the outlaw motorcycle gangs. The *Gold Coast Bulletin* newspaper reported that the gangs were accusing police of harassment, hiring top Queensland lawyers to take vexatious cases against the police; as a consequence, it was claimed that police had been ordered to back down.

It all came to a head when a gang of 29 bikies, including members of the Finks, Black Uhlans, Lone Wolf and Nomads, rode their bikes into the heart of the Surfers Paradise entertainment strip. Police followed routine orders and set up a random breath-test site, testing the bikies as they drove past. It was claimed that within minutes a police inspector arrived, telling the officers to let the bikies go unchallenged. A police union spokesman said, 'Police are supposed to be enforcing the law, not pandering to criminals'.

A despondent Utah was beginning to wonder if the Queensland police's reluctance to use him in operations against the Bandidos was not part of some misguided strategy to appease the gang. He decided it was time to visit his bolthole at a location in North America one final time because it was obvious his role as a police informant was becoming untenable. As Stevan Utah headed out of the country, what he had no foreboding of was one final appalling failure in the police turf wars that would very nearly see him dead.

23

THE TIMELY PRESS RELEASE

What else could you expect from an oxymoron like
'Police Intelligence'?
Guardian, 19 September 2007

It's not rocket science to work out that one of the lynchpins of running an informant is secrecy. Blabbing can lead to your informant becoming very dead very quickly and, of course, to your operation going up in smoke.

For reasons unknown—perhaps ego, positive public relations, political opportunism, an honest mistake or just plain stupidity—someone at the Australian Crime Commission decided to blab to the media about their great work. In April 2006 they bragged about their authorisation of an intelligence operation against outlaw motorcycle gangs that had started in about July of the previous year—the same time as Utah really got into the swing of things. The brag was almost Utah's death warrant. The story was reported in the *Sunshine Coast Daily* newspaper on Saturday 22 April 2006 under the arresting headline: 'Drugs, guns and vicious assaults. Just where do bikie gangs fit?' The article began:

The woman's injuries were horrific. A broken nose and cheekbone. Concussion. Gravel grazes and cuts all over her body. Staples were needed to stitch a gash together, which ran from one side of her head to the other.

Blood freely ran down her face and dripped on the road, where she lay moaning.

But it wasn't a car which caused these injuries, it was something almost unthinkable.

The woman, believed to be in her 40s, had allegedly been badly beaten before being dragged behind a motorcycle. She was found near Bronwyn Street in Caloundra's industrial estate around 9pm last Saturday. But despite the shocking experience, the woman has not lodged a complaint with police.

The *Daily* learnt of her experience after an anonymous woman, claiming to be the victim's friend, rang to express her anger at the alleged attack. The friend claimed the injured woman had been drinking at the nearby Bandidos clubhouse earlier in the evening and that the alleged assault was a payback for an earlier incident.

She said the person responsible for the attack had links to the motorcycle club, but while police are investigating, at this stage no arrests have been made. A Bandidos spokesman said he had been at the clubhouse on the night of the alleged assault, but was unaware of any incident.

A dreadful enough story. The journalist, on a roll, then went on to recap some Bandido history, in particular the Milperra Massacre. Not content with local news, he then went offshore to recount the recent find of eight bodies in the tiny village of Shedden, Ontario, Canada, believed murdered as a spot of Bandidos 'internal cleansing' and reported by the local media as Canada's worst mass murder. All this would have been sufficient to get the attention of the local Bandidos, who would have loved the clincher that followed:

> But the Australian Crime Commission (ACC) com-
> menced an Outlaw Motor Cycle Gangs (OMCG)
> intelligence operation in July last year, looking into the
> dealings of the 35 identified OMCGs in Australia.
>
> Two of those clubs have chapters on the Sunshine
> Coast, the Bandidos and the Rebels.

The Bandidos on the Sunshine Coast would have spluttered their bourbon and coke at this point; and perhaps it was then that they decided it might be an idea to do a bit of their own 'internal cleansing'. The list of new entrants who might have enjoyed significant access to the gang since the middle of the previous year was not terribly long. The sleuthing skills of Sherlock Holmes were not required. In fact, only one name stood out. Stevan Utah. His attempts to go straight had not been wildly successful but he had tried. At the behest of the ACC and their partners in crime fighting, Utah had hurled himself back in to the bikie world, ramping up his efforts in the middle of 2005. There was, in Utah's view, no-one else who fitted the profile.

The Bandidos on the Sunshine Coast were thinking along similar lines. Utah was in the clubhouse at Caloundra when the story was published. As Utah tells it, one of the bikies slapped the newspaper onto the bar in front of Utah, pointed his thick finger at 'July' and said sarcastically to Utah, 'Nice story Steve'. Luckily for Utah they had not quite settled on him being public enemy number one at this point, so he waffled and bullshitted his way through the visit and got out in one piece. The bikies were also aware that he was heading overseas on one of his frequent junkets. What they did not know was the junkets were to do some tweaks on his escape plan.

What was also troubling the bikies was the public allegation of the brutal assault against a woman. Very bad public relations. Utah knew precisely who was responsible. When the woman was assaulted in the clubhouse, Utah was 'standing ten feet away', and powerless to do a thing. He had known the bikie responsible since about 1999. He recalled the woman suffered broken facial bones and had needed almost two hundred stitches. The Bandidos were still smarting after their clubhouse had been raided in December 2004 during a police investigation into an attempted murder involving a samurai sword. The Bandidos were not too keen on more bad publicity. It got in the way of business.

THE TIMELY PRESS RELEASE

It was simply lousy timing for Utah, who had recently found himself in a spot of bother with the Bandidos over another, though comparatively smaller, matter ... and once again, it was the Crime Commission's fault. He had borrowed a CD that had some photographs on it of many of the Bandido members. Utah thought it might have had some intelligence value and had arranged with the gang to borrow it. All reasonable, but they did want it back within seventy-two hours. Utah took the CD and some other information he had collected and left the lot at a police 'dead drop' he used in a locker at a Brisbane bus terminal. Utah reckons the records show the CD was collected at 4 am. It was never seen again by Utah. When he met with Plod, his undercover associate, at Morayfield Tavern, Utah was expecting to get the CD back, as he'd been promised earlier. However Plod gave him another digital recorder but knew nothing about the CD. Utah was in strife. Punishment for this minor crime was a swiftly administered black eye and a fine of $250 payable to the club. All things considered, his planned overseas trip to do a bit more work on his escape route came just at the right time.

When Utah returned to Australia on the morning of 19 May 2006, he was met at Brisbane International Airport by Tank's girlfriend who, in that quaint incestuous way of some bike gangs, had been Hombre's mistress. All was looking quite rosy. And then it was a pleasant motor north along the Bruce Highway toward Caboolture, a little over half an hour away. On the drive north, they stopped for fuel, with Utah giving her $50. At that point Utah's sixth sense kicked in. She had a pay-as-you-go phone but told him it was out of credit. Yet at the service station while Utah was filling the car, she ducked around the corner, where she thought she was out of sight, and made a call. His unease grew when she returned to the car. 'I didn't like her body language.' The conversation wasn't exactly bubbling along either.

Through Caboolture and then left onto the D'Aguilar Highway toward Woodford. Australian country towns are justly famous for their fine old pubs. Sweeping verandahs to offer shade in the hot months, wide windows to catch the breeze and architecture that captures the time of the building. The Delaneys Creek Hotel has none of these features. It is a ramshackle pile, with only cold beer and pleasant staff to offer. Not a bad spot for the local bikies to have a quiet ale or ten. It was also where Tank's girlfriend turned left for the last few kilometres of the drive.

Utah was getting very very edgy, and the temperature in the car was dropping like a stone. The car rounded a bend, motored over the bridge which crossed the heavily wooded creek and then swung left into the driveway. The house, nestled in the lee of a hill at the end of a driveway about one kilometre long, was the perfect lair for those with criminal endeavours on their mind. After they had negotiated the gate the car drove very slowly along the drive. Far too slowly for Utah's taste. The hairs were standing up on the back of his neck. At that point he recalls, 'I sensed something was horrifically wrong. I asked her what was going on as we drove up the driveway. She said nothing.'

Utah's army training and a fair amount of rat cunning kicked in, and he opened his door and jumped out of the car. The car just kept going. Then, Utah says, 'I saw a couple of shadows and the next thing I know I was set upon'. The reason for the slow motoring was that Tank and a few of the lads were waiting in the bushes on the north side of the driveway. Utah was scheduled to meet with a very nasty demise. There would be no need to take his body to Beerwah cemetery. The remote woods on the side of the driveway would make a perfectly discreet last resting place for the late ACC informant.

Utah recalls, 'All hell broke loose! I didn't see the first hit coming. You know that busted my eye open!' His old meth-cook 'mate' Tank was responsible for that first powerful blow. His compatriots joined in kicking and punching his now-battered frame curled up in the foetal position on the roadside. The position did not offer him much protection from the assault. Teeth were knocked out and blood was splattered everywhere. A convincingly horrible scene. One of the bikies yelled at him, 'You're a second from losing your miserable fucking life'. Another offered, 'dog cunt' as he went about his work. Utah recalls, 'A lot was said but you know at the time I wasn't really caring'.

When they had contented themselves that a good beating had been administered and that Utah wouldn't be heading anywhere in the near future, they moved to one side for a chat. He could hear the subject of the chat was about how they were going to kill him—something slow and painful in retribution, or just quick and be done with it. Fortunately for Utah, though he looked badly injured, it was nowhere near as bad as his assailants had hoped for. A little bit of blood goes a long way. In his words: 'I was pretending I was out of it. I got blood coming out of me everywhere. There's bits hanging off me everywhere and I like realised they were around the corner and I'm gone!' With the bikies distracted, chatting about their grisly plans, Utah seized his only opportunity and bolted into the nearby bush, heading down a rough path that led to the creek. He remembers: 'I didn't stop running. I'm in the middle of nowhere. I was in the middle of nowhere!'

A bit of luck finally came the way of the bruised and bloodied Utah. He ran through the bush and onto the road near a farmhouse that had been empty for the past twelve months or so. However, as he ran toward it, he noticed tradesmen were on site giving the place a spruce-up. As he said, it was 'just one of those things. You know, not your time or whatever. There were about ten tradesmen there renovating this place on this day. They've seen me coming running up and I've got blood and stuff hanging off me everywhere and they've like, they've all just stopped.' The sight of a bloody and bashed Utah bolting towards them would have caused anyone to pause.

The pursuing bikies also paused. Too many potential witnesses for any further grief. Utah says, 'And I knew—I saw one of them coming along the roadway in his car getting ready to intercept me and I knew there was someone behind me but all of a sudden there was no-one chasing me!' The tradesmen did not hang about either, nor did they step back from doing the right thing. Utah was bundled into a car and rushed to the Caboolture Hospital. The ACC would later interview the tradesmen who had come to Utah's aid.

At the hospital, Utah contacted a Queensland-based ACC member and told him what had transpired. According to Utah, the ACC then sent two people to hospital to watch and see what might or might not happen. The people let Utah know that a black Mercedes was lurking in the hospital car park. There was a fair chance that the Bandidos had sent watchers as well. Utah was quite right to believe he was still in peril.

Rather than trust either the Queensland police or the Crime Commission, who at this stage he says were not moving heaven and earth to help him, he called a friend who only he knew about. She literally was the prostitute with a heart of gold. At about 1 pm that day, she arrived at the hospital. Utah was still waiting for treatment. A discreet departure was in order, so both left via the back door and drove to a service station ten kilometres away, where the ACC operatives were waiting. Utah gave them a quick briefing, and then he and his friend drove on.

All Utah had were the clothes on his back and a mobile phone. No passport, no money, no credit cards. His friend loaned him $500 and her car, and sorted a short-stay apartment in Brisbane for him. He reckoned this cost a further $600. By that time it was around 4 pm, and Utah took himself to Royal Brisbane Hospital for treatment. Seven hours of waiting and no treatment later, he went back to his apartment. He called Laurel and asked if Laurel could use his ACC credit card for a private doctor to treat him. Laurel declined the request. Utah patched himself up as best he could and got a bit of rest.

In the middle of the morning of 20 May, Laurel arrived in Brisbane and he and the local ACC representative met with the still untreated Utah. At least Laurel came with $400 cash in his hand. Better than nothing and enough to do a partial restock of the depleted wardrobe. Laurel also agreed to reimburse him for the accommodation, however Utah reckons that he is still waiting for that cheque. As for treatment, no offers were forthcoming from Laurel.

During their meeting Utah got a call on his mobile from the Bandido responsible for the assault on the woman that had triggered the whole disaster. He tried to sweet-talk Utah into popping down to the Bandidos' East Brisbane chapter. Utah wisely declined. He did agree to meet with police at the Roma Street headquarters of the Queensland Police Service later that day for a lengthy debrief. In the interim, his friend took him to a private doctor in suburban Sandgate. Utah's face was x-rayed, and the doctor noted a bruised kidney, bruised spleen, multiple lacerations, facial swelling, a very black eye and missing teeth. It had been a brutal and comprehensive beating.

At police headquarters later that day, Utah met with a Queensland police officer who took a brief statement about the assault and some photographs of his injuries. Utah alleges that the report was not formally generated or given a file number, at the request of Laurel. He had overheard the phone conversation between Laurel and the police officer. It was a pretty fair call to think the ACC had been thrown by what had happened, and that damage control was in full swing. Sadly, Utah's welfare was obviously not a prominent part of that control.

The following morning Utah went with the local ACC gentleman to a storage unit in Brisbane that he'd been using to keep documents safe. As for a comprehensive debriefing of Utah about the attempt on his life, the brutal assault in the clubhouse, and of course more than a year's worth of work as an informant, nothing whatsoever happened.

Utah was bruised and battered both physically and mentally. He stewed in the rented apartment for a couple of days before he finally decided to do something positive. His first act was to call a copper he knew in the Queensland police to give his eyewitness account of the assault on the woman at the Caloundra clubhouse. The detective arranged to meet Utah back at the Roma Street headquarters two days later. On his way to the meet, Utah's mobile phone rang. It was Laurel and he wasn't happy. According to Utah, Laurel's opening was: 'What the fuck are you doing?' Utah was a bit confused, and responded, 'What do you mean?' The Crime Commission handler replied, 'We have a contract and the QPS does not want to deal with you!' Laurel went on to tell Utah that the detective had contacted the ACC representative in Queensland and told him about the arranged meeting. It was not going to be a good day for either Utah or the public, it would seem.

When Utah got to Roma Street police HQ, he found the meeting would not be one-on-one as he'd been led to believe. In the room waiting for him was the detective, his superior and one other person. Utah's distrust of the Queensland police was at full tilt seeing this, so he told them this was not what he had agreed to. However he did the right thing and gave them a brief synopsis of his evidence before leaving the meeting. He tried to contact Laurel but hit a brick wall. He was in strife, in pain and very much alone.

Laurel finally got back to him two days later. The conversation wasn't enjoyable. Laurel allegedly told Utah, 'You're off the payroll, you won't be getting any more money or assistance'. Utah was blackly amused considering how little money or assistance he'd actually been given in the last year, and in particular the last few days. When the going had gotten tough his handlers had been conspicuously absent, he reckoned.

Laurel did offer one cheering thought for Utah, telling him, 'You can still have your sealed document for the fraud matter in Queensland'. However that nicety was immediately qualified when he said: 'Just don't shit on me and I won't shit on you'. The ACC obviously thought there might be a few curly questions heading their way.

On 15 June 2006, with a newly issued passport, a ticket paid for with borrowed money and just $50 in his back pocket, Utah boarded a plane for his overseas bolthole. He remarks, 'I had nothing. There was no due diligence. There was absolutely nothing. I was left flat out in the cold.' The sealed document has yet to turn up. However, the offer of the document, which was intended to be a 'get out of gaol free' card if he was convicted, was recorded by him, on the ACC issued digital recorder. It is a recording Utah is still hanging on to, tightly.

In his new country he got the medical attention he'd needed. He says: 'I mean I've had to pay my own dental expenses, my own medical expenses, my own relocation. I was literally left with $50 in my pocket. Not bad for a guy who had $86 000 in his bank three years ago.' Utah does not step back when asked who is responsible for his predicament. He points his finger straight at the ACC, saying, 'They blew their own informant!' In a late 2006 email exchange with ACC members and a Victorian detective involved in the

Mooring murder inquiry, Utah alleges things got a bit fiery. The ACC got a little defensive: 'Oh, like that's our fault?' To which Utah tersely replied, 'Well it's not fucking mine!' The ACC's response was predictable: 'That's [the press report from the *Sunshine Coast Daily*] not our fault.' The Victorian detective rather dryly offered, 'That certainly didn't help matters'. Utah had the last words: 'You don't need to be Einstein to work it out. It's really simple. They gave me up.'

Despite now knowing full well that Utah reckoned their public relations had nearly cost him his life and effectively ruined their undercover operation, the ACC reprised its boast in its 2005–2006 Annual Report. The report opened with a letter dated 13 October 2006 from Mick Keelty, the commission's chair and also head of the Australian Federal Police. Mick was quite pleased and noted, 'approval of an intelligence operation on Outlaw Motorcycle Gangs to collect intelligence on members of motorcycle clubs, and persons associated with these members or clubs, involved in serious and organised criminal activity'. On page 43 in a chapter headed 'Report on performance', they offer the grateful Australian public a little more information on their good deeds:

> Intelligence Operation—Outlaw Motorcycle Gangs
> Overview and background
> The Outlaw Motorcycle Gang (OMCG) intelligence operation was authorised by the ACC Board on

25 July 2005. It aims to develop and implement a national intelligence and information collection and coordination capability to improve the national intelligence picture and understanding of the threats posed by OMCGs. It also provides Australia's law enforcement with intelligence that informs and supports the development of strategies to reduce the impact of the OMCG threat.

OMCGs exist in a dynamic environment; members are involved in a large number of serious and organised criminal activities designed to generate income and protect gang interests. Such offences include murder, firearms, illicit drugs supply and production, extortion, prostitution, serious assault, sexual assault, arson, robbery, theft, vehicle rebirthing, receiving stolen property, fraud, money laundering, corruption and bribing officials and perverting the course of justice.

The old joke about 'police intelligence' that appeared in the UK *Guardian* newspaper on 19 September 2007—'What else could you expect from an oxymoron like "Police Intelligence"?'—comes to mind.

Though their relationship was in tatters, Utah, out of some sense of loyalty, morality, desperation or a combination of all three, still kept in occasional contact with Laurel. He had asked the ACC for some support with the local authorities, and had also offered to send Laurel the mobile phone

Gronk had given Utah for safekeeping before he headed off to prison. It came complete with text messages and all manner of potentially fascinating telephone numbers—a kind of who's who of Australian organised crime. The responses from Laurel were along the lines of, 'I'll get back to you next week'. That week has yet to arrive.

What would later add further insult to his existing injury was that the bikie whom Utah alleged had committed the assault at the clubhouse would soon turn informant for the Queensland Police Service. That bikie was a gentleman we'll call 'Butch', who collected his 'get of gaol free' card for his agreement to turn on his Bandido colleagues over a little matter of arson. On 27 March 2007, six members of the Bandidos were alleged to have headed to the Rebels' clubhouse in the Brisbane suburb of Albion. Those Bandidos were Butch, another gentleman we'll call 'Sundance', local president Ivan Glavas, sergeant-at-arms Kenneth Whittaker and Blair Thomsen. The alleged wheelman for the adventure was former and rather disgruntled Rebel John Debilla. Debilla was driving his Ford station wagon. The prosecution alleged the Bandidos were very displeased after a few of their lads were tipped off their bikes on nearby Bribie Island during a clash with the Rebels about a month earlier. Unfortunately for the Bandidos, some of the Rebels had used baseball bats, and there were reports of shots being fired. Burning down the Rebels' clubhouse seemed to be the punishment that fitted the crime, if a little exuberant perhaps.

Sadly for the Bandidos, the police reckoned they had CCTV footage of Thomsen carrying firearms at the scene of the arson, and vision of Whittaker buying petrol shortly before the fire. The six were soon scooped up by police and charged. Debilla quickly admitted his role, telling police he waited down the street, and after the explosion he drove his co-accused from the scene. Sundance did a quick roll and gave up his mates. A delicious touch of irony about Sundance is that Utah alleges that his father is a lifetime member of the Rebels. As he mentioned, 'No shit, a patched Bandido has a father who is a patched Rebel'. Family gatherings at the Sundances's must be interesting affairs.

Butch rolled shortly after. At a court hearing the prosecutor noted that Butch and Sundance had not wanted to be involved in the arson but 'understood to refuse would result in them being expelled from the club'. In return for his evidence Utah reckons Butch got an indemnity from prosecution on the assault, formal acknowledgement of his role as an informant, a new identity with a nice clean record, and the possibility of the $25 000 reward for information on the fire offered under the Arson Reward Scheme. Utah observed, 'You gotta love the QPS [Queensland Police Service]. He does it and rolls and gets protection. He was the main instigator on the attempt on me. They spend all this money on these two assholes for an "arson" and I am left out in the cold. If this wasn't so serious they would make a comic book from this. Butch couldn't lie straight in bed.'

Though Butch wasn't much of an arsonist by all accounts, he seems to be an extremely good negotiator. Consider the arson prosecution. Two of the principals caught on camera, one buying petrol shortly before the arson and one at the scene. Add to that the evidence of the getaway driver and the evidence of Sundance against his co-accused. Tasty stuff. Yet for his contribution to the prosecution he gets immunity from the arson charges, and what for him must be a glorious silence regarding Utah's allegations of assault and complicity in what Utah surely believes was a serious attempt at murdering him. Utah is adamant his complaint about the assault was lodged with the Queensland police. Butch was very definitely a skilled negotiator.

Utah, when seeking help from his ACC handlers, says he got absolutely nothing. He asked for assistance to relocate to somewhere less hazardous than Queensland. He reckons his handler was less than helpful, saying something along the lines of, 'You got a little flogging, get over it'. Though Queensland has its problems, it seems to do a better job of looking after its informants. Utah's allegations regarding the assault of the woman at the clubhouse and the attempt on his life do not appear to have been vigorously pursued. No formal statements were ever taken from Utah. The evidence, including the photographs of the battered Utah taken the next day, are probably gathering dust in a quiet corner.

In its 2005–2006 'Illicit Drug Data Report' the ACC said the 'strong prevalence of Outlaw Motorcycle Gangs involvement in the ATS (amphetamine-type stimulants) has been identified, particularly with small and versatile laboratories'. If the bikies and their drug endeavours were listed on the Australian Stock Exchange, share prices would no doubt benefit from another positive little snippet in the ACC's publication: 'Domestic manufacture has advantages over importation: a higher profit margin, laboratories can be versatile and easily relocated to satisfy market demand, and fewer people are required to be involved thereby reducing the risk of exposure.'

With Stevan Utah now out of the way, that risk of exposure was reduced even further.

24

GOING PUBLIC

They'll come after me. I really am a dead man running.
Stevan Utah

It is a lonely life living on the run as a hunted man, hiding from people who want you dead. Stevan Utah found himself in another country, broke, homeless and constantly looking over his shoulder. The normal pleasantries of social discourse—'What's your name?', 'Where are you from?', 'What do you do?'—were and still are for him constantly loaded with menace. 'I don't sleep. I don't talk to anyone. I don't go out and enjoy myself. I don't like people getting too close to me. I hate being touched. I don't trust anyone. I don't love. I just exist', Utah says.

After his horrific near-death experience at Delaneys Creek, thousands of kilometres away, he was deeply traumatised. Soldiers call it combat stress. Psychiatrists call it PTSD—post-traumatic stress disorder. In an instant, a curious look or shout across a crowded bar, the crack of a backfiring car or the slam of a door could jolt him back to the awful moment when Tank and the other Bandidos thought they had beaten him to death.

It was hard—very hard—going in his new country. Dumped by his Australian police handlers, there was no witness protection program or any money to help him survive. He had no entitlement to health support to help fix the bones and teeth still damaged from the severe beating he had suffered. He had no formal work visa, no money, no friends, and no identity documents with a name other than the one that, ominously for him, the mob of gleefully homicidal Bandidos chasing him already knew: Stevan Utah.

A few months after he had been in hiding overseas, though, curiosity got the better of him. He picked up a phone and rang one of the most senior leaders of the Bandidos in Australia. He wanted to know just how much they suspected. It was a bit like a big fat juicy steak disporting itself in front of a lion's cage at the zoo. A frosty conversation, at best:

He said, 'Do I know you, Steve?' I've known this guy for twelve years. 'Do I know you?' The last time I heard him say something like that he accused the person of being an informant as well. Yeah, he didn't say, how are you doing, Steve? I spoke to him eighteen months ago—no, not that long ago, it was May last year, and he said, 'You know, no matter what happens I don't have a problem with you'. Here we are twelve months later and he's saying do I know you, Steve?

Do I know who you are?

They knew all right. And there was no doubt in Steve's mind what would happen to him if they found him. 'I never have a good night's sleep. Never', he says. 'They'll come after me. I really am a dead man running!'

Back in Australia, fears of a national bikie war were rising after a spate of tit-for-tat shootings and bombings between clubs, especially in Utah's home state of Queensland. A few weeks after Bandidos burned the Rebels' Brisbane clubhouse to the ground, the same thing happened at the former Sunshine Coast home of one of the Bandido arsonists responsible—Sundance. For good measure, his car was smashed and shot at on a suburban street as well. Problem was, no-one knew if it was the Rebels who did it, taking revenge for his now admitted role in the bombing, or his old Bandido 'brothers', furious that he had rolled in return for an indemnity. Whichever, there was an unsubtle implicit message for Stevan Utah there about what happens to those who roll to police.

From the other side of the world, Utah, who freely admits he was initially attracted to that often brutal one-percenter culture, now finds the time to ponder the folly of it all: 'You know, I don't think they even know what they want. I think they just enjoy fighting. And killing each other. Tit for tat. Won't be over until the last fight is won. It's pretty senseless. Police will tell you it's a turf war. They'll tell you it's because members of one club will defect to another. They'll tell you it's drug related or petty jealousies. I think maybe if you add a little bit of all of that and eighty per cent of nobody knows, you might have the truth. I have seen it so many times and why, I don't know.'

Despite the hard evidence that the state's bikie gangs were enjoying a booming trade in supplying the nation's hunger for illicit drugs, there were mixed messages coming from the politicians. In a submission to a federal parliamentary inquiry into organised crime in February 2007, the Queensland government reportedly played down its booming methamphetamine trade as 'merely a cottage-based industry'—this despite the state having the largest number of detected illegal drug labs in the country, and many more, on Utah's account, that the police know nothing about. The notion of it being a cottage-based industry conjures up, for some reason, images of jolly lederhosen-wearing bikies standing behind a picturesque cottage's white picket fence, with bubbling vats of drugs in the cellar.

Down a phone line, Utah guffaws at what he labels a 'pathetic attempt at damage control'. When also told that a senior Australian Crime Commission official had boasted in a recent report to parliament about the wonderful cooperation it enjoys with state and territory police forces, including Queensland, he cracks up: 'I don't know if he's been eating funny coloured food or what the story is there but if he calls that wonderful cooperation . . . maybe he should go and see a neurosurgeon because he's had a bad head knock.'

Queensland's anti-corruption body, the Crime and Misconduct Commission, for once seems to agree with Utah about their state government's rose-coloured glasses. It had heard days of secret in-camera evidence from bikie insiders, including Utah while he was working for the ACC. Embarrassingly for the politicians, in early 2007 its highly respected chairman Robert Needham warned the public that the drug market in Queensland had in fact become 'diverse and entrenched' as organised crime groups, including bikie gangs, changed their methods and networks to avoid detection.

Its head firmly in the sand, the Queensland government chose to downplay the link between organised crime and the drug trade. Amusingly, in light of Utah's experiences with Queensland's reluctance to allow the Australian Crime Commission to use him inside Queensland, the Queensland government boasted in a press release that its police were successfully targeting repeat drug trade offenders and that they were leaving federal agencies to take the lead on cross-border investigations. That one must have had the ACC investigators slapping their sides with laughter, the multiple knock-backs of their requests to use Utah in Queensland still painfully fresh in their minds.

Just to make things especially hard for Queensland police investigators, they were also hobbled by another extraordinary curb on their powers. In a historical throw-back to the era of Queensland politics when all too many police and politicians were generally crooked and did not want their phones tapped, that state was still, in early 2007, resisting calls for its police and anti-corruption body, the Crime and Misconduct Commission, to be given the power to bug phones. This time, though—one hopes—the political objections were not made because, as in the past, the politicians feared their corrupt conversations would be tapped. The then premier, Peter Beattie, said the reason for his resistance to the change in law was because he wanted an independent safety monitor to curb abuses of phone-tapping powers. It demonstrated a laudable and refreshingly original concern for civil liberties in Queensland, but one that surely could have been overcome long before now.

Utah had provided police with the private phone numbers of most of the senior echelons of the Australian Bandidos—but no-one, it seems, was listening too closely. In fact, he had of course taken with him to his overseas bolthole the old mobile phones and SIM cards of both Gronk and Stoat, two senior Bandido gang members. The phones contained a veritable who's who of Australian crime. Utah offered them to the Australian Crime Commission, in an email to Laurel—but he got no reply. Another bewildering missed opportunity by Australia's finest. 'They'd have the phone numbers of most of the major crims in Australia. I just don't understand why they didn't want them. I wasn't asking for money or anything. They just weren't interested.'

In the pages of the local newspapers, the news that bikie gangs were now big-time players in organised crime was a laughable non-issue, even if it was disputed by the government. One wit offered this comment about Queensland Police Minister Judy Spence: 'Bikie gangs involved in major crime—YOU THINK? Maybe we should rename the police minister Judy Dense?'

Opposition governments generally win power by whipping up public hysteria about crime (only to have the same thing done to them when they're in power); but this time they had been beaten to the pulpit by the anti-corruption watchdog. So Queensland's state opposition made what Utah believes is actually a smart suggestion. They recommended the state bring in anti-racketeering laws, similar to those successfully used in the United States to control the mafia. In the United States, there are around thirty-five such stipulated racketeering crimes where, if two or more are committed in a ten-year period, they can be deemed to form a criminal pattern and lead to organised crime syndicate members being charged as a group.

Just like the mafia, however, the bikies are getting very shrewd at counter-spin and insinuating themselves into the mainstream—witness the embarrassing revelation for the Queensland opposition a few weeks later when it emerged that the son of a former National Party member of parliament had joined one hundred mates in an after-school formal at the Bandidos' Mermaid Beach clubhouse. Police Minister Ms Spence thundered: 'The former MP was quoted as saying the matter was just "storm in a teacup" stuff, and that he thought it was a good idea and [was] prepared to give people [like bikies] the benefit of the doubt. This is a shocking message to give to our young people. The truth is these gangs contain dangerous criminals, and they are subject to increasing targeted police operations in Queensland.'

Around this same time, the minister forgot her own cautionary advice and came a cropper through a few of her coppers earning a bit on the side. She had criticised charities and hospitals for accepting money or gifts from bikie groups trying to sanitise their image—a spin-tip the bikies use straight from the Sonny Barger Hells Angels public relations guide book. The bikie thinking seems to be, give a sick child a stuffed bunny and maybe Mummy and Daddy will forget about the ice the bikies hooked their daughter on during Schoolies Week on the Gold Coast. Maybe the bikies' giving-to-charity strategy is working after all and maybe the reader who earlier opined on Ms Spence's denseness had a point, because a few weeks later came the revelation that members of her own police force were being paid to work as security officers at a charity event sponsored by the Bandidos.

Every Easter on the Sunshine Coast, the Caloundra Hot Bike and Rod Show raises money for local community groups. It is an opportunity for local rev-heads to burn rubber and show off their souped-up cars, as well as a chance for the colours-clad, tattooed Bandidos to strut their stuff in a wholesome family atmosphere. For the tens of thousands of 'normal' mums and dads who flock to the show with their kids, it is a bit like going to the zoo—wide-eyed kiddies watch on in awe as swaggering bikie wild animals walk past. Such events are very shrewd marketing for the one-percenters, normalising them in the public eye and making the baying warnings of the politicians and police sound specious and shrill, however valid. It is also a huge money-earner for the Bandidos.

The minister sought to minimise the damage by claiming that her moonlighting police were paid by a local Australian Rules club, and not by the bikies. Queensland Police Commissioner Bob Atkinson promised an investigation but reportedly said he believed 'nothing untoward occurred ... My understanding is the same as the minister's, that the money came from the football club.' Utah laughs at this suggestion, saying the real deal is widely known within the clubhouses:

> The deal is this ... the football club offers the club facilities and land to the Bandidos for the show. The proceeds are 50/50 Bandidos–football club, after costs, so this is 'net'. So if the costs are absorbed then the money most certainly did also come from the Bandidos. I know this as I have seen it, heard it, been there, dealt

with it ... Oh, and the local surf lifesaving club also
gets a 3k donation. Eighty per cent of the 50/50 take
then goes to the national club for the Bandido fund set
up to provide legal defences for members and money
for families etc while they are in jail.

It is a staggering thought that the Queensland Police
Service is indirectly and unwittingly funding the defence
of some of the organised crime figures it supposedly seeks
to restrain.

By April 2007, Stevan Utah had made another
momentous decision. Still bristling from his treatment by
the ACC and Queensland police, he was incredulous at
what he sees as the load of 'political fucking shit' which
he strongly felt was restricting police from combating
the bikie gangs. There was also more than a little bit of
seething anger with his former Bandido buddies who had
tried to kill him. Utah wanted to get square.

He knew his claims about the way police were dealing
with the bikies with one hand tied behind their back
would no doubt attract a snide political response. He
knew from the whistleblowers he had seen go public
before that politicians generally appease public concern
about an issue by calling for an 'investigation' into the
allegations, of which they are supposedly unaware. (Slap
hand to forehead in surprise: 'Oh, that multi-million
stuff-up', 'That paedophile minister', 'That undeclared
donation' ...) Such a call usually means it's hoped the

allegations will go nowhere—or, more cleverly, they will eventually be discredited a few months down the track by a compliant lawyer or bureaucrat hoping for a judgeship or a cosy tenure on a government committee, and who knows what his masters want.

Unlike in America, which often reveres its whistle blowers, there is a great and proud tradition in Australia of shafting 'dobbers'—especially those who tilt at public institutions like the police. Utah fully expected to be shafted but he wanted his claims to be heeded; and he did not want the responsible politicians to have any wriggle room. So in late April 2007, he sent an extraordinary letter marked 'confidential' to the Queensland police minister.

Formal notification of QPS' failure to properly investigate organised crime

My name is Stevan John Utah. I am currently living overseas after fleeing Queensland because my assistance to Police, in combating extensive organised crime inside the Bandidos motorcycle gang, resulted in an attempt on my life in May last year . . .

I am writing directly to you because I am extremely concerned that you are not being fully advised, if at all, by your senior police management about what they have done to hinder and frustrate both a Victorian Police and an Australian Crime Commission investigation into extensive criminal enterprises involving senior members of the Bandidos.

Both I and senior Federal and Victorian Police believe that the actions of senior Queensland Police have jeopardised perhaps the biggest blow against organised crime in this country in the last twenty years. This could be confirmed by you if your staff were to ring [name deleted] in ACC.

I believe you are being misled by some in your senior Police administration about the reasons why the Queensland Police Service has elected to veto an operational certificate which would have allowed the ACC to run a major operation in Queensland. The plan was to use me to use my existing contacts with the Bandidos' senior hierarchy to obtain admissible evidence of serious crimes.

As the ACC would tell you, even preliminary intelligence suggested this operation could have achieved a massive blow against organised crime, including illicit drugs manufacture and importation; solve at least three unsolved murders, and resolve other serious crimes committed across this country.

I freely admit I am a convicted criminal—although not involving crimes of violence—and I have witnessed some terrible crimes. The Queensland Police—notably [name deleted], who is primarily responsible for this decision—will no doubt claim that I am raising this matter with you simply because I am due to face fraud charges in the District Court in Brisbane early next month. I expect that when you as

Minister send this letter down the line for comment, your advisors will be led to the view that I am just an opportunistic criminal who is trying to escape a possible jail sentence.

I could tell you that nothing could be further from the truth. I could tell you how I could just have walked away from Australia and put what I know behind me—and you would have been none the wiser. I could tell you how I have made a decision, as a concerned member of the public, to acknowledge my knowledge of serious crimes and to help the authorities bring bad people who have committed these terrible crimes to justice. I could also tell you I am totally innocent of the charges I am due to face next month.

But I won't even bother doing that.

Whatever you think of me and my motives, I just urge you to consider the following indisputable facts.

I think that any reasonable analysis of these facts would lead you to the conclusion that a serious mistake has been made by a senior member of your Police executive that may well thwart an extremely important operation.

On 10 October 2000 a Victorian man known to me, Earl Neil Mooring, was murdered in a horrendous manner by senior members of the Bandidos Motorcycle Club. I know about this murder because I was an accessory after the fact in disposing of the body.

It is not publicly known, even now, that that body was recovered. Victorian Police Detective Tony Thatcher will tell you that he believes my continued cooperation with Police, if it was facilitated on Queensland soil through the granting of an operational certificate, could well bring the murderer to justice . . .

You should ask your senior Police, notably [name deleted], whether it is true that when Victorian and ACC investigators asked for this operational certificate to be issued he stated that this would be done 'over my dead body'. You should clarify with him whether it is the case that he directed Det Sgt [name deleted] to re-arrest me for fraud charges that had been withdrawn in November the previous year—against the wishes of both the ACC and the Victorian State Police.

I ask whether the reason why some in Queensland Police want me jailed is because I have personal knowledge of corrupt Queensland Police who have provided confidential information to bikie gang members.

I ask whether the reason why some in Queensland Police want me jailed is because Queensland Police failed to act quickly enough on a tip I provided in 2004 about the locations of two underground bunkers in Queensland used for the production of methamphetamine and the storage of a substantial shipment of heroin from Vietnam.

I know that in the 17 weeks between my initial tip and the eventual QPS 'bust' on those properties the drugs were moved and sold on the open market. I find the failure to act on this tip alarming; and so do Federal and State Police with whom I have spoken.

I would not be surprised if people died from the heroin and methamphetamine that was allowed to be sold on the open market through the negligence of senior Queensland Police.

I notice that you, as Minister, announced on 16 November 2006 that Queensland was spearheading a national amphetamines crackdown. I note that on 17 October 2006, you boasted that the Beattie Government takes 'a hard line on drugs.' I wonder whether, when you said this, you were aware that just two years earlier the Queensland Police threw away an opportunity to bust a major methamphetamine and heroin racket?

I wonder whether you know that I assisted the ACC in covertly recording a conversation with a very senior Bandidos official who made admissions about an unsolved murder in Caboolture and his involvement with 100 pounds of pure methamphetamine. I later met with another contact that provided one pound of this pure methamphetamine.

This intelligence was provided to Queensland Police by the ACC with a request for an operational certificate which would have allowed them to operate inside Queensland Police's jurisdiction. This certificate was declined.

The only reason that I can think of for why this operational certificate was declined is that Queensland Police resented a Federal operation being run on their 'patch' which might have revealed their short-comings in drug interdiction and intelligence . . . whatever you think about me, take a moment to think about the consequences of the decisions made by Queensland Police [name deleted].

His vetoing of an operational certificate has single-handedly thwarted what would have been a massive blow against organised crime in Australia.

His decision to have me charged with fraud means that my assistance to Victorian and ACC investigators will now almost certainly be made public. This will end any opportunity for me to assist Police investigators in bringing to justice the perpetrator of at least three murders; major drug importations and illicit drug manufacture.

It may also result in my being killed in jail—if I am convicted for an offence I did not commit.

This is because I do believe that the Queensland Police Service has been hopelessly compromised and infiltrated by bikie gangs, including the Bandidos. I have personally witnessed improper, if not corrupt, relationships between QPS officers and bikie gangs which have seen criminal investigations thwarted.

It is inevitable, I believe, that if this fraud charge proceeds then my assistance to Queensland, Victorian, New South Wales and Federal ACC investigators will be publicly revealed.

Of course Minister . . . I don't really expect you to do anything about this. I just want this letter on record so when the inevitable does happen, you and the Beattie Government cannot claim you did not know anything about it.

Yours sincerely

Stevan John Utah.

Whatever you might think of Utah, he has one very solid point that neither the federal ACC nor the Queensland police seem too interested in investigating. A bunch of bikies tried to kill him because they suspected—correctly, as it turned out—that he was a secret police informer. That fact alone should surely be worthy of intense investigation.

If it truly was the case that a reckless comment to the media by the ACC jeopardised his safety then procedures need to be changed to ensure such a thing never happens again. If the explanation is more sinister, if either Queensland police or the ACC have been penetrated by organised crime, the need for independent inquiry is all the more urgent.

25

THE DAY SOCIETY LOST

It's going to get bad, and people will die!
Stevan Utah

One day Utah made the approach he had been weighing up for months. Through an intermediary he contacted one of the authors of this book, a reporter with the Nine Network's respected *Sunday* public affairs program. Utah asked if he could get any money for telling his story and it was explained to him that the program would not pay for such a story. We expected that would be the end of the matter. It often is when someone claiming to be a whistle-blower has more mercenary financial motivations. But we kept on talking with Utah, building up a strong relationship by email.

It was very clear that Utah had weightier reasons than money for wanting to tell his story. He had decided he wanted his story told properly. Maybe it was the distance from Australia that had made him hanker to make a difference. Maybe, he laconically suggested, it was the blow to his head or his desire to make a difference before his imminent demise at the hands of vengeful Bandidos. Whatever it was, by mid 2007 Utah had written hundreds of emails explaining what he wanted to say to a national television audience and how to check out the extraordinary claims he was making. Very slowly, that is what we did.

The outlaw motorcycle gangs were also becoming a major public issue, mounting clashes between Rebel gang members and the Bandidos putting the fear of a national bikie war on the front page. Public brawls between the two gangs had become more brazen over the last few years, including one memorable fight right on the steps of the Sydney Local Court building. 'If the Bandidos are prepared to storm the stairs of the Downing Street Centre a few years ago and bash Rebels in front of police and the public on the stairs, then a few fire-bombings and bashings where detection is unlikely will reoccur. It's going to get bad, and people will die! Yes, war has been declared', Utah said in one email. Ominously, he warned in another email that more turf wars between the Rebels and the Bandidos were inevitable:

> When the Rebels made the comment about everyone should leave the 'Gold Coast', make no mistake about it, there was an alliance between the Bandidos and the Hell's Angels to square up on them. Rebels are and have always been declared 'Bash on Sight' ... A war is 'when' not 'if'. You make no mistake about

this, THE NATIONAL MISSING PERSONS LISTS ARE ABOUT
TO GROW. Most will be covert murder. Some will be
brutal bashings. The public should know the ACC
is being hampered. The problem is this, the criminal
code in Qld federal legislation restricts their power
in that, to obtain an operational certificate it must
be approved by the CMC, the Queensland Police
Service and senior management of the ACC. If one
doesn't sign it then it's a no go. On a federal basis, an
operational certificate cannot be granted to someone
who has any form of criminal record. Obviously I
do, and we could not get one on a federal level. The
ACC was extremely tenacious in their resolve to get
an operational certificate, but at all stops Queensland
police wouldn't do it. For all the power the ACC may
have with hearings and oppression, they have none
when they enter another domain. It's sad, and the
public should know. The respective attorney generals
should change these laws so personality issues never
get in the way again.

'I am not pissing in my own pocket here, but society lost
when they lost me', Utah ever so slightly immodestly
claimed.

A few weeks before Utah's television interview was due
to air in July 2007, Queensland's *Courier-Mail* newspaper
ran a story confirming Utah's claims about corrupt police
giving information to bikies. Documents obtained by

the paper showed that a policeman had sex with a bikie gang associate before giving her information about a drug operation. It was a typical example of just what Utah had already warned was happening. A senior constable, Peter Chapman, had only been detected because the drug dealer he tipped off was being investigated by the Australian Federal Police. He was sacked when the dirty dealing was revealed to Queensland police but he fought a court battle in the Queensland Supreme Court to be reinstated. Incredibly, the Queensland police force's own internal disciplinary hearing had only fined him $150 to be paid over six weeks. That is what a copper in the Queensland police force gets for selling information to criminals.

Mercifully, the Crime and Misconduct Commission deemed the judgement too lenient and it appealed to the Misconduct Tribunal, which ruled he should be sacked. 'It is reasonable to infer that Chapman was not a naive police officer', the tribunal said. 'It is clear that any police officer engaging in conduct of this nature ... should be dismissed from the service. His conduct in accessing official and confidential information in Queensland Police Service databases without official purpose ... and the passing on of that information to someone he believed was an amphetamine dealer with links to outlaw motorcycle gangs ... is deserving of the ultimate sanction.' At the time of writing, Chapman was still appealing, seeking reinstatement.

The week before broadcast, the *Sunday* team preparing Utah's story approached the Queensland Police Service, the Australian Crime Commission and Victorian police seeking comment about his claims. Most of the allegations in this book were put to each agency in great detail, with an offer to include any response in the broadcast. It was their opportunity to tell us—even off the record—why Utah was wrong. The silence was deafening.

The Crime Commission, which, to be fair, operates under strict secrecy constraints, sent a carefully worded statement in response to Utah's claims that they had compromised his role as a police informant inside the Bandidos. They said:

> The Australian Crime Commission (ACC) can confirm that intelligence about illegal firearms and drugs was disseminated to relevant agencies. The ACC refutes the suggestion that it provided information to the *Sunshine Coast Daily* that compromised any individual. The information reported in the *Sunshine Coast Daily* on 22 April 2006 was in relation to the establishment of the ACC's national intelligence operation into Outlaw Motorcycle Gangs (OMCGs). The intelligence operation into OMCGs was established by the ACC Board at its scheduled July 2005 meeting to enhance law enforcement's understanding of the nature and extent of the OMCG threat to Australia nationally.

The ACC statement also suggested that anyone with a concern about it could make a complaint to them, the Commonwealth Ombudsman or the new Australian

Commission for Law Enforcement Integrity (ACLEI), which had recently been established to investigate and report on corruption in the ACC and other federal government policing agencies. Utah took the view that it was not even worth bothering because he had received so little response from his ACC handlers since fleeing overseas that he no longer trusted them. He knew how the ACC story had been interpreted inside the clubhouse despite a perhaps well-meaning investigator who said it had not meant it to compromise him.

The Victorian police also declined to answer questions about whether it knew of the ACC's rebuffed efforts to stop heavy calibre handguns being sold by a Bandido on the Queensland black market. They said it would be 'inappropriate' to comment on whether the weapon allegedly used by Christopher Wayne Hudson in the Melbourne city shooting in mid June was the same or in any way connected to the Queensland criminals selling the weapons Utah had wanted taken off the street. They also refused to comment on Utah's assistance to police in relation to the murder of Earl Mooring. Behind the scenes, though, there was little doubt that more than a few senior officers in the Victorian police would be cheering Utah's criticisms of the ACC from their lounge rooms.

Queensland police and Police Minister Judy Spence also declined to go on camera to discuss Utah's allegations. The minister sent *Sunday* a one-line statement sniffing: 'If Mr Utah wants to allege corruption or impropriety by the Queensland Police Service, or he wishes to make a complaint about the actions or inactions of Police, he should contact the Crime and Misconduct Commission.' This response drew more chortles from Utah down the phone line: 'That's the most stupid response she could have made to me. Did you know that myself and the ACC made three complaints to the CMC? I still have the emails.'

Utah believed that his complaints to the Queensland Police Service about his outstanding criminal charges and, in particular over the tens of thousands of dollars of items stolen from his property, had been ignored by police and inadequately investigated by the Crime and Misconduct Commission. He set this out in one of his many emails: 'Simply, when an allegation of corruption or misgiving is made against the QPS the CMC has 14 days to write to the Minister's office and the Commissioner's office. That is a statutory requirement. They then have 6 months to reply. That is also a statutory requirement. Well, let's do some maths here, March 2005 to July 2007 . . . Yes, that is longer than 6 months. Seems they are a law unto themselves in that area.'

To put it bluntly, Utah did not trust any Queensland government agency to fairly investigate its own dirty laundry. He did not see any point in trying:

To make a complaint against the Queensland Police to the Crime and Misconduct Commission for misconduct, hang on I can't do that anyways. LMFAO [Laughing My Fucking Arse Off]? The ACC got the intercepts from me and a version of events. They went to the QPS and got knocked back several times—how can I make a complaint? I can only ask for an inquiry or seek the Ombudsman's injection [investigation] to the allegations. Since there are broader issues, this would have to be done on a federal level.

Sometime in June 2007 Utah and the television crew met at his now former overseas location. He knew he would have to move on once the interview was done. Bikies had contacts in the airports and media. It was too easy for a flight manifest to be checked on the quiet. When the film crew arrived in his peaceful suburban street, he was already waiting at the door. Even when he stood inside his house he was always watching the comings and goings outside. Behind the laconic, self-deprecating Aussie humour, his eyes were always very alert, half expecting Brutus to be coming towards the house with a sawn-off shotgun.

On camera, his chilling account of what he had seen in his years hanging with the Bandidos was part-apology, part-confessional:

What have I seen? I have seen people bashed to the point where you can't actually work out what their face is. I have seen people tortured with hammers. I have seen fingers broken. I have seen toes broken. I saw a girl who was in an unconscious state bashed and kicked so savagely that she got 184 stitches and seven broken bones in her face. Ah, but there's not too much I haven't seen . . . It changed me in the head. I am not normal. It changed me.

When he had finally said what he wanted to say, Utah looked relieved, as if a load had been lifted from his shoulders. There was no doubting the momentous nature of what he had just done. He had unloaded on his former 'brothers'. If Brutus and Tank were not chasing him before, they would surely be doing so when they saw this interview. So why had he done it? 'Well, there's been people all over the country that for years have seen me as a person who won't talk. And a lot of people listening to me now, and wouldn't quite understand it, listening to what I am saying now. But you know like—I've had enough.'

When asked on camera whether he thought the Bandidos would eventually find and kill him, his answer was not an idle boast:

Utah: Oh, I will be killed . . . Unfortunately if they
          try that and I have to defend myself then I am
          going to go to jail for defending myself.
Interviewer: You really believe that they'll come after
          you even on the other side of the world where
          we are at the moment?
Utah: Why wouldn't they?
Interviewer: Well, why would they?
Utah: Loose lips sink ships. Shut him up.

That was his final answer after hours of interviewing. Then, following a brief pause as the camera was turned off, he tipped his head back and laughed: 'That'll really fuck 'em off.'

Back in Australia, there was one final task to complete before broadcasting the interview. It was nearly a year since Stevan Utah had fled Australia. He knew Bandidos were looking for him and perhaps the last thing they would expect would be to see Utah's face on national television, revealing the extent to which some of their members are heavily involved in organised crime. We dialled a number that Utah had called many times before; the mobile phone of one of the most senior Bandidos in Australia. We will call him 'Mort', for reasons that will become obvious. Just a year earlier, Mort had offered Utah a full patch inside the gang, so highly was he respected within the group. Now, when told of Utah's allegations and asked for comment, he feigned not to know him. As well as being one of the principals of the Bandidos, Mort has a little business on the side with another gang member. They make memorial tombstones. The irony is not lost on Utah: 'Wonder if they'll give me a free one.'

When Utah's story finally aired nationally on Sunday morning, 8 July 2007, the media coverage was intense and, as predicted, the counter-spin against Utah from Queensland began with a vengeance. *Sunday* had gone to unusual lengths prior to the broadcast, putting out a press release to all media warning that Utah was facing unrelated criminal charges in Queensland and that to protect his chances of ever getting a fair trial he would be called 'Joe Florida' in any broadcasts or transcripts in that state. It can be a serious contempt of court for media to publish information which compromises a defendant's fair trial by jury. In Australia, Utah's bikie connections and details of his past criminal convictions would likely be seen as highly prejudicial to any juror.

Many media heeded the warning, but the *Brisbane Times* excelled itself by not only publishing Utah's real name but by breathlessly treating as news the criminal charges he had already acknowledged in the broadcast. What was most extraordinary was that the *Times* had spoken to Queensland police, who might surely have been expected to caution the paper about the risks of contempt of court:

Bikie whistleblower facing charges

July 9, 2007, 9:57AM—A former bikie whistleblower who has accused Queensland police of turning a blind eye to the criminal activities of outlaw motorcycle gangs is himself facing criminal charges.

The Queensland Police Service confirmed this morning that Stevan Utah (not his real name) was being investigated by the Crime and Misconduct Commission over a number of 'serious', but as yet un-named, offences.

Utah, a former Bandidos member-turned Australian Crime Commission mole, used the Nine Network's

Sunday program to allege widespread police corruption and inter-agency bumbling which was allowing murder, drugs and gun-running to go unchecked in south-east Queensland.

He said police had tipped off the gang about imminent drug raids, had failed to act on information he provided as an informer and blasted QPS for refusing to cooperate with the ACC on four occasions due to 'pathetic, petty jealousy'.

QPS has refused to officially discuss the allegations, but a spokesman told brisbanetimes.com.au earlier today they were being treated seriously and had referred the matter to the CMC.

'The person making these allegations is well known to QPS and is facing serious criminal charges,' the spokesman said.

'QPS is supportive of determining whether there is any truth to these claims and will assist the CMC in any possible manner,' the spokesman said.

'QPS encourages anyone with information that could assist in establishing the truth in this matter to provide it to the CMC.'

He said he was unable to furnish further details about the exact nature of charges levelled against Utah. 'That's in the hands of the CMC, we don't even know,' the spokesman said.

Utah was a member of the Bandidos for more than a decade before turning ACC informer in 2004. He

THE DAY SOCIETY LOST

told the program of at least two murders, the bashing of a woman and a 'flogging' which left him fearing for his life.

According to Utah, members of the Bandidos were responsible for:

- The shooting murder of 54-year-old Geelong security guard Earl Neil Mooring, who he said was tortured to death with a hammer in October 2000. Utah said he helped dump Mr Mooring's body in Goulburn, south of Sydney, and he later led ACC investigators to the body's location.
- The murder of a former Bandidos member four years ago, who Utah said was forced to hang himself rather than be beaten to death after a corrupt Queensland Police informant told gang members the Bandido was helping them.
- The beating of a woman, who Utah said was dragged by her hair and kicked while unconscious outside a Bandidos clubhouse on Queensland's Sunshine Coast. She had up to eight broken bones and 184 stitches.

He said the QPS refused an ACC request for permission to send Utah undercover to buy methylamphetamine, after he had been offered the drug by a Bandido member.

Utah said he drew a map outlining the locations of two Bandido drug labs in Queensland but QPS did not raid the premises until six months later.

He said he was forced to flee overseas after a

newspaper article tipped off the Bandidos to his role as an informant and was 'flogged' by Bandidos members who were trying to kill him. He said his requests for help from the ACC had fallen on deaf ears.

'I feel total betrayal', he said.

'Last time I looked, regardless of what anyone thinks of me, I did the right thing and I'm still a citizen of Australia.

'Why wasn't I looked after?'

There is an old saying in investigative journalism circles: 'Always assume a fuck-up before a conspiracy.' It is a handy rule of thumb for young journalists (and coppers for that matter) who tend to assume the sinister explanation before the banal. It was tempting to see the reported statements from the Queensland Police Service as a conspiracy to white-ant Utah, but what is more likely is that, in the scramble to respond, there had been a major fuck-up by either the Queensland Police Service or some journalists.

Or was the explanation more sinister? For if the *Times* story was correct, then a Queensland Police Service spokesman had asserted several serious falsehoods to the press. Stevan Utah, contrary to the story, was Utah's real name. Surely a police spokesman did not tell the media this without a warning that naming him could jeopardise his chance of a fair trial? Utah was also not, as the story claimed, being investigated by the Crime and Misconduct Commission for several 'serious but as yet unnamed' offences. Utah has that assurance in writing from the CMC. There was more than a whiff here of either a journalist wanting to diss a rival's story or the more likely possibility that someone in the Queensland Police Service wanted to rubbish Utah's claims before they got traction in the press.

The police spokesman's statement that Utah was 'well-known' to police and the false implication that his outstanding charges were not disclosed in the broadcast were clearly defensively pejorative, if not calculated smears. Utah had expected as much. But what he had not expected was the stupidity of whoever it was in the Queensland Police Service who decided to issue a statement so prejudicial to his forthcoming trial.

All politicians know about the risks of incurring the wrath of a judge for breaching the sub-judice rule and some have been prosecuted by zealous prosecutors for jeopardising a case. Unlike the jury system in the United States, where the media regularly comment on ongoing trials, digging up dirt on witnesses and defendants alike, the English legal system likes to pretend a juror is a blank slate—not prejudiced by any other evidence than what is tendered in court. So it came as something of a shock to see Queensland Premier Peter Beattie, himself a former lawyer, apparently being quoted in an article that also referred to Utah by his real name linking his criminal past to the current charges against him. If ever Utah had any chance of a fair trial in his home state, the combined comments of the Queensland Police Service and the premier had blown it:

Qld: Corruption whistleblower no Mother Teresa—Beattie

BRISBANE, July 8 AAP—A former bikie turned informant who has made claims of Queensland police corruption is no Mother Teresa and his allegations should be taken with a grain of salt, Premier Peter Beattie says.

A former Bandidos member known as Joe Florida (aka Stevan Utah) told Channel Nine that moles within the police service were tipping off outlaw motorcycle gangs, warning them before drug raids.

Queensland's Crime and Misconduct Commission (CMC) is investigating.

'As the police have indicated, the person involved is known to police so we are not talking about Mother Teresa,' Mr Beattie said today. 'But having said that, it doesn't matter who makes the complaint, the CMC will investigate it. There's no cover-up, it's not like the bad old days. I don't know the circumstances of this case, but you've got to remember just because an allegation is made doesn't mean it is true ...'

A Queensland Police Service (QPS) spokesman told News Limited today that 'the person making these allegations is well known to the Queensland Police Service and is facing serious criminal charges'.

Mr Beattie said he had total faith in the QPS. 'I believe our police service is one of the best in Australia. I think it is one of the best in the world,' he said.

There is a fascinating site on the internet which could only prosper in the legal and moral free-for-all that the internet represents: a web-site called bikernews.net. In between the innocuous information one would expect on a biker website, there is an area on it called 'One-Percenter News'. Enter, and the tender reader is taken into a kind of mafia bulletin board where one page entitled 'Cops Gone Bad' reports on police who have themselves been caught doing crooked things. There is also an area called 'Donut Gang', listing convicted paedophiles, which some might interpret as an open invitation for gang members to exact vicious retribution on those named within it.

At the very top of the 'One-Percenter' page there is an area called 'Who's a Rat'. It features the photos and details of all known police informants in the world, including those who have ratted on bikie gangs. The implicit threat behind such a page is obvious. Within a few hours of Utah's appearance on Australian national television, the transcript of the whole story was uploaded to the bikernews website, with Utah's real name and details. The volume of comments about what Utah had done was enormous. So was the bile directed at him from angry bikies across the world. One comment posted by someone called 'Drillin' read: 'Gee fuckhead utah now you know how the Bandidos feel about you!!!!!!!!!! THE ONLY GOOD SNITCH IS A DEAD SNITCH!!!' Another, unsubtly dubbing himself 'El Diablo', wrote: 'Isn't it funny how they all look the same . . . snitches . . . i watched this STORY . . . weazley little rat . . . lookin for sum [sic] discount for his impending incarceration . . . you will get your OWN headlines shortly no doubt . . .'

'Magnoliaprinces' wrote: '"Why wasn't I looked after?" LOL oh poor snitch boy, the coppers didn't look after you. Waaa Waaaa. What a big freakin surprise. You should have known better you moron. They got what they wanted and you [sic] life don't mean shit to them. Have fun enjoying a life and paranoia and looking over your shoulder. Be sure to duck when you hear a loud noise. LOL . . . AMEN.' Another wrote: 'RAT FUCKER. We need to have PICS of ALL the RAT MOTHER FUCKERS in this WORLD. DIE YOU RAT FUCKERS.'

There was a lot of mocking of Utah's quoted comments that he felt 'total betrayal' by the Australian police: 'Awwww . . . Poor little rat feels betrayed . . . Kinda like those that you used to call "BROTHER"?' Another bikie, calling himself 'Ironduke', wrote: 'He will get what's coming to him! Rats never have a long life cause they use every-one and at the end no one will be there for him! Have fun running the rest of your life you piece of shit rat motherfucker! If your [sic] smart you'll kill yourself!'

Scanning the names on the message boards, Utah realised he knew several of the posters, including one known as 'Squid' from the Geelong Bandidos. Then there was this seemingly innocuous message among all the violent threats, sent by a gang member from Salt Lake City in the United States: 'Just wanted to sent [*sic*] out a big red and gold hello to all of the Bandidos in Australia. The Hermanos are a Bandidos support club and welcome any red and gold visitors from down under! SYLB [see you later brother].' To Utah, that message meant only one thing: 'That's an offer to help the Aussies find me. It's the classic way they do it. Hey brother, I can help you find this guy. It's exactly how they work. In all likelihood the people they will send to try to kill me will not be Australians. It will be a favour, done by a local club. Makes it very hard for the police to track them down if and when it happens.'

Utah's story also drew a huge response from other viewers who not only supported his allegations about police corruption or impropriety in relation to bikie gangs, but had stories of their own they wanted investigated. A consistent theme from dozens of emails and phone calls to the program was that police were too scared to act against the outlaw motorcycle gangs. One commented:

It is almost funny watching straight people try to realise how bad crime is in our country. I teach security guards in [deleted]. We have been having problems over winter with bikers carrying GUNS.

Calls to police have gone unanswered. Now the boys just search the guys to know how many guns are in town. I have forwarded this info' on to local council, who forwarded it on to local police. No one has made any contact to me, other than the [Hells] Angels, who would like some training. Your story may open some eyes to all the straights, but it will not open the real eyes. The police are scared, out-gunned and paid off.

Another viewer wrote with detailed information about a particular police officer based near the country area of Queensland where Utah had lived. In what was an eerily familiar complaint from many viewers, he alleged the officer seemed unwilling to prosecute bikies involved in the manufacture of illicit drugs:

This scumbag was informed of a certain bikie member making speed in the garage of a property 2 ks from town at the time. He was shown photos of the lab and given the names of the people involved. This copper refused to take a statement . . . 2 hours later [the policeman] visited the house and warned the bikie that he had to move everything as there could be a raid within 24 hours. One of the other people involved had been acquitted of murder due to a false statement given by a girlfriend. His residence was also visited that afternoon by [the same policeman] and he was warned of involvement and warned of possible

raids. This is the same corrupt dog that takes 9 weeks
to question a paedophile after complaints were made.

Utah knew the officer well: 'He is a well known lazy ass
fuckwit!'

Yet another emailer wrote:

I myself have been used as a pawn by the [Queensland
Police Service—QPS]. They call it a drug war, but
when they use people for information and those
people have reached their use by date the QPS then
turn these poor souls onto [the] street for live bait.
The worst thing of all is the QPS will promise all the
protection, funding to relocate. But unless you get [it]
in writing . . . the QPS never hold up their end of the
bargain. In a nutshell, [the] majority of these people,
that the underworld call DOGS, are left to their [own]
devices to protect themselves against these organised
crime groups. When you do protect yourself and love[d]
ones then you can expect to be charged and if the
crime is bad enough then you can expect to be sent to
jail where these groups can and will get access to you.
The way the QPS sees it they get two for one . . . Final
note, I myself will never help the QPS, in any shape
or form. The QPS' only aim is to look good in the
eyes of the public. They have done squat about motor
cycle gangs, considering the gangs started to reach out
and recruit people during the early nineties. It makes
you wonder what the QPS has been doing for the last

seventeen years or at least how much B/S they have told [the] public. One thing is for sure, what they teach you as [a] child, that you can trust the POLICE then my experience BEGS TO DIFFER. You can bet that if my wife and I live long enough and manage to have a family MY children will be taught NEVER TO TRUST POLICE . . . I will make sure of that. The worst thing in my case is that . . . information that was given . . . was never acted upon or never investigated. I was left wondering why I had even bothered in the first place. Considering I now have a bounty on my head. I had great problems with this because I was informed by a QPS member who happens to be a relation. This person could not defend me because they were silenced [by] senior QPS members. I know that not all police officers are dirty, but money talks and bullshit walks. Police agencies all over Australia need to pool resources because the bike groups do.

Utah was gratified to hear of the positive response supporting his allegations, if not a little sobered by the brazen threats on bikernews.net. But he was also now a man on a mission to warn the public about the risk of outlaw motorcycle gangs:

I have seen and heard many media reports that refer to me as brave, good bloke, honest and even betrayed. I don't care about any of that shit. To use my old saying, let's do the maths on this: Australia has what? Twenty-five million people and 400 Bandidos? America has ... 265 million people and 800 Bandidos? Europe has ... 1.7 billion people and 1400 Bandidos? Canada has ... 27 million people and 14 Bandidos? Seems to me based on the international averages we shouldn't have any more than 60 Bandidos. That to me is pathetic, ineffective, inefficient policing and society and our next generation will pay for the failures of today's law enforcement. How many drug dealers will be made in that time? Jesus! A lawyer once said to me, 'Steve, fight only the battles you can win'. Well, you can't win a fight unless you fight it, right? I admit it's hard, mate, I stand alone, and I have no-one and have nothing. But I am alive; there isn't a day that goes by that I [don't] wish my life would end through natural causes. I even dream of it. Once when I felt this way the ACC would fly a counsellor to see me. Now I simply don't exist. You gotta love that fucking due diligence shit, hey?

Utah was staggered by comments that Queensland Police Commissioner Bob Atkinson had made to the media following the broadcast. At the same time as politicians were promising independent and impartial investigations into his allegations, the commissioner had dismissed one unspecified allegation Utah made by saying: 'I have personal knowledge on this matter and it's absolute nonsense.' As Utah commented: 'So much for a fair inquiry. My life will be over probably sooner than later, but I won't shut up! Sometimes I want to cry, but I can't, I can't allow myself to be beaten.'

Meanwhile the numbers of young Australians suffering from the burgeoning quantities of ice coming out of the illicit bikie labs mounted. The same Queensland government which had repeatedly knocked back federal and state police requests for an operational certificate to use Utah to stem the drug rackets announced a month or two later that it had 'declared war on the "brain frying" drug ice'. The then Queensland premier told attentive media that: 'Parents have lost their children to this drug, lives have been lost and thousands of users have inflicted serious damage to their mental and physical health as well as resorted to violent crime to feed their habit', he said. 'We've got to say to young Queenslanders, "if you use ice it will fry your brain".'

One news story summarised a spate of tragic incidents involving ice users on the Gold Coast. A man charged with killing his father was believed to have been revved up on ice at the time of the alleged attack. A man charged with ram-raiding a Bunnings Hardware store told the court he was desperate for a fix of ice. Another man was charged with stabbing his pet dog fifteen times with a kitchen knife after taking ice for the first time. Ice was found in the car of those charged with a vicious attack on a Gold

Coast police officer. 'And in another terrifying example of the tragic effects of ice, a Labrador [Queensland] man cut off his own testicles with a craft knife in April while high on the drug', the paper luridly recounted.

In the lofty offices of the Crime Commission, federal police and various state police agencies, there were more than a few investigators feeling similarly emasculated—but for a very different reason.

26

ANOTHER WITNESS BURNED

If you oppose him you are opposing the Bandidos.
Sam

Among the many tips and pieces of information which flowed in following the broadcast, one new source stood out. He was another former associate of the Bandidos who had become a police witness; someone also burned by police. We will call him 'Sam'. Sam used to own a custom motorcycle shop located in a popular Queensland tourist spot. The way he told it, a senior member of the Bandidos stood over him—took over his business and then demanded huge amounts of money for nonexistent 'debts'. 'I was beaten up when I first met [him] in 2005. I used to go to bike auctions and when I wanted to buy a bike the bikies would come and tell other people to fuck off. I wanted to get out of my relationship with them earlier but it wasn't going to happen', he said. Sam went to the police. While local police wanted to help, senior police shut down the investigation, preferring to buy peace with the gangster, who has a reputation as something of a local crime lord. We will call that Bandido 'Vulcan'. 'Organised crime squad Queensland had full telephone recordings of [Vulcan] threatening us', Sam says, 'but my problem was [Queensland Police Service]. They came to me and said you will have a lot of problems if you won't stand at your counter and work undercover in your shop for us to catch them. I refused, and I paid the consequences. I was cut off completely by QPS.' When he and his family fled Queensland, Vulcan and other Bandidos stripped his shop of all its stock as police watched.

The police's failure to act on Sam's mistreatment by Vulcan was one thing; but what Sam also knew about corrupt police assisting the Bandidos was deeply worrying. Vulcan had a very senior source in New South Wales police whom Sam says he witnessed tipping Vulcan off on imminent operations against the bikies on more than one occasion. 'He boasted to me that if there [were] any problems with police he would get to know about it—through that connection', Sam says. 'The big problem in the QPS is that the ones who are trying to do the right job against the bikies are getting hamstrung . . . I also witnessed [name deleted], an old-time crim and [Vulcan] assistant, ring a Queensland cop. He was able to find out if an undercover was one of theirs.'

Sam's account of his shabby treatment by his police handlers was remarkably familiar to Stevan Utah, who knew of Sam—and who knew Vulcan all too well. 'His aura is so cold, his demeanour. He, he's like . . . You know he's a strange guy. When he's standing with his dad you know butter wouldn't melt in his mouth. He comes across and he just has this feel about him, he's just the nicest guy you could ever meet. When he's by himself, fuck. He just . . . it just chills you. You have to be careful . . . but it's always in your head—don't mess with this guy, don't mess with this guy', Utah recalls.

Vulcan is a former nightclub bouncer from Sydney's Kings Cross who earned a fearsome reputation along that notorious entertainment strip as a local heavy. The son of a priest, he appears to have inherited none of his father's religious moral code. Instead, like all too many Bandidos, he used the club as a shelter for sophisticated and high-level organised crime—biffing, bashing and, on his own account, killing his way to the upper echelons of the club.

Patched early, he landed in a senior position in the Bandidos when one club principal was sent to gaol for drug dealing. In the years since, he has never looked back. In defiance of supposed bikie bans on moving heroin, Vulcan was, and still is, according to Utah and Sam, a big-time dealer in 'H'. He is also a bully as well as a thug . . . an all-round nice guy. One of his favourite ways of making extra cash is to claim false 'debts'. And that is the rort he pulled on Sam and his family: 'QPS wouldn't give me a new identity. They refused protection', Sam says. 'No money for airfares. I was a family of five on the run. My wife was six months pregnant. [Vulcan] threatened her. [Vulcan] plays a very cunning game and if you oppose him you are opposing the Bandidos.'

Utah had also been the victim of an extortion attempt by Vulcan. '[Vulcan] is a gangster, not a bikie', he says. During the time Utah was working for the Australian Crime Commission Vulcan once claimed he had lost $200 000 worth of drug chemicals and accused Utah of having something to do with it. 'But I was with [Brutus] the day they went missing', Utah says. 'It was basically an extortion attempt by him. He was expecting me to agree to do a cook-up to buy peace with him.' Utah and his alleged accomplice in the drug theft, a member of a powerful local Queensland crime family, were summoned to a meeting with Vulcan at a local motorbike shop. He went with some trepidation. He had alerted his police handlers in the Australian Crime Commission, who knew Vulcan's formidable reputation for sadistic violence. Concerned back then for their new witness's skin, they had enlisted the help of the Queensland police to protect him. Utah recalls:

The police had a team outside ... ready to come in if things got nasty. The arrangement was I'd get a call on my phone and if I felt things were getting out of hand then I had to say the keywords 'Osama Bin Laden is a fuckwit', to save my arse ... 'Dennis Lillee is a shit cricketer' meant everything is fine. What was amazing about this meeting was that [Brutus] knew [the debt] was crap and he'd left a weapon there ... for me to take out [Vulcan] if necessary ... At the meeting they asked me what happened that day and I explained. [Vulcan] said you owe me $100000 both of you. I walked out. I said [Vulcan] can go fuck himself.

Utah recognised Vulcan's request for a cook-up as a great opportunity for the ACC investigators. If he did what Vulcan had ordered and manufactured illegal methamphetamine, it was another prime opportunity for the federal investigators to nail a Mr Big in Australian organised crime. 'I rang [Laurel] and explained I had been asked to pay over $100G, what should I do? He said I don't know, what *are* you going to do?'—perhaps a variation on the old saying, 'Who's "we", white boy?' Yet again, the ACC had failed to seize an opportunity. Just why is anybody's guess. They are not talking. Utah says, 'What amazes me about this decision is that the ACC could have got me to cook the drugs and they could then have arrested everyone. Two hundred thousand pills would probably have got them—[Vulcan] included—two years in gaol. Can somebody please tell me why they didn't use me?'

Sam also knew a lot of things which confirmed Utah's accounts of his time inside the Bandidos. He claimed, for example, that the assault by Butch on the woman outside the clubhouse was in fact filmed by one gang member on his mobile phone. 'Every Bandido member had footage of that. The reason that chick got it was that she was an associate of the Rebels. She got beaten because she said Rebels' parties were much better than Bandidos' parties', he claims.

What disgusts Sam most of all is that some of the senior Bandidos involved in the takeover of his bike shop along with Vulcan, despite having criminal convictions, travelled recently to a 'Biker-Build-Off' competition in South Dakota in the United States. Senior police and immigration officials in Australia were told of these connections, but nothing was done to stop it. 'They're appalling criminals and how come they're getting visas to the US and not me? You aren't supposed to be able to get into the US if you are a member of an outlaw motorcycle gang. Yet four are going over from each club in Australia.'

Efforts to prosecute Vulcan for his extortion and murder threats against Sam were made by police, but several witnesses all of a sudden developed amnesia prior to the trial, after a visit from a Vulcan associate we will call 'Big Mac'. Sam recalls:

Five people witnessed Vulcan trying to kill me. The police held coercive hearings [a hearing where investigators can compel a witness to answer questions with no right to silence] to make sure nobody would lie. Bandidos, though, knew all the witnesses. I handed the business to an administrator to get out of the deal. But the Bandidos came in for four days and took everything out of the shop. The people who witnessed this were too terrified to give evidence. The Bandidos put my wife's picture in the window of the shop—as the contact for creditors. We were told it was going to trial and then we were told the prosecution wouldn't proceed. [Name deleted] from the Finks told me [Vulcan] had told him he'd made sure it was not going to go to trial.

Police subsequently raided Big Mac's home and, according to Sam, they found stolen machine guns and cocaine there. Sam alleges 'all charges were dropped'. Whether true or not, the perception that both Stevan Utah and Sam have is that the police prefer to buy peace with Vulcan and other senior outlaw motorcycle gang members involved in criminal activity rather than fruitlessly attempt to prosecute. 'My Queensland Police Service handler, ex AFP, told me that because I had a wife, kids, family, I didn't want to be looking over my shoulder for the rest of my life', Sam claims.

Intriguingly, Sam also claims that Vulcan even boasted of having played a role in killing Earl Mooring. 'We were sitting in a coffee shop . . . and he said, "Sometimes people around me do stupid things. Sometimes these are consequences of bad information. Like the guy down in Melbourne." [He] told me he was a security guard. He was sitting on a drug stash. He said, "We tortured the guy until he was dead". He told me how he drove nonstop to dump the body', Sam recalls.

Both Victorian police and Stevan Utah believe Vulcan was not involved in the murder of Earl Mooring at all; he was simply using what he had heard about it around the clubhouse to bully his extortion victim into doing what he asked. What did ring true, however, was Vulcan's claim to have also been involved in the murder of Milad Sande, the Sydney drug dealer killed at Malabar—the killing that sparked the deaths of both Russell Oldham and Rodney Monk, the Bandido president. Sam says:

> They told me about another guy in Sydney they killed—Sande. They tortured him and killed him. The conversation about this was just before [Vulcan] got married in 2005. The murder of Sande was all about an offer from the Nomads to do the dealing in methamphetamine and give a cut of the dollars to the Bandidos. [Vulcan] said Oldham was using the gear and bringing disrepute to the club. A year later, when the Nomads decided to come over into the Bandidos in Sydney, [Vulcan] presided over the merger. [Vulcan] told me that he killed Sande. He said I shot the guy so many fucking times.

Sam also has other evidence to substantiate his belief that Vulcan was telling the truth about being involved in Sande's murder. With his permission we ensured Sam's evidence got to the New South Wales homicide squad.

At the time of writing police are still investigating the killing.

Sam also knew about Vulcan and other Bandidos getting help from a crooked local Brisbane accountant with fake paperwork, enabling them to get multiple bank loans to buy property. The property was used to launder huge sums of money from illegal drug dealing. Not only did the accountant allegedly get tips from Queensland police about imminent investigations into his clients, his wife worked at a senior level in the tax office.

Sam alleges that the bikies got well over a thousand of such dodgy loans through a well-known mortgage lender—the big banks only too happy to turn a blind eye to the illegal source of funds because the bikies were prompt payers. All of this was coordinated by Vulcan's crooked accountant:

> They created fake paperwork for everyone. They would get them a home loan and put them into a house. [Vulcan]'s wife was working in a real estate agent's office and she knew the houses that were coming up. She knew their bottom line price. No-one has ever acted on the fraudulent mortgages. Some of them had eight or nine houses. I know of 1600 home loans done ... with the bikies. They bought one house for $1 million and the guy put up $1000. His payments are $6500 per month. He doesn't work.

A search for Vulcan's and his wife's names in the Queensland Land Titles Office shows only one property registered, jointly, to them. But other sources in the banking industry have also alleged that some big banks are indeed turning a blind eye to the provenance of monies funding many bikie-connected property purchases. It is the sort of inquiry only a police or anti-corruption agency can make; but whether any such agency has done it is anyone's guess.

Once again the outlaw motorcycle gangs are not the only worry for witness Sam. Just as in Utah's case, there is a strong suspicion that police turf wars over Sam's use as a witness seriously compromised the safety of Sam and his family. He recently attempted to flee overseas to escape Vulcan and his homicidal mates, but he says someone falsely tipped off Canadian authorities that he was a drug mule. He found himself deported back to Australia—unprotected and exposed.

Utah was fortunate. He has made it overseas and he decided to tell his story to police and immigration officials in the country where he is now hiding. As luck would have it, he was put in touch with one of that country's top experts on outlaw motorcycle gang organised crime. The official soon recognised just how useful Utah's inside knowledge of the bikie gangs could be, and then he made an extraordinary invitation. That senior policeman asked Utah if he would be prepared to speak to police officers about the bikie gangs at official training courses. It is hilarious to think of Professor Utah taking wet-behind-the-ears coppers through recipes for crystal meth. But in fact what the overseas police had recognised was Utah's value as an insider. They wanted to hear how to look after an informant of such value—how to protect a source and how to infiltrate an organised crime gang like an outlaw motorcycle club.

Irony of ironies, the very same criminal whom those in Australia had spurned was now so highly valued by his new country, they wanted to hear what he had to say about organised crime inside the bikie gangs. 'I am humbled by the efforts of policing elements in the country I am currently in', Utah says. 'They owe me nothing, I gave them nothing, yet they guide me, take time to ask me how my day was. You know what, mate? Australia should be fucking embarrassed, this is shameful. Law enforcement in Australia will be an embarrassment in the western world . . . Maybe then law enforcement may have better budgets, estimate committees will allocate resources correctly and laws will be enforced.' But there was more to what Stevan Utah knew, much more. When he sat in front of the television lights in the middle of 2007, he had hinted as much:

Interviewer: Is there information that you haven't yet
            told the police about?
Utah: Yes.
Interviewer: Of more criminal activity?

Utah: Mmm.

Interviewer: Why haven't you told them that?

Utah: Why? What's the point? They won't do anything. They don't communicate with each other. I mean, some people would see me as being quite flippant about the whole thing. It's not like that. They DON'T talk to each other. They just don't.

Ever cunning, Utah had kept something in reserve. Within months we were to learn just what he meant.

27

BIKIES AND TERRORISTS

*Offer enough money, you can have anything you
fucking want.*
Stevan Utah

There was one major nightmare haunting Australian
counter-terrorism investigators in early September 2007.
They had done all they could to protect US President
George W. Bush and twenty other of the world's leaders
who were in Australia's harbour city for the APEC
meeting. But a worst-fear scenario was playing heavily on
their minds.

On the other side of the world a former Australian
Crime Commission witness was wrestling with his
conscience. Stevan Utah had a guilty secret. There was
something he had seen inside the outlaw motorcycle
gangs which he had not told his police handlers about.

Sydney was in an unprecedented security lock-down.
A huge chunk of the city's CBD had been fenced off from
normal citizenry and was now the exclusive preserve of
solid, unsmiling, menacing men with wires in their ears,

guns and bulletproof limousines. Extraordinarily powerful new laws had been pushed through parliament to allow police to detain terrorist suspects, and to shoot to kill if necessary. The security goons cocooned their leaders around the city in long speeding motorcades with police helicopters circling overhead. It seemed the entire city had been taken over by the kind of unpleasant male who makes his living as a night-club bouncer—snarlingly officious types who angered city workers with their all too smug enjoyment of the nation's temporary lurch towards fascism.

The whole ridiculously self-important event left itself wide open for a noble Australian tradition—the 'piss-take'. In much of the Australian news media the security was derided as overkill; a very unAustralian stomping on traditional civil liberties. One edict that angered protesters most of all was that they were to be allowed no closer than three hundred metres from POTUS—the US president. As Iraq sank further into the abyss and anger about US stalling on climate change hotted up, there was a lot of steam many protesters wanted to vent at George W. Bush. Ironically, the outsiders who got the closest were a bunch of comedians from the local ABC television, who created a fake motorcade and were—to the great embarrassment of police—waved through security cordons to a street just outside POTUS's luxury hotel.

Behind the scenes, though, there was a very good reason for the security clamp-down. For months prior to the APEC meeting, in the offices of New South Wales and federal police and Australia's domestic spy service, ASIO, a top-priority secret operation was under way. A major reason protesters were being kept so distant from the president and other leaders was because security services had discovered there were at least nine military rocket launchers somewhere out there in Sydney's underworld. They could destroy any of the toughest armoured vehicles. The M72 L1A2-F1 light anti-tank weapon fires a high-explosive warhead at one hundred and fifty metres per second. On impact, its copper liner liquefies, piercing up to twenty-eight centimetres of solid steel armour. Anyone inside is shredded with molten metal.

The rocket launchers had been stolen by a trusted soldier from within one of Australia's most secure military facilities—a weapons storage depot at Orchard Hills in Sydney's west. In a shocking betrayal of trust, they were allegedly sold to a Lebanese–Australian crime gang who then onsold some or all of them to Lebanese–Australian Islamic fundamentalists. The 66 millimetre M72 rocket launchers are a terrorist's dream weapon. Easily concealable, they can fold-down into a backpack. Designed to knock out tanks and armoured vehicles, they would make short work of any of the impressive-looking armoured limousines whisking world leaders around the city that APEC week. While the maximum effective range is about two hundred metres, the rocket motor can propel the warhead as far as one thousand one hundred metres.

Small wonder the US secret service and the Australians were paranoid. For, despite months of searching, only one of the weapons was recovered prior to the APEC conference. Numerous parks and areas of bushland around Sydney were secretly excavated in a search for the rockets, which were believed to have been secreted inside buried PVC piping.

Two men were charged with offences relating to the theft. Former soldier Dean Steven Taylor, and a highly decorated army ammunitions technician officer, Captain Shane Malcolm Della-Vedova. In April 2007 police raided both their homes at dawn, telling a court hearing that Della-Vedova sold one of the rocket launchers in 2003 through a member of an outlaw motorcycle gang, now a protected witness codenamed 'Harrington' in the court hearing.

At Taylor's committal proceedings in November 2007 Harrington told the court that while he was in Long Bay prison in July 2001, on drug offences, Taylor had come to visit. Apparently his wife and Taylor's wife were old friends. Harrington alleged that during the visit Taylor offered him the weapons, bulletproof vests and night-vision goggles. It just so happened that the first person Harrington thought of to move the pilfered rocket launchers, grenades and other army ordnance was none other than Milad Sande—the young man who was to meet an untimely demise in a lonely Malabar park just two years later. Though his grieving family had publicly described him as having a 'heart of gold', Harrington's evidence suggests he was nonetheless a major league Sydney criminal.

It turns out that the Crown's chief witness in the rocket launcher prosecution, Harrington, was a long-time illicit business associate of Sande. One of Harrington's tendered statements provided to the Crown as part of his roll-over admitted:

> I knew Milad through our involvement in supply of illegal drugs. We had previously sold and bought prohibited drugs to each other including amphetamine and pseudoephedrine. Our usual involvement was when I supplied him with pseudoephedrine based tablets that he would later use in the manufacture of amphetamines.

Harrington knew he had nothing to lose by dobbing his old, now deceased business partner so he put him right in it: 'I contacted Milad because I was aware he was widely connected through the criminal community and that he would be able to find a buyer for the weapons.'

Milad had agreed to buy the weapons but he first wanted a 'taste'—and, according to Harrington, he offered to buy just one of the rocket launchers at first for $20 000 plus a couple of grenades for $1000 each. When he turned up to make the buy he had another villain with him from central casting whom we will call 'Sinbad'.

Sinbad was Milad's muscle . . . in Harrington's statement he was described as 'of large muscular build' with 'tribal or celtic tattoos down one arm'.

A day after Harrington had handed over the rocket launcher for $20 000 Milad turned up to say that whoever he had sold the weapon too was not happy with it. Harrington revealed, 'They didn't realise it was only a single shot weapon. The buyer wanted to return the weapon and wanted their money back.' In the interests of good customer relations, Harrington took the rocket launcher back.

Milad still wanted the grenades and even asked for more although he later complained to Harrington that 'two of the grenades had been thrown and they didn't go off and he wanted his money back'. No light is shed in Harrington's evidence on whom or what exactly Milad or his associates were throwing the grenades at but with Milad Sande returning the rocket launcher, Harrington now had to find a new buyer.

Selling rocket launchers on the black market is a difficult thing. You can't exactly put an ad on eBay. But it just so happened that Harrington had done another young fellow a favour a while back. A couple of Lebanese criminals in his particular western Sydney suburb had been having trouble with a person whom we will call 'Farouk' who, Harrington told the court, was 'threatening them'.

As bikies like him are often asked to do, Harrington had been asked by Farouk's adversaries to 'come around to help sort it out'. It was the beginning of a beautiful relationship. Farouk had then allegedly steered Harrington to a source who could steal large quantities of pseudo-ephedrine tablets from a local factory. Harrington admitted he had arranged for the sale of 500 packets of pseudo-ephedrine Actifed tablets from Farouk to Milad Sande for $23 000—whacking $5000 on top of that as a profit for himself.

Harrington admitted that during this time Farouk had also boasted a lot about selling guns, so it seemed perfectly natural to offer the rocket launchers to him. He offered them to the illicit gun-dealer for $12 000 each. 'In the end we agreed on seven for $12 000 each', his statement acknowledges.

Of his wholesale business Harrington told the court, 'I was just onselling them to whoever I could, I don't know what [Farouk] wanted them for. I just supplied them to him.'

The police also alleged that, a month later, Della-Vedova sold another seven rocket launchers to Farouk through Harrington for at least another $70 000. Farouk allegedly onsold the weapons to an underworld figure called Adnan Darwiche. He in turn allegedly passed them on to a terror suspect who was dubbed by his criminal associates 'The Psycho Cunt'. It's as good a name as any and in the circumstances—as you will see—probably right on the money. The Psycho Cunt cannot be named because at time of writing he is facing charges in relation to other matters. However, an extremely colourful statement provided to the court by one of his alleged criminal associates—a person we will call 'Bling'—offers an insight into the integrity and good character of the persons to whom the Crown witness Harrington now negotiated the sale of the purloined rocket launchers.

In his own words Bling and his criminal associates '[c]ontrolled a few drug runs in the South-west of Sydney. Because of our business we did shootings, bashings, knee-cappings, attempted murders and murders.'

One of Bling's associates who can be named is Adnan Darwiche, who is mercifully now incarcerated in NSW's notorious supermax prison at Goulburn, serving double life terms for killings arising out of an extraordinarily bloody feud with a neighbouring family, the Razzaks. Nine people died in brazen shootings that turned the south-west of Sydney into a virtual wild west. There were differing claims about what caused the carnage—either drug turf wars or a marriage gone wrong. But for a few frightening years from mid-2003 things got terrifyingly out of control.

In November 2006 Adnan Darwiche and two other men reportedly laughed and shouted 'God is Great' as they were sent to gaol for the drive-by shooting at the Sydney suburb of Greenacre, which killed a woman sleeping in her bed and a member of the Razzak family. Around a hundred bullets were allegedly fired at the house. But that court also heard how Adnan Darwiche—also known by his mates as 'Eddie'—had also discussed using a rocket launcher to attack the house; but that he had ruled it out because of fears the explosive projectile might have just gone straight through the fibre-cement walls without exploding.

What to do with a bunch of rocket launchers? We know now because of Harrington's statement to the court that the rocket launchers Adnan Darwiche and his maniacal colleagues had in their possession were onsold to them by the illicit gun dealer Farouk, who in turn had got them from Harrington. More disturbing are the revelations in Bling's statement of how Adnan Darwiche was slowly becoming radicalised under the influence of a very religious friend—the man he and his colleagues dubbed The Psycho Cunt—because of his expressed desire to blow up bits of Sydney in a terrorist jihad. According to Bling's statement: 'About mid 2002 we all became religious.' Adnan Darwiche, aka Eddie, grew his beard long and hassled Bling to go to the Haldon Street Mosque in Sydney every Friday. Disturbingly Bling says: 'Eddie had a different view in relation to the law of self-defence. He agreed that we wouldn't go to heaven if we killed another human being unless it was in self-defence. However he told me his view was more along the line that if you thought someone was going to kill you it was okay to find them first and kill them.'

At least five of the rocket launchers bought by Darwiche were then allegedly sold by him to The Psycho

Cunt. It was a horrific worst-case scenario: stolen military weapons had found their way through a bikie gang to an alleged terrorist.

But when the first news of Adnan Darwiche's involvement in the rocket launcher transaction broke in 2007, the Darwiche family patriarch, Albert Darwiche, strenuously denied his family's heavy involvement in criminal activity. Intriguingly he did make one comment to Chris Zinn of the ABC television's *7.30 Report*: 'They're saying there's six rocket launchers. How do we know there's six? What we're hearing is there's probably 20, 30, maybe even 100 rocket launchers around', Albert Darwiche said.

Officially there are only nine stolen Australian Defence Force rocket launchers at large. But Mr Darwiche clearly was better placed to know than most just how many weapons are in circulation. As you will see, there are very good reasons to be sceptical that the nine so far disclosed are the only ones out there. And that is where we return to Mr Stevan Utah.

As it happens, Stevan Utah used to know Shane Della-Vedova extremely well. They were mates up at Lavarack Barracks in Townsville during his time in the Australian army. Both Della-Vedova and Utah did the specialist training as ammunition technician officers within a year of each other in the late 1980s and they became good drinking buddies. It was very dangerous work, learning not only how to blow things up and how to handle dozens of different military weapons and explosives, but also how to safely dispose of them when they reached their expiry date. Utah says:

> Della-Vedova was with the assault pioneer platoon of the 1st Battalion of the RAR. I could literally see it from my office. In the late eighties, early nineties, the defence budgeting was so fucked that we couldn't even fire a live round down range, have any money to buy shit. People like, I was known as this little wheeler and dealer. If I needed something like bags of cement, I would go and get them off the assault pioneers. Because they were assault pioneers they couldn't get black pens and shit like that, believe it or not. I had boxes of them. So I would be swapping boxes of black pens for bags of cement. I have very intimate knowledge of what an ammunition technician does. It is a tri-service trade meaning only the army has them but the navy and air force are allowed to apply for the course. Each year they have about a thousand applicants. Out of those thousand applicants only twelve people make the course. I have done the course. My father, my natural father, is a very well-known ammunition techie.

But as Utah is now willing to testify, and as police alleged in the Della-Vedova court hearing, it is clear things had got very sloppy inside the military when it came to ensuring that such dangerous weapons were in fact destroyed as claimed. Putting it bluntly, you could drive a truck through the poor security protecting these weapons—and, by the looks of it, that is pretty much what Della-Vedova did. Utah says, deftly ensuring he speaks hypothetically, careful not to imply he is speaking from personal experience:

> Let me put it this way, it would be the easiest thing in the world to take a pile of rocket launchers for disposal behind a hill with a bit of plastic explosive to help the big bang along. Cordon off the area. Keep everyone away for safety reasons. All everyone on the base sees is a big fucking bang. No-one's any the wiser and no-one's sure as hell doing any checks if the techie puts the launchers in the back of his private car and drives out [of] the base with them. It was that slack in the military in my time there sadly . . . and it sounds like it still is.

The evidence in the Della-Vedova prosecution only involves charges for the alleged theft of ten rocket launchers during 2001, nine of which have yet to be recovered. But Utah's descriptions of what he saw in the Bandidos—grenades, machine guns and at least one rocket launcher—included stolen weapons that pre and post dated any of the offences which were the basis of the current charges against Della-Vedova. The obvious question is whether, when Utah became an ammunition technician, he too was a player in the illicit trade. Utah adamantly denies any such role, but as the revelations about stolen military weapons became increasingly significant during 2007, it also became obvious that Utah knew a lot more than he was letting on.

Like any criminal Utah is evasive and forgetful on things that could still come back to bite him on the behind. Early in his original 2007 television interview Utah admitted that during his time as a hang-around in the Bandidos he had witnessed a rocket launcher being fired by bikies at a farm tractor: 'I don't want to open a can of worms . . . There was an incident where a tractor, or a bulldozer, was shot with a 66 rocket launcher in New South Wales back in the mid nineties.' Military weapons do not just fall off the back of a truck into the hands of bikies. It would be fair to say that on the speculative issue of just where these weapons come from, former ammunition technician Stevan Utah was curiously vague.

When challenged on what he knew about the illicit trade in military weapons between army personnel and bikies, Utah initially said: 'I am not aware, despite the fact that there are a number of former military personnel in outlaw motorcycle clubs across Australia, I am not aware of military involvement, regardless of what the media said. And I would be aware of it.' That assertion never quite made sense when, on Utah's own admission, the bikies were clearly getting military weapons from somewhere. If there was one issue about which we had always felt Utah was being especially evasive, it was what he knew about stolen military weapons.

As the date of the APEC conference neared, we pressed him repeatedly. He was obviously not letting on about something very important. There was a twenty-four-hour pause and then he called back. Stevan Utah had clearly had a long hard think. This time he said he would be prepared to tell what he knew to police, not just because it might be good for him in the long run, but also because he said he was appalled the weapons had found their way to alleged terrorists. What Utah claims he knows raises a huge new headache for Della-Vedova, who finally pleaded guilty in November 2007, presumably in the hope of a reduced gaol sentence. Utah's allegations open a whole new line of inquiry for counter-terrorism officials.

At first blush, some police might take the view that Utah's sudden recollection is just an opportunistic attempt by him to boost his own usefulness as a police witness by claiming to know something about the missing rocket launchers. But Utah realised that, in making the decision to tell what he knows, he is just buying into more unwelcomed heat from the police he had left behind. 'I could tell you shit that would honestly make you fall off your chair', he finally admitted in late 2007. But he knew the risks in telling what he knew. Not only was he worried about implicating himself in more criminal charges, the last thing he wanted was to be hauled back to Australia to face coercive interrogation by the Crime Commission: 'I don't want anyone knocking on my fucking door. I don't want anyone forcibly taking my arse out of this country. And if I go back there I don't want to be arrested for anything. I want an undertaking saying come back and help us with this and fuck off again.'

Utah surprised no-one when he failed to show at his fraud trial in late 2007. A warrant for his arrest is outstanding and a return to Australia is not high on Utah's agenda. He believes that with what the bikies know he has in his head any time in an Australian gaol is a death sentence. He maintains his innocence on the fraud charges. But what was playing on Utah's conscience was that he had witnessed Captain Shane Della-Vedova transact a completely separate arms deal with bikies two years after the matter for which Della-Vedova had just pleaded guilty.

Nothing that he knows implicates Dean Taylor, Della-Vedova's co-accused; Utah has never met him and knows nothing of him. At the time of writing, Taylor was still pleading not guilty and it should be emphasised that nothing Utah says he knows about the stolen military weapons reflects on the guilt or innocence of Taylor. But what Utah claims to know about Shane Della-Vedova has never been publicly disclosed before and, from what is allowed to be seen of the court files, there was no mention of it during the hearing.

At Della-Vedova's sentencing hearing in May 2008, the statement of facts read into the court record by the Crown prosecutor appeared to leave open the possibility that Della-Vedova's thieving of rocket launchers and other dangerous army kit might have happened on more than one occasion. The court heard how 'Della-Vedova would write the rocket launchers off as destroyed but actually take them home or elsewhere.' That certainly did not sound like they were talking about a once-off theft.

But in Della-Vedova's record of interview with police he maintained that his theft of the ten rocket launchers was accidental; that '[t]hey were part of a consignment given him to dispose of. He just panicked.' To further play down his criminality, the court was told that Della-Vedova denied removing the identifying markings on any of the rocket launchers he took, and that 'Harrington told him he wanted the rocket launchers for trophies'. He also admitted knowing Harrington was a member of an outlaw motorcycle gang and, 'I know he's not a nice dude ... I understand that he may have people ... this is a nasty world. Sydney's a nasty place.' As for the profits from the sale, he played it down, suggesting it was more like $5000.

Della-Vedova asserted the theft that had landed him in very hot water was a one-off. When asked whether he knew of other defence force personnel stealing ordnance, he took the Sergeant Schultz line—I know nothing, 'not a skerrick', he said.

The Crown too was at times curiously at pains to minimise the gravity of Harrington's and Della-Vedova's appalling alleged crimes, suggesting that there was also a good chance the rockets still at large might not go off if they were used. 'The particular rocket that was recovered was apparently part of a batch of rockets to be decommissioned due to a high failure rate', the Commonwealth Prosecutor told the Court. More of a whimper than a bang it would seem.

A picture was also painted by Della-Vedova's defence counsel, John Stratton SC, of a now contrite offender with a previously distinguished service record in the military. A wad of references were presented to the Court on his behalf. Then, crucially, this assertion: 'He is before your Honour because of a single very stupid mistake which has left his career in tatters.'

A single stupid mistake. No mention of Stevan Utah's allegations made to police eight months earlier. Any observer sitting in the court would have gone away with the distinct impression that Della-Vedova's crime was indubitably a one-off. The court also heard there was also no record of army disciplinary charges and no prior convictions. And, of course, Della-Vedova's defence team had no evidence before them to suggest anything different.

On 15 May 2008 Della-Vedova stood before his Honour Judge Williams of the NSW District Court and learned his fate. The judge wasn't buying the story he'd been told. He observed:

I find it extraordinarily difficult to believe that these ten rockets and launchers could somehow have been overlooked by Della-Vedova in the first place. I find it even more difficult to accept that if they had indeed been overlooked and not destroyed when they were supposed to have been that Della-Vedova could not have speedily and easily rectified this situation within Army guidelines, with little or no censure from those who mattered within the Service.

The next step taken by Della-Vedova, even if the initial scenario was accepted, is even more incomprehensible. The suggestion that ... he thought they would end up in the cow cockey's trophy cabinet is with respect wholly unbelievable given that the World was still reeling from the 9-11 terrorism.

He then gave Della-Vedova the really bad news. Ten years imprisonment with a non-parole period of seven years.

But, if Utah is right, then Della-Vedova was not just a one-time player who fell into weapons dealing by accident, for he had seen the army captain selling rocket launchers before, on at least one occasion, at the western Sydney home of the Bandido bikie we have dubbed 'Steed' in early 2005.

When Utah went back inside the Bandidos for the Australian Crime Commission from late 2004, he regularly visited Steed as he gathered information for police. Steed had become a good buddy but it is also clear from the way Utah talks about him that he was not someone to be fooled with: 'Smooth talker. Likeable guy. You feel really good around him. When he has a few drinks he can be an arrogant little cunt. About five foot ten, 70–75 kilos. Likes using meth. A bit on the skinny side. Won't hesitate to fight. Always has a handgun near him. No exception to that rule. Always.'

Steed's family are Bandido royalty. His father was one of those gaoled after the Milperra Massacre. Steed's father 'is one of the founding members of Bandidos Australia. He's a life member. His kids do whatever they fucking want . . . That's how far he goes back. [Steed's family] are very well known, very well trusted. [Steed] has a rap sheet in New South Wales for bulletproof vests, restricted firearms, tazers. He's a pretty connected little prick', Utah says.

One of the people he met through Steed was a man whose name he did not know, possibly of Lebanese extraction. 'I am just not the sort of guy who asks names. I am just not that sort of person', Utah explains. The man was not a Bandido but clearly a close criminal associate of Steed's. According to Utah this unidentified man turned up at Steed's house one February morning in 2005 with Della-Vedova. They were carrying five rocket launchers wrapped in a blanket. The connection to Della-Vedova was through Cleaver, the brother of Queensland Bandido Brutus, who had also served in the army with Utah and who also knew Della-Vedova in Townsville. 'He and [Cleaver] were friends before he even done the ammunition technicians course', Utah says.

Utah admits he never told his Crime Commission handlers about this incident, explaining that they never asked him about it. 'The only suggestion that's been put to me was by the Australian Crime Commission in late 2004, if I was responsible for helping [the Bandidos] blow shit up . . . they weren't interested in investigating anything. They just wanted an informant in Bandido circles, so why would I give them information?'

Utah says he was out of the room having a swim in Steed's backyard pool when Della-Vedova did the deal, so he does not know how much money was discussed. But he knows the rocket launchers were sold that day because the army captain left without them. 'I would probably suggest a hundred grand. And knowing [Steed] as well as I do and I have known him for a very long time, I suspect he would have swapped a couple of kilos of meth or something like that because he doesn't like playing with cash.'

Utah did witness Steed's brother taking the rocket launchers away to be hidden somewhere else. He was not asking any questions about what he had seen: 'Because if you involve yourself in that business you get a bullet in your fucking head real quick . . . When you are sitting with three or four very well-known, higher echelon criminals like that there's no loose ends lying around them, mate.' What Utah did not doubt was that the Bandidos who now had the weapons would sell them for a good price to whoever was offering enough money. 'I'll give you a very common phrase that's used—"Money talks. Bullshit walks". Offer enough money, you can have anything you fucking want. I can buy fucking Uzis in that country [Australia] for $24 000.'

Utah's information, with his permission, was immediately passed on by the authors to the same counter-terrorism police who had investigated Della-Vedova's separate sale of weapons to the Rebels outlaw motorcycle gang. By then they had already charged Della-Vedova and Dean Taylor and their committal hearings were due in a few weeks. This was a late complication in the Crown case against Della-Vedova, to say the least. Utah had also agreed to talk to the New South Wales and federal police on one condition: 'I don't want to be paid. [But] if I even sniff the ACC near me I will get selective amnesia.'

It was inevitable that the police investigating Utah's claims would contact the Australian Crime Commission, no matter what he demanded. They would not have been doing their job if they had not contacted the ACC to check out his story. The mistake they made was to allow him to find out about it. Worse still, Utah claims he discovered that Australian counter-terrorism officials made a formal request to the country where he is currently hiding, asking for him to be deported immediately to Australia for questioning.

Late in 2007 Utah stopped talking to the Australian police investigating the rocket launcher thefts—or maybe they just stopped talking to him. It is not entirely clear what happened. But at the time of writing Stevan Utah has never been formally interviewed by any Australian police agency about what he knows of either the stolen military weapons trade or Captain Shane Della-Vedova's part in it. That failure is more than a little puzzling. Some might say mind-boggling.

Stevan Utah bristles at suggestions that his claims about Della-Vedova are a concoction. He is adamant he is telling the truth. One possible explanation for why the New South Wales and federal police have not taken his allegations further is because they think he is lying. It may be that they are sceptical because he never told his ACC handlers about the weapons deal. But that does not explain why he has never been properly and fully questioned about what he knows. There is a lot Utah never told the Crime Commission, possibly because he was worried about implicating himself in criminal activity they did not know about.

To put it mildly, given a bit of careful and respectful handling, Utah would doubtless love to tell more about his former Bandido brothers' involvement in weapons dealing. They tried to kill him once and he knows they will try again. To get square, he would like to help police find those rocket launchers and he thinks he knows enough to help track them down: 'My knowledge of every one of their dirty fucking deeds is so extensive that they couldn't hide shit. They would literally have to exterminate each other because I just know everything that went on. I think they're sitting there going, "Let's just hope the fucking cunts don't believe you".'

Court evidence reveals that Della-Vedova was supposedly responsible for the demolition of at least one hundred and fifty-four M72 light anti-tank weapon systems, including rocket launcher tubes and warheads, on 8 June 2001. But the blood no doubt drained from the faces of investigators when they realised that no-one had actually witnessed that demolition. Worse still, Della-Vedova was also responsible for the further destruction of one hundred and sixty-nine rocket launchers during August that same year. How many of these supposedly destroyed weapons actually ended up in the bikie underworld is still anyone's guess. Officially only ten went missing and just one was recovered in a controlled operation involving Harrington.

On the evidence that is publicly available, it seems nobody has any real idea how many stolen weapons are out there. There is more than a whiff to Della-Vedova's activities that suggests the weapons dealing had been going on for quite a while. Utah's account would suggest a much wider racket than has previously been disclosed. So why do police not seem all that interested in investigating it? And then there are other questions— again to do with the selective morality behind giving indemnities to serious criminals. Time to take a closer look at the Crown witness codenamed Harrington.

BIKIES AND TERRORISTS

From the committal hearing evidence it is clear that through early 2007 Della-Vedova and Taylor were allegedly growing increasingly concerned about media revelations that at least one of the rocket launchers had been recovered and was now being closely examined by police. Their big worry was allegedly that Harrington, their bikie intermediary with the criminals buying the weapons, might talk.

Excerpts from bugged phone calls suggested Della-Vedova had assured his mother that Harrington was 'keeping his ears and eyes open and won't let his guard down'. But what the army captain had not contemplated was that Harrington would roll to police. Clearly, in the all-out effort to track down the missing rocket launchers police had put the fear of god into the bikie and he had been made an offer he could not refuse. To Della-Vedova's later horror, it emerged that Harrington had worn a wire as he met with Della-Vedova and Taylor. Their muffled alleged conversations were highly incriminating. 'Is there any way they [the stolen weapons] can be traced back?' Harrington allegedly asked both men during the taped conversation. 'No way', Taylor allegedly said. 'There's no fucking way', Della-Vedova echoed. But, oh, yes there was. Their alleged co-conspirator had rolled.

Court orders forbid the publication of Harrington's real name. The ban cannot be because his bikie 'brothers' might find out he has become a police informer because they most definitely know. It is presumably because police are still investigating those criminals to whom he sold the weapons, and the terrorists who then bought them latterly.

As was disclosed in the court hearing, Harrington is a former senior member of a major outlaw motorcycle gang. It is always a difficult issue for police and prosecutors to decide whether any criminal should be given indemnity from prosecution in return for their evidence, as we have already seen from other controversial cases, including Peter Klarfeld in the Queensland murder trial. But the decision to give Harrington a full indemnity for his crimes under the Commonwealth Crime Code, but not any NSW criminal offences, was more fraught than most. He was a major bikie criminal, allegedly responsible for selling the deadly weapons to other criminals, which had ended up in the possession of terrorists. In the end, police chose to prioritise shutting down Della-Vedova, hopefully with a view to exposing whatever other rackets in stolen military weapons might be going on. There was also no doubt considerable relief in the military and security services to be able to allay public concern that those allegedly responsible for stealing the weapons would be brought to justice. If that meant supping with the devil and giving Harrington a 'get out of gaol free' card, then so be it.

It is normally a condition of any such indemnity that the witness makes a full statement of their crimes. Full disclosure is essential. It is vitally important also for police agencies to be seen to be scrupulously fair and open in their handling of indemnities. This is why it can only be hoped that when the state and federal attorneys-general were asked to approve his indemnity, they were told about another serious criminal incident involving Mr Harrington several years earlier. It was as compromising for police as it was for Harrington.

Sometime from mid 2001 onwards the New South Wales police set up a confidential strikeforce dubbed 'TUNI'. Its role was to investigate bikie associations with police. The concern inside the force about outlaw motorcycle gang members who were also serving or had been police officers had arisen when a uniformed sergeant with the state's tactical response group had left the police in 1998 and immediately joined a major outlaw motorcycle gang on a full colours patch. The obvious implication was that he had been a bikie for some time before he left the force, a concerning thought considering the number of sensitive operations in which he was engaged.

As we can reveal, investigators on another NSW police strikeforce, this time rather confusingly called TUNO, also turned up some very worrying whiffs of police criminal complicity with bikie gangs. Another now retired police officer was a known close associate of the Rebels—often seen drinking with them at a notorious Sydney bikie pub—and he became a suspect in the murder of a man whose body parts were found distributed along the Hastings River on New South Wales's North Coast.

Bits of his body took months to float to the surface in seven different bags—an unpleasant surprise for local fishermen.

The victim had just made a plea agreement with police to testify against other bikie members. On day release from gaol, while serving time for a drug offence, the victim had gone to work at a garage in that police officer's then local area command, reporting to that station. The victim's workmates described how one day several men, including two wearing police uniforms, had arrived and taken him away in an unmarked car. He was never seen alive again. Police investigators were strongly suspicious the officer who was friendly with the bikies had tipped them off. He had also given evidence for the victim's wife in an apprehended violence court order, and was rumoured to be having an affair with her. As well he had a part-time job as a driver with a trucking company owned by a senior outlaw motorcycle gang member. But the murder investigation got nowhere.

In another alleged security breach, the wife of a Rebel gang member was working in the section of a major bank which received all requests from the New South Wales Crime Commission for access to financial data of bikies under surveillance. Though she has never been prosecuted, sources believe she may have passed on information that compromised a few investigations.

The last straw for the internal affairs team was when, very recently, police discovered a bikie had deliberately enrolled as a police cadet in the New South Wales Police Academy at Goulburn. Bikie penetration and counter-surveillance of police was now a huge issue. One job the police internal affairs Strikeforce TUNI team investigated involved a stolen police Glock handgun. Somehow, the gun ended up in the possession of none other than Harrington—now the chief Crown witness against Della-Vedova. As fate would have it, when one of Harrington's relatives was on work placement at the station as a student police officer, an informant allegedly tipped police off that the gun was at his home. Before the police raid, a discussion had taken place between two detectives about the search warrant with Harrington's relative listening on. When the search warrant was served—surprise, surprise—the gun was no longer there at the house. As the late self-described 'gangster' and colourful Sydney identity Tim Bristow often commented, 'You can't help bad luck'.

Sources say the evidence suggested the gun had been there but that it was removed because someone had called the house that day to give Harrington a warning. The finger of suspicion pointed very strongly at Harrington's relative in the force and subsequent inquiries by the TUNI strikeforce bolstered that view. A report was prepared and sent to the old internal affairs department of NSW Police for investigation. The level of criminality in allegedly tipping off Harrington was such that it 'could not be ignored'. But the police complainants never heard another word about the complaint—and they then heard that the suspect had been confirmed as a probationary constable at the same police station.

The stolen police weapon was eventually recovered by police but, at time of writing, no charges have been laid against Harrington for possession of the stolen police weapon and his relative is still in the force.

Should it affect the veracity of Harrington's evidence in the rocket launcher case? Probably not. But by not investigating it and prosecuting both Harrington and his relative inside the force, police have left themselves wide open to the perception that Harrington's indemnity deal was inordinately generous. Did they ever offer him just a reduced sentence rather than protection, freedom and a possible reward? And why was that not a more appropriate offer to such a seriously implicated criminal than a full indemnity? Was he ever questioned about the missing handgun? Was it allowed to be quietly returned, no questions asked? And when he was given indemnity, were those who made the decision told about this incident? Probably not. As for the investigation of Harrington's relative—it has allegedly gone nowhere. Harrington was not identified under NSW law but, at the time of writing, outstanding charges against him have not proceeded to trial.

For the same reasons, Stevan Utah believes he has a right to see his allegations about Shane Della-Vedova fully investigated. By not doing so, the police and security services open themselves up to the perception that they just want the whole embarrassing saga of stolen military weapons to go away. The full terms of Della-Vedova's negotiations with police to plead guilty have not and probably never will be disclosed. But has he been questioned about any other sales of weapons to bikies? Has any effort been made to question Steed or to put him under surveillance since we alerted police to Utah's allegations in September 2007? How many of the rocket launchers, grenades and explosives stolen by Della-Vedova are still out there in the hands of bikies, other organised crime groups and terrorists? And where are they?

Yet again, the police seem to be missing a perfect opportunity to rigorously investigate bikie organised crime. Stevan Utah is not the only person asking why that is.

EPILOGUE

Late in 2007, a man called Stevan Utah, living somewhere on the other side of the planet, ceased to exist. With the help of a now-friendly overseas police agency he was finally able to get identity documents in a new fake name—a name we are delighted to say we do not even know ourselves. We do not want to know. It is probably better for both of us. Because his old Bandido 'brothers' will be hunting him forever.

Stevan Utah, as he used to be known, will spend the rest of his life looking over his shoulder. Not just because of the bikies on whom he informed, but also because of the Queensland police. He failed to appear in a Brisbane court in late 2007 on the fraud charges to which he pleads his innocence. The warrant for his arrest is still outstanding, but even if Australian police do move to extradite him, the process could take years. The person formerly known as Stevan Utah has applied for refugee asylum in his overseas hiding place, alleging he would be murdered by vengeful outlaw motorcycle gang members if he returned. He is probably right on that score. He has done a lot to upset them.

He is also concerned that his knowledge of corrupt former and serving officers inside state and federal police agencies makes a safe return to Australia or a fair trial impossible. This claim will no doubt draw shouts of angry indignation from police, in Queensland in particular. And indeed there can be no doubting the desire of most men and women in law enforcement to do their best to fairly investigate and prosecute organised criminals. However, even some inside the various Australian police agencies agree that a few of their own have got too close to their targets inside the outlaw motorcycle gangs.

The story of the man who used to be known as Stevan Utah also raises some very unpleasant truths about how police turf wars, petty politics and old-fashioned testosterone are hindering Australia's battle against organised crime. The one-percenters—the outlaw motorcycle gang members fingered by Utah—will doubtless also strenuously deny his claims, despite recent arrests in New South Wales, Queensland, Victoria and South Australia for drug and firearms offences. What they have in their favour is that some in Australian law enforcement seem unwilling to take the bikies on—be they cowed by threats or hamstrung by legal restraints and petty politics.

But perhaps the most corrosive and dangerous thing about the furore over the one-percenters is that a large slice of Australian media and culture chooses to glamorise them. Unlike several western countries which have slowly woken up to the fact that outlaw motorcycle gangs are all too often by definition organised criminal franchises, too many commentators have written about the romance of the bikies, the freedom of the open road, the freedom of life without the constraints of many of we 'normal' types. It is all very post-modern, with a blind eye turned to the beatings, the murders, the drugs and the guns.

Such romantic notions are completely and utterly wrong and a tribute to the public relations skills of men like Sonny Barger and the rose-tinted glasses of the commentators. The same can be said of much of the outpourings of law enforcement bodies who talk about cooperation between agencies, between states and between like-minded countries. All very nice, all very palatable and reassuring. It is the sort of reassurance designed to help us sleep comfortably each night. However, like the bikies' public relations, it is a triumph of spin over reality.